Savoring China

WILLIAMS-SONOMA

Savoring China

Recipes and Reflections on Chinese Cooking

Recipes and Text
JACKI PASSMORE

General Editor
CHUCK WILLIAMS

Recipe Photography
ANDRE MARTIN

Food Stylist
SALLY PARKER

Scenic Photography
JASON LOWE

Illustrations
MARLENE McLOUGHLIN

Oxmoor
House.

KAZAKHSTAN

MONGO

KYRGYZSTAN

TAJIKISTAN

AFGHANISTAN

XINJIANG

GOBI DESERT

GANSU

PAKISTAN

NINGXIA

CHINA

QINGHAI

XINING ·

LANZHOU ·

TIBET

SICHUAN

SH

NEPAL

LHASA

CHE

BHUTAN

INDIA

BANGLADESH

YUNNAN

KUNMING ·

MYANMAR
(BURMA)

VIETN

BAY OF BENGAL

LAOS

THAILAND

SSIA

HEILONGJIANG

JILIN

INNER
MONGOLIA

TIANJIN   LIAONING

NORTH
KOREA

SEA
OF
JAPAN

40°

BEIJING

HEBEI

SOUTH
KOREA

JAPAN

TAIYUAN

SHANXI   JIN·AN

YANTAI

SHANDONG   YELLOW SEA

NAN

KAIFEN

JIANGSU
YANGZHOU

30°

NANJING

ANHUI   SUZHOU

HUBEI

HANGZHOU·
SHAOXING

SHANGHAI

JIANGXI

EAST
CHINA
SEA

HUNAN
·DONG'AN

FUJIAN

ZHEJIANG

PACIFIC OCEAN

GUILIN

GUANGDONG

GUANGZHOU

TAIWAN

HONG KONG

20°

SOUTH CHINA SEA

KM
0   100 200 300 400 500

0   100   200   300
MILES

PHILIPPINES

Contents

INTRODUCTION

The Chinese Table

SO MUCH ABOUT CHINA is vast and overwhelming that it is sometimes hard to see beyond its sheer scale to the everyday aspects of life in the world's most populous nation. Yet it is the cameo glimpses of this amazing country that tell its story: the cormorant fisherman isolated in his little wooden boat on a wide sweep of one of the country's immense rivers, alone save for the birds that have worked with him since they were old enough to swim; the grandmother squatting on a wooden stool at the back of a stall in the vegetable market patiently peeling a mountainous pile of garlic cloves; strings of dried fish sunning at a beachside; a stone bridge curving over a lotus pond; a congregation of old men with their pet birds in bamboo cages, gathering at a teahouse to gossip and sip mugs of steaming black or oolong tea; the small child at a street-side restaurant slurping noodles noisily from a large bowl; the red tiles on the curved roof of a pagoda reflecting the afternoon sun; a cage of live snakes near the door of a restaurant announcing the eagerly awaited specialty, snake soup; a street-side vendor frying crisp scallion cakes in a blackened wok for hungry passers-by; the farmer delivering a live pig to market in a wire cage strapped to his bicycle pillion seat; the old woman sinking toothless gums into the soft dough of a freshly steamed *baozi* as she trudges home from the market.

Left: An old woman of the Zhuang tribe peers from behind a screen. Numbering 15 million, the Zhuang are China's largest minority group. **Top:** Street stalls display abundant fresh vegetables in China's warm south. **Above:** Noodles are cooked to order at Shanghai's street stalls.

These are the images that endure, even as China rushes headlong into the twenty-first century. No amount of development will obscure the treasures, both natural and crafted over millennia, of this magnificent country. Progress has meant the Chinese are now enjoying a resurgence of interest in their unique cuisine: the nation's chefs are dusting off the neglect of two generations of internal upheaval, rediscovering and reshaping classic dishes, and guiding the cuisine to new heights.

With each visit, China reveals more of itself to the visitor. It is a measured unveiling. As our boat floated between the mist-shrouded volcanic peaks and ridges that follow the course of the Li River, east of Guilin, one of my travel companions, in a flash of poetic insight, commented, "this country is like a virgin bride, shyly divesting layers of silk to expose herself in all her raw beauty." Nature indeed worked on a grand scale in shaping

China, and the diversity of its terrain, climate, and cultures reflects eloquently in a multi-faceted cuisine. The country's eastern border stretches over two thousand miles along a coastline framed by three seas, to northern reaches that wrap around the high, windswept grasslands of Mongolia. Heilongjiang, the most eastern province, probes north to an icy 50 degrees latitude, while in the northwest towering mountain ranges taper off into the dead expanse of the Gobi.

The subtropical provinces of the south border Vietnam, Laos, and Myanmar, yet share no culinary directions with them, save for the ubiquitous rice paddies terraced around the mountain foothills and cascading in ribbons of emerald, jade, and gold down the sides of plummeting gorges. Rice crops are the main-stay of the southern and central provinces. In the north, vast fields of wheat cover high plains whipped by winds sweeping in from the west.

Some of the world's longest and largest rivers carve through China's landscape, roaring down treacherous gorges and snaking along valleys and croplands to spread into brown-silted coastal deltas. The craggy limestone peaks and imperious, granite mountain ranges that fringe these rivers have inspired painters and poets for tens of centuries.

China is enthralling in so many ways that it has lured me back time and time again. I have experienced it on the run and at leisure. On one whirlwind food tour, our erudite guide made the wry comment that to see China in such a rushed way—eight cities in two weeks—was to "admire flowers from a galloping horse." I prefer not to visit China on such a frantic schedule. My own travels there began in the early 1970s, and although Mao Zedong's regime, at the height of its zeal, restricted my itineraries on those first visits, by the end of the decade I was able to travel further afield.

One of my most memorable and fruitful trips was a lengthy stay at the tea-growing commune of Yingteh, about one hundred miles (165 km) north of Guangzhou. Besides acquiring an enduring addiction to Chinese tea and an invaluable, hands-on education on all facets of the tea industry from cultivation to packing, the visit presented me with an unequaled opportunity to observe and participate in life from the perspective of rural Guangdong and Fujian.

It was to be a half decade, and very changed times, before I would visit the north and west, and intensify my fascination for China and its food. Learning about the cuisine and its etiquette became a fascinating voyage of discovery into the sensory pleasures of taste and texture. What could be more whimsical than an appetizer of ducks' tongues glazed with honey? More practical than the shared pot? As economic as rice gruel or as deliciously, decadently extravagant as a banquet dish of whole braised sharks' fins and abalone? What could be more perfectly balanced than a salty oyster sauce over a silken crabmeat omelet, the crunch of bamboo with tender braised mushrooms, or stir-fried tender pork on crisp noodles?

Left: A one-hundred-foot (31-m) reclining Buddha is but one of the elaborate, thirteenth-century wall carvings at Baoding in Sichuan. The extensive carvings took over seventy years to complete and narrowly escaped destruction by the Red Guards. **Top:** A farmer in Guangxi, using methods that have stayed the same for hundreds of years, prepares his rice terraces for planting. **Above:** Goods are taken to market the quickest way possible. These hens have just arrived at a local village market in Sichuan.

Below: Dried starfish, snakeskins, and frogs make striking wall decorations as they hang in a stall in the Qing Ping Market in central Guangzhou, Guangdong province.
Bottom: Women bundle green (spring) onions for the day's customers at a vegetable market in Chengdu.
Right: The peaceful environs of the Summer Palace in Beijing are not disturbed by these early morning practitioners of tai chi. Once reserved solely for the emperors and their retinue, the palace grounds have become a favorite relaxation spot for Beijing residents.

Naturally I've developed a fondness for particular destinations. It's often the small things that count—the discovery of a unique teapot for my collection, a special dish, a spectacular sunset or starry night, or an adventure, like borrowing a bicycle and jostling for a place in the handlebar-to-handlebar throng of Shanghai's cycling workers. I love visiting Guangzhou, where the local dialect washes over me in vast waves of nostalgia, and where I can walk for hours in its expansive food market, down aisles between hessian bags brimming with dried mushrooms of a dozen varieties, sweet-smelling spices, and pungent dried seafoods.

Chengdu always intrigues me. It is a city that epitomizes the precept of contrasts, the duality of yin and yang. It's a principle based on opposites and harmony, on one element balancing another. Tiny, ancient shops and houses survive in streets almost transformed by development, where rickety, age-old bamboo scaffolding encases massive, modern construction sites. It is polluted, noisy, and bustling. Yet, away from the broad new avenues and hustle, you can still find remnants of a city with two thousand years of history, where rickshaws aren't just for the tourists

and medicine vendors hawk their esoteric fare of dried tiger's legs and mountain-gathered herbs.

I never visit Shanghai without crossing the zigzag bridge to the famous Hu Xin Ting teahouse in the Yuyuan Garden, and in Beijing I wander the precincts of the Forbidden City in search of a special curved roofline, or an ornate window frame or doorway to add to my photographic collection of architectural cameos.

While China is vast and richly rewarding for the tourist, as a culinary destination it is unsurpassed. Four main geographical areas—northern, southern, eastern, and western—attempt to break down the huge diversity of regional dishes and cooking styles. The east has superb seafood, and its flavors progress from the characteristic lime-scented dishes of Fujian on the southern coast, to the elegant and sophisticated dishes of the northeast. The port city of Shanghai is perhaps the most assertive exponent of the eastern style.

In the south, Guangdong and neighboring Guangxi are the original homes of dim sum and subtle seasonings. The reverence of the local chefs for the freshest of ingredients is clearly defined in the crisp textures, bright colors, and natural flavors they capture in their stir-fries and steamed dishes.

The bold seasonings and complex flavors of Sichuan cooking dominate the central and western regions, where chefs have abundant local ingredients to draw on: freshwater fish and shellfish, rice and vegetables, fungi and herbs, game and exotic meats.

It was in the eastern part of northern China that the imperial cuisine developed over several millennia. Northern cuisine retains much of the diversity and creativity of those distant times. Wine sauces and marinades, herbal seasonings, perfection in baking and roasting, and a dazzling array of appetizers characterize the food of the north.

China's minority ethnic groups, the Muslim population, and those living in the remote western and northern regions of this massive country have all contributed to regional flavors. But, of these groups, it was the Manchus, China's rulers for more than three centuries (1644–1911), who had the greatest impact on the country's cooking. All of these influences contribute to the fascinating culinary cocktail that is China's cuisine today.

Left: The Great Wall of China is an impressive reminder of China's traditional might and of its periodic weakness in the face of nomadic invaders. Stretching for more than 1,500 miles (2,500 km), it crowns the ridges that formed the northern border of China with Mongolia. **Below:** Shellfish are presented in gaily colored bowls in a Shandong market stall. **Bottom:** A farmer carries his piglets to market in handmade, woven cages.

APPETIZERS, DIM SUM, AND SOUPS

An array of small dishes – hot and cold – stimulates the appetite for the plates that will follow.

FROM THE FIRST BITE, a Chinese meal is a shared experience that does not necessarily begin with appetizers and rarely starts with soup. In fact, you don't have to wait for mealtimes to enjoy the small bites and bowls of the Chinese cuisine. Small dishes make the crossover from street food to the table and back with practiced agility. Just about any of the snack foods served at food markets or cooked up by mobile food vendors make delicious first courses on the home table. The sliced, roast red pork you snack on while shopping would be a welcome appetizer served over boiled peanuts or marinated bean sprouts. Pork dumplings are as appealing on the plate as they are eaten out of hand as you wander a marketplace. Wontons are a popular on-the-run snack, yet floating in a clear soup in your best bowls they make an elegant first course.

Hong Kong presented a young cadet journalist with many reasons to consider a career in food writing—its thousands of restaurants and their exciting and extensive menus, its crowded *yum cha* halls and *da pai dang* (street-food stalls) where the food is inexpensive and sensational, the fish restaurants where the catch swims blithely in plastic tubs and aquariums, unaware of impending fate, and the markets with their throbbing life and mix of malodorous and tantalizing smells. There was inspiration everywhere for the eyes, ears, and nose.

But the final catalyst for me was the intoxicating aroma of black mushrooms. One chilly winter day I ordered in chicken and mushroom soup for lunch. Three plump black discs floated in a well-made stock, imbuing it with their heady fragrance. I sniffed the steam deeply and fell in love. Anything that could smell that good must be written about, taught

Preceding pages: Every dim sum restaurant must have bamboo steamers filled with piping-hot, succulent morsels ready for the morning's diners. **Left:** The labyrinthine Stone Forest in Yunnan is a popular tourist destination. Local Sani women act as guides through the maze of intriguing limestone pillars. **Right:** In the busy streets of Kunming, Muslim street vendors, in their traditional embroidered caps, do a thriving trade with their lamb skewers and other local delicacies.

Top: Vendors weave traditional baskets while they wait for customers at their vegetable stalls. **Above:** An elderly Chinese couple share a plate of dumplings in one of Shanghai's crowded eateries. **Right:** Delicious aromas waft from every slow-simmering pot in Chongqing's old town. These simple, outdoor woodburning stoves are a common sight in the older corners of Chinese cities.

of, talked about . . . and eaten often. The direction of my career was set that day. Incidentally, I haven't yet tired of that alluring aroma. I am sure I never will.

Chinese soups are a sensation—with or without mushrooms, hot or cold, winter or summer. Their thick soups are chunky and full-bodied, their clear soups never insipid. No self-respecting Chinese chef would prepare a soup without using freshly made stock. They are adept at drawing deep flavor into a soup stock and are happy to share their secrets— slow, gentle simmering over a low flame, ginger for flavor and clarity, and pork hocks for richness. And, for strongly flavored stocks, local hams add pleasing saltiness and unique flavor, while star anise lends its distinct taste and wonderful aroma.

At a restaurant, soup usually is not ordered individually or served as the first course. But there is no reason why you should follow this custom. In a typical menu, soup comes midway through the main meal as a palate cleanser. However, when a host wants to impress his or her guests with a special soup it comes

to the table first, so it can be appreciated without distraction. Soups with rare or expensive ingredients, such as shark's fin, abalone, or seasonal specialties such as snake or bamboo fungus, are given this honor.

Soup is important in the everyday diet—as comfort food for the elderly and unwell, as a nutritional meal for children, and as a sustaining snack eaten at any time of the day. From dawn to dark in any Chinese city, town, or village you will always find a small restaurant or street stall with a simmering pot of soup at the ready. Soup is sucked noisily from porcelain or metal spoons. To slurp is to show due appreciation that the soup is hot and delicious—and you won't burn your tongue as you eat.

The art of the appetizer platter is unique to Chinese cuisine. It is a specialized skill demanding artistic and culinary flair, and an understanding of the mythology of the culture. Bite-sized cold appetizers are assembled on large, ornate platters in scenes symbolic of the occasion. The five-clawed dragon of myth and legend offers congratulations, good luck, and happiness. The mythical phoenix expresses wishes of good fortune. The peacock is a symbol of business success, and the pine and crane stand for longevity.

These elegantly composed appetizer platters, accompanied by rice wine, are to be nibbled during the toasts before the main courses begin to arrive on the table. On formal occasions, waiters may serve the appetizers using silver chopsticks, but at casual dinners everyone reaches for their own choice from the plate in the center of the table.

The majority of appetizers are cold dishes, and traditional favorites include pickled cabbage redolent of chile, salt-sweet marinated cucumber, slivers of crunchy jellyfish or dry-fried duck, crisp-fried dried fish, salty razor clams, marinated mushrooms, and cold meats. Morsels of tender, pink duck with glazed amber skin have universal appeal, as do candied walnuts. But some prefer their appetizers hot and exciting—small bites, such as Sichuan dumplings in a fiery chile sauce, steamed or fried chicken wings, fried spring rolls, and steamed dumplings. And if tastes tend to the

Left: A water buffalo wallows in the Li River. Buffalos are widely used to pull the plows that till China's vast farm fields. **Below:** Corn cobs are stripped of their kernels at the Wednesday market in Lunan, Yunnan. The normally quiet town is packed with donkeys, carts, and bicycles when market day arrives. **Bottom:** Meat-filled dumplings are made fresh every day.

exotic there are flash-fried duck tongues, jumping live shrimp to subdue with hot rice wine, "chrysanthemum" chicken gizzards, and even crisp, roasted scorpions.

I find Chinese cold cuts and pressed meats particularly appealing as appetizers. The range is not immense, but the textures and flavors are impressive—the simplicity of plain, boiled pork with a pungent, garlic sauce, the enticing aroma and pleasing crunch of pork shanks slow-poached with soy, sugar, and star anise, or the delicacy of steamed pork sausage or pressed pickled goose.

In the southern provinces, cold, cooked meats are enjoyed as appetizers. But the Cantonese tend not to place great importance on pre-meal nibbles, preferring to move straight on to the main course dishes. In the north it's different, in a restaurant at least. No meal would begin without at least one dish to titillate the taste buds and it is not unusual for

as many as a dozen or more different appetizers to be ordered at a dinner—depending, of course, on the number of diners, the budget, and the significance of the occasion.

Most dim sum dishes are perfect to serve as a first course with a home-prepared Chinese meal. I regularly undertake a big cooking day, stocking up on *shao mai*, spring rolls, and other such small foods that take time and patience to prepare.

When dinner is not a celebratory occasion, simplicity usually prevails. Appetizers are served on small plates, often without garnish or affectation. Virtually anything that can be served or savored in small bites is a contender for the appetizer repertoire. The choice of ingredients is as endless and varied as the imagination of the chef and the availability of ingredients. The objectives are to arouse the olfactory glands, tease the taste receptors, and stimulate the appetite—in short, to prepare the palate for the main dishes to come.

Top left: Plump *cha shao bao* (pork buns) originated in the south of China. **Bottom left:** In western China, duck is a favorite ingredient in spicy stir-fries and clay pot cooking. **Top:** A traditional game of checkers is hotly contested, while aspiring players look on. **Above:** An array of woks for sale. The wok has been a vital part of the Chinese kitchen armory for over a thousand years.

Southern

Songshu Yuanzhuiti Youyu

fried cuttlefish "pinecones"
with pepper-salt

*Chinese cooks treat seafood with reverence.
At the market they buy only the freshest, and in
the kitchen prepare it with care and cook it in ways
that highlight its natural goodness and flavor.
Creative chefs also seek imaginative presentations
for all fresh seafood, from the humblest of the catch
to the most prized and exotic species. Scoring the
firm, snow white flesh of cuttlefish or squid
makes it exquisitely tender, and, once cooked,
the pieces curl up to resemble miniature pinecones.
The finished dish, with its crisp-fried parsley
leaves, becomes a bonsai on a plate.*

*Several important fish dishes use a similar
scoring technique. Thick fish fillets, scored right
down to the skin, are coated liberally with
cornstarch (cornflour) or a cornstarch batter.
When deep-fried to a golden crispness, the
segments stand out proudly from the curling
skin. Close crosshatching, as in this dish, gives
a brushlike effect. Wider-spaced crosshatch
scoring results in a grape-bunch effect.*

7 oz (220 g) cleaned cuttlefish or large squid
bodies (about 10½ oz/330 g before cleaning,
page 249)

2 teaspoons fresh lemon juice

½ teaspoon salt

½ teaspoon crushed garlic

PEPPER-SALT

2 tablespoons salt

2 teaspoons ground Sichuan pepper

¼ cup (1 oz/30 g) cornstarch (cornflour)

vegetable or peanut oil for deep-frying

leaves from 1 bunch fresh parsley

❀ Rinse and thoroughly dry the cuttlefish (or squid)
bodies. Using a sharp knife, slit each body lengthwise
to open it flat. Using the sharp knife, score a ¹⁄₁₆-inch
(2-mm) crosshatch pattern over the inside surface.
Cut into pieces 1 by 1¾ inches (2.5 by 4.5 cm).

❀ In a bowl large enough to hold the cuttlefish, stir
together the lemon juice, salt, and garlic. Add the cuttlefish and stir to coat evenly. Marinate for 20 minutes,
stirring occasionally.

❀ To prepare the pepper-salt, place a dry wok over
medium-high heat. When it is hot, add the salt and
warm for about 40 seconds, stirring constantly. Add
the pepper and remove immediately from the heat.
Stir to mix, then pour into a shallow dish to cool.

❀ Drain the cuttlefish and dry on paper towels. Put
the cornstarch into a shallow dish and lightly coat
the cuttlefish pieces with the cornstarch, tapping off
the excess.

❀ Pour the oil to a depth of 2 inches (5 cm) into a
wok, and heat to 375°F (190°C), or until a piece of
the cuttlefish dropped into it sizzles immediately.
Working in batches, add the cuttlefish and fry for
only about 15 seconds. It will remain white and
should be very tender. Do not overcook, or it will
toughen. Using a wire skimmer or slotted spoon,
transfer to a rack placed over paper towels to drain.

❀ Add the parsley to the hot oil and fry until crisp,
bright green, and you hear a rustling sound, about
1½ minutes. Be careful that the oil does not spatter
you. Using a wire skimmer, transfer to paper towels
to drain.

❀ Arrange the cuttlefish on a platter, sprinkle with
about one-third of the pepper-salt, and surround
with the fried parsley. Serve at once with the remaining pepper-salt in small dishes for dipping.

serves 4

*If seafood does not reach
the market in pristine
condition, it is salted
or dried.*

SAVORING CHINA

Dim Sum

Dim sum restaurants are the daily precinct of millions of enthusiastic diners in many parts of China, and in particular the southern provinces of Guangdong and Guangxi. But it wasn't always that way. During the Ming dynasty, *yum cha*, or "taking tea," was a privilege of the wealthy, leisured classes, who lingered for hours in ornate teahouses exchanging social and business gossip while they sipped tea and nibbled exquisite snacks. Many of the delicious snacks had originated in the kitchens of the royal households, where they were served as palate refreshers between the ostentatious courses of imperial banquets.

As the teahouse became accessible to everyone, the food came to be known as dim sum, meaning "dot-hearts" or "heart's delight." These names poetically describe the diminutive portions of a panoply of dumplings, buns, meaty tidbits, cakes, and pastries, which collectively offer an unmatched spectrum of tastes, aromas, and textures. Elegant teahouses were replaced by gargantuan, multistoried canteens, some accommodating over a thousand at a

seating, and speed of service became as vital to commercial success as variety and quality were to customer satisfaction. The ingenious dim sum cart solved the problem, and the tradition was exported. Steamer baskets and plates of steaming hot snacks are piled high on the carts, which hostesses push between the tables advertising their fare in singsong voices. The diner takes a peek beneath the lids, makes a selection, and the plates are transferred to the table with dipping sauces of chile and soy, mustard and red vinegar.

A pot of steaming-hot Chinese tea, which is never allowed to run empty, accompanies dim sum. A wave of the hand or the lid laid askew on top of the teapot is the signal for a roving water carrier to top it up. *Pu er* (black tea) is preferred in the south, while jasmine tea has universal appeal.

When it's time to pay, the waiter simply adds up the number of serving plates on the table, or totes up the entries made by the serving staff on a paper chit.

Southern

Shao Mai

steamed pork and shrimp dumplings

The acknowledged master chefs of dim sum usually come from Guangzhou, in Guangdong province, training in restaurants like the Pan Xi Jiujia, with its dining rooms and pavilions set beside Li Wan Lake. At this famous restaurant, you can order direct from the chefs, then watch them prepare the mounds of fresh dumplings that will be lined up in gigantic bamboo baskets and stacked to steam over huge woks of simmering water with roaring gas fires below. Two of the restaurant's specialties are xia jiao, crisp-tender shrimp dumplings in elegant translucent wrappers, and shao mai, an international favorite. These "open-face" dumplings are the archetypal dim sum. The tender dumplings of moist pork and succulent shellfish, lightly seasoned with green (spring) onions and oyster sauce, are encased in a soft, parchment-thin wrapper that leaves the filling exposed, so the eyes can appreciate even before the first bite.

Pork and shrimp are two ingredients the southern Chinese hold in particularly high regard, so much so that they use them together in many dishes. Tender, finely sliced marinated pork and whole shelled shrimp with crisp and colorful fresh vegetables feature in stir-fries and noodles, sweet-and-sour dishes, and steamboats. Satiny smooth minced pork helps to bind and enrich fillings for buns, pastry rolls, and dumplings, like those in this recipe.

FILLING

4 large dried black mushrooms, soaked in hot water to cover for 25 minutes and drained

½ lb (250 g) coarsely ground (minced) fat pork such as pork butt

6 oz (185 g) shrimp (prawn) meat or crabmeat, finely chopped

2 green (spring) onions, including tender green tops, finely chopped

1 teaspoon superfine (caster) sugar

4 teaspoons oyster sauce

1 tablespoon cornstarch (cornflour)

½ teaspoon ground white pepper

1 tablespoon vegetable or peanut oil or 1½ teaspoons each vegetable oil and sesame oil

24 round wheat-flour dumpling wrappers

2–3 teaspoons vegetable oil

light soy sauce, mild mustard, or chile sauce

☝ To prepare the filling, remove and discard the stems from the mushrooms if necessary and very finely chop the caps. Place in a bowl and add the pork, shrimp or crab, and green onions and mix well. Mix in the sugar and oyster sauce, then stir in the cornstarch, pepper, and oil. Let stand for 20 minutes.

☝ To shape each dumpling, make a circle with thumb and first finger of one hand and position a dumpling wrapper centrally over the circle. Place about 2 teaspoons of the filling in the center of the wrapper, and gently push the dumpling through the circle so that the wrapper becomes pleated around the sides of the dumpling filling. You should have a cup-shaped dumpling with the top of the filling exposed.

☝ Brush the rack of a steamer basket with the vegetable oil and place the dumplings in the basket, leaving some space between them. Bring water to a simmer in a steamer base. Set the steamer basket in the steamer, cover tightly, and steam the dumplings until the filling is firm, 7–8 minutes.

☝ Serve the dumplings in the steamer basket or transfer to a plate. Accompany with soy sauce, mustard, or chile sauce in small dishes for dipping.

makes 24

Southern

Huntun Tang

wonton soup

It is typical of Cantonese chefs to bring creativity and invention to even the simplest dish. Wontons are no exception. With deft fingers, chefs can convincingly replicate the shapes of aquarium fish, with flowing tail fins, to showcase their skills and impress diners. Wontons lead a double life. As a snack or first course in a clear soup they are a satisfying favorite. Slide them into hot oil, and they emerge as golden, crunchy hors d'oeuvres that beg a hearty appetite and a sweet-and-sour sauce dip.

The Chinese believe in the rejuvenative qualities of freshly made chicken soup. With its nutritious soup and tender wontons, this is the dish every Chinese mother turns to when nursing a sick child or an aged relative. A good homemade chicken stock is a vital ingredient in the Chinese kitchen, being the base of sauces for most stir-fries and noodle dishes, and for clay pots and hot pots, imparting flavor, richness, and goodness to them all.

WONTONS

¼ lb (125 g) diced pork, chicken, or shrimp (prawn) meat

1½ teaspoons peeled and grated fresh ginger

2 tablespoons chopped water chestnuts

1½ tablespoons chopped green (spring) onion, white part only

1 tablespoon chopped fresh cilantro (fresh coriander)

1 tablespoon light soy sauce

1 teaspoon rice wine (optional)

1 small egg

large pinch of salt

large pinch of ground white pepper

24 wonton wrappers

SOUP

2 or 3 dried black mushrooms, soaked in hot water to cover for 25 minutes and drained

6 cups (48 fl oz/1.5 l) chicken stock (page 250)

¾ cup (1¾ oz/50 g) small bok choy leaves

1½-inch (4-cm) piece carrot, peeled, thinly sliced lengthwise, and then finely julienned

1 green (spring) onion, tender green tops only, finely julienned

❀ To prepare the wontons, in a food processor, combine the pork, chicken, or shrimp and the ginger and process to a smooth paste. Add the water chestnuts, green onion, cilantro, soy sauce, rice wine (if using), egg, salt, and pepper and process again until a smooth paste forms.

❀ Working with 1 wonton wrapper at a time, place it on a work surface and moisten any 2 edges with cold water. Place 2–3 teaspoons of the filling in the center and fold over into a triangle. Press the edges firmly to seal, then fold the two outer points across the top of the mound and pinch the edges together. If they do not stick, moisten with a little water. Repeat until all the dumplings are filled.

❀ To prepare the soup, remove and discard the stems from the mushrooms if necessary and slice the caps. In a saucepan over medium heat, bring the stock to a boil. Add the bok choy leaves, carrot, and mushrooms and simmer for 2 minutes.

❀ Meanwhile, bring a saucepan three-fourths full of water to a boil over high heat. Add the wontons, reduce the heat to medium, and simmer gently until they float to the surface and the skins are tender, about 3 minutes. Using a wire skimmer, carefully lift out the wontons and divide evenly among warmed individual bowls.

❀ Divide the julienned green onion tops evenly among the bowls, and then ladle the soup over the wontons, again dividing evenly. Serve at once.

serves 4–6

China's best water chestnuts are harvested from the banks of the waterways that surround Guilin.

Western

Chun Bing

vegetarian spring rolls

Black "wood ear" fungus introduces an appealing crunchiness to the filling of these crisp, golden snack rolls.

FILLING

3 large dried black mushrooms, soaked in hot water to cover for 25 minutes and drained

1½-inch (4-cm) square dried black fungus, soaked in hot water to cover for 25 minutes and drained

¾ cup (2½ oz/75 g) finely julienned carrot

½ cup (1¾ oz/50 g) finely julienned celery

¼ cup (1¼ oz/40 g) finely julienned bamboo shoot

¾ cup (2 oz/60 g) finely sliced napa cabbage

¾ cup (1½ oz/45 g) bean sprouts

2 green (spring) onions, including tender green tops, cut into 1½-inch (4-cm) lengths and then julienned lengthwise

2 tablespoons hoisin sauce or oyster sauce

1 tablespoon tapioca starch or cornstarch (cornflour)

20 spring roll wrappers, each 5 inches (13 cm) square

vegetable or peanut oil for deep-frying

Sweet-and-Sour Sauce (page 108) or light soy sauce

To prepare the filling, remove and discard the stems from the mushrooms and the woody parts from the fungus if necessary. Finely slice the mushroom caps and fungus. Set aside.

Bring a saucepan three-fourths full of water to a boil, add the carrot and celery, and blanch for 1½ minutes. Using a wire skimmer, lift out the vegetables and drain well. Add the bamboo shoot, cabbage, bean sprouts, and green onions to the same boiling water, blanch for 1 minute, and drain well.

In a bowl, combine all the well-drained vegetables and the hoisin or oyster sauce. Mix well, then stir in the tapioca starch or cornstarch to absorb any excess liquid.

❦ To assemble each spring roll, place a wrapper on a clean work surface, with one corner pointing toward you. Place about 2 tablespoons of the filling in the center of the wrapper and fold the point nearest you over the filling, tucking the end in and nudging the filling with your fingers to form the roll shape. Fold the 2 side edges in over the filling. Moisten the tip of the remaining flap with cold water and roll up, giving the spring roll a gentle squeeze to secure the end flap. The roll should be about 2½ inches (6 cm) long and ¾ inch (2 cm) in diameter. Repeat until all of the rolls are formed.

❦ Pour the oil to a depth of 2 inches (5 cm) into a wok or large, heavy saucepan, and heat to 325°F (165°C), or until a small cube of bread dropped into it begins to turn golden in 5–10 seconds. Slide in half of the rolls and fry, turning several times, until golden brown, 1½–2 minutes. Using a wire skimmer or slotted spoon, transfer to a rack placed over paper towels to drain. Fry the remaining rolls in the same way.

❦ Arrange the hot spring rolls on a platter and serve immediately with the Sweet-and-Sour Sauce or light soy sauce in small bowls for dipping.

makes 20

❦ To prepare the stock, rinse the chicken legs (drumsticks and thighs) under running cold water. In a saucepan over high heat, combine the chicken legs, ginger, and stock or water and bring to a boil over high heat. Reduce the heat to low and simmer gently, uncovered, skimming the surface as needed to remove froth, until the chicken is cooked, about 35 minutes.

❦ Meanwhile, in a small bowl, combine the sliced chicken breast, soy sauce, and rice wine and let marinate while the stock simmers.

❦ When the stock is ready, remove the chicken legs from the pan and reserve for another use.

❦ Add the marinated chicken breast to the simmering stock and simmer briefly until cooked through. Using a slotted spoon, lift out the chicken and divide evenly among warmed individual bowls. Divide the spinach leaves or pea shoots and the ginger, if using, among the bowls.

❦ Season the stock with salt and pepper, then pour through a fine-mesh sieve into the bowls, dividing it evenly. Serve at once.

serves 4–6

Southern

Qing Tang Ji Bocai

clear soup with chicken and spinach

This soup exemplifies the duality of yin (light and bland) and yang (dark and flavorsome).

STOCK

2 or 3 whole chicken legs

½-inch (12-mm) piece fresh ginger

6 cups (48 fl oz / 1.5 l) chicken stock (page 250), superior stock (page 251), or water

2 oz (60 g) chicken breast meat, thinly sliced

1 teaspoon light soy sauce

½ teaspoon rice wine

1½ oz (45 g) young, tender spinach leaves or pea shoots

1 tablespoon peeled and finely grated fresh ginger (optional)

salt and ground white pepper to taste

Ma Ti Niurou Gao

water chestnut and beef cakes

*Guilin's sweet, large, crisp water chestnuts are the
best in China. The poetic name for this dish
means "triumph and exultation."*

7 oz (220 g) ground (minced) lean beef

2 oz (60 g) ground (minced) fat pork such as
pork butt

2 tablespoons water

1 teaspoon peeled and grated fresh ginger

1 teaspoon garlic-chile sauce

1 tablespoon light soy sauce

½ teaspoon salt

½ cup (3 oz/90 g) finely chopped water chestnut

¼ cup (¾ oz/20 g) finely chopped green
(spring) onion, white part only

⅓ cup (1½ oz/45 g) cornstarch (cornflour) or
tapioca starch

vegetable oil for frying

ground white or Sichuan pepper to taste

light soy sauce or sweet chile sauce

☗ In a food processor, combine the beef, pork, and
water and process to a smooth paste. Add the ginger,
garlic-chile and soy sauces, and salt and process until
well mixed. Add the water chestnut and green onion
and pulse to mix them in without crushing them.

☗ Shape the mixture into about 16 small balls about
1¼ inches (3 cm) in diameter. Spread the cornstarch
or tapioca starch in a shallow bowl and coat the balls
evenly, tapping off the excess. Lightly press each ball
to flatten into a cake ½ inch (12 mm) thick. If time
allows, cover and chill for 1 hour before frying.

☗ Pour the vegetable oil to a depth of ¼ inch
(6 mm) into a shallow, wide pan, and place over
medium-high heat. When the oil is hot, add the
cakes, in batches, and fry until golden brown on the
first side, about 2½ minutes. Turn and cook on the
second side until golden brown, 1½–2 minutes
longer. Using a slotted spoon, transfer the cakes to
paper towels to drain for about 1 minute, then
arrange on a warmed serving plate.

☗ Sprinkle the cakes lightly with pepper. Serve hot
with soy sauce or sweet chile sauce for dipping.

makes about 16

Yumi Xierou Geng

creamy corn and crab soup

*The Empress Dowager Cixi (AD 1835–1908)
loved tiny steamed cornbreads. In central China,
corn kernels are stir-fried with chiles. Southern chefs
prefer miniature ears of young corn as visual elements
and crushed corn for creamy soups. In the far north,
it is a valued grain for thick, sustaining gruels to ward
off winter's fierce cold. Cornstarch is the thickener
in countless sauces and glazes.*

1 can (14½ oz/455 g) creamed corn

4 cups (32 fl oz/1 l) chicken stock (page 250)

1–2 teaspoons chicken stock powder

2 teaspoons light soy sauce

salt and ground white pepper to taste

2 tablespoons cornstarch (cornflour) dissolved in
⅓ cup (3 fl oz/80 ml) chicken stock (page 250)
or water

¼ lb (125 g) crabmeat

3 egg yolks or 2 whole eggs

2 tablespoons finely chopped green (spring) onion,
including tender green tops

Wonton wrapper garnish (page 246) (optional)

☗ In a saucepan over high heat, combine the
creamed corn, stock, chicken stock powder, and soy
sauce and bring to a boil. Season with salt and pepper. Stir in the cornstarch mixture, reduce the heat to
medium, and cook, stirring, until the soup thickens,
about 1½ minutes.

☗ Meanwhile, in a small bowl, combine the crabmeat and egg yolks or whole eggs, mixing well.

☗ Remove the soup from the heat, add the crabmeat
mixture, and let stand for 30 seconds, then slowly stir
into the soup. The eggs will form short strands.
Reheat gently if the egg has not set sufficiently or if
the soup has cooled too much to serve. Do not allow
to boil.

☗ Ladle the soup into warmed individual bowls and
garnish with the green onion, the fried wonton
wrappers, if using, and a dusting of pepper. Serve
immediately.

serves 6–8

Northern

Hai Zhepi Lengpan

seafood appetizer platter

Appetizers are delicious tastes to savor over drinks. They are designed to stimulate and tease the palate in readiness for the multicourse meal to follow. Small servings mean just a few bites each, and at an informal meal everyone uses chopsticks to reach the appetizer plates at the center of the table, or spins the lazy Susan until the plate of choice is within reach. The number of different appetizers served varies according to the budget and the occasion.

Using unusual ingredients is customary. The edible mantle of giant sea jellyfish dries into thin, semitransparent amber disks. Salty and tough as leather, they are sold presoftened to eliminate lengthy preparation.

JELLYFISH

2 oz (60 g) dried salted jellyfish

1½ teaspoons sesame oil

salt and ground white pepper to taste

3 fresh cilantro (fresh coriander) sprigs, cut into 2-inch (5-cm) lengths

2 thin slices fresh ginger, peeled and finely julienned

SQUID

3 oz (90 g) cleaned squid bodies (about 4½ oz/140 g before cleaning, page 249)

1½ teaspoons sesame oil

½ teaspoon chile oil

salt and ground white pepper to taste

2 pieces canned abalone, drained

oyster sauce

☸ To prepare the jellyfish, in a bowl, combine the jellyfish with cold water to cover and let stand for 1 hour. Drain, return to the bowl, add fresh water to cover, and let stand for another hour. Drain.

☸ Using a sharp knife, cut the jellyfish into fine strips. Place in a bowl, add warm water to cover, and let soak for 20 minutes. Drain, rinse with cold water, and then drain thoroughly. Return to the bowl, add the sesame oil, salt, and pepper, and mix well. Add the cilantro and ginger and mix well again.

☸ To prepare the squid, bring a saucepan filled with water to a boil, add the squid, and blanch for 20 seconds. Do not overcook or the squid will toughen. Drain in a colander and immediately place under running cold water to cool completely. Drain well again. Using the sharp knife, cut on the diagonal into paper-thin slices. Place in a bowl and add the sesame and chile oils, salt, and pepper. Toss well.

☸ To cut the abalone, one at a time, press each piece flat against a cutting board. Using the sharp knife or a cleaver, and working parallel to the cutting board, cut horizontally into paper-thin slices.

☸ To serve, arrange the jellyfish, squid, and abalone in separate piles on a platter. Serve at room temperature or very lightly chilled with oyster sauce in small dishes for dipping.

serves 6

Worry less and eat well and your heart will be preserved.

Tea

"First, warm the pot with boiling water and pour off. Next, add tea leaves, allowing about one teaspoon per person. Pour freshly boiled water onto the leaves. After thirty seconds, pour it off. Allow the dampened leaves to expand and release their flavor. Again, add freshly boiled water—preferably spring water—to the pot. Warm and rinse porcelain tea cups in a bowl of hot water and pass them around. Drink the first two pots quickly, simply for refreshment. It is not until the third lot of water has been added to the pot that the tea is just right."

This was my first lesson in Chinese tea making, more than twenty-five years ago. China was emerging from the stifling yoke of the Cultural Revolution, and I was a working guest at the showcase tea commune plantation at Yingteh, about a hundred miles (165 km) north of Guangzhou. Over six weeks I learned to identify tea varieties by aroma and taste, to select only the top three tender leaves of the tea sprigs for picking, and to understand the stages of the process that gives us China's three premier types of tea—green, black, and oolong.

Green tea (also called white, for its pale color) has the fresh flavor of a natural, unfermented tea. It is light and fragrant, and when fresh picked can be a strong stimulant. The leaves are gently fired in ovens to prevent fermenta-tion and to dry them. For China's finest *Longjing* (Dragon Well) tea, named after a spring near Hangzhou, each leaf is rolled by hand to ensure it is of the very highest quality. The delicately flavored green tea can be good enough to eat: in the Hangzhou specialty Stir-Fried Shrimp with *Longjing* Tea, plump, male, freshwater shrimp are stir-fried over a roaring flame, then quickly tossed with the freshest of morning picked, tender *Longjing* tea leaves. Less specialized, but internationally popular, is jasmine tea, made by infusing green tea leaves with the fragrance of whole jasmine flowers.

Black tea (*pu er*) (popularly called red after its amber-red color) is a mellow-tasting, dark-colored, fully fermented tea. Before drying, the leaves are spread on trays to wilt and ferment, which transforms their color and flavor. In Guangzhou, mellow black tea is the favored beverage with dim sum, and in warm weather it may be served at room temperature in drinking glasses.

Oolong is a distinctive, spicy-flavored, and intense green tea. After 70 percent fermenta-tion, the leaves are fired to dry them and cease the fermentation. Some of the best oolong grows in the high elevation tea plantations of Jiangxi. One of these, *Tie guan yin* (iron goddess of mercy) is a fragrant oolong, sometimes served extra-strong in thimble-sized cups.

Jinqian Xiabing

sesame shrimp toast "coins"

This festive hors d'oeuvre of shrimp toast,
shaped to resemble old Chinese coins, symbolizes
luck and prosperity.

7 oz (220 g) peeled and deveined shrimp
(prawns) (about 1 lb/500 g unpeeled)

1 teaspoon peeled and grated fresh ginger

1 tablespoon water

2 teaspoons light soy sauce

1 teaspoon rice wine

1 egg white

1 tablespoon cornstarch (cornflour)

½ teaspoon salt

6 large, thin slices white bread

24 small fresh cilantro (fresh coriander) leaves

2–3 tablespoons sesame seeds

vegetable or peanut oil for deep-frying
Sweet-and-Sour Sauce (page 108)

♨ In a food processor, combine the shrimp and ginger and process to a smooth paste. Add the water, soy sauce, rice wine, egg white, cornstarch, and salt and process until well mixed. Evenly spread the shrimp mixture over the bread slices.

♨ Using a round cookie cutter 1¾–2 inches (4.5–5 cm) in diameter, cut out 4 rounds from each bread slice. Place a cilantro leaf in the center of each round, and evenly sprinkle the still-visible shrimp mixture on each round with the sesame seeds, pressing them on lightly with your fingers.

♨ Pour the oil to a depth of 1½ inches (4 cm) into a wok, and heat to 350°F (180°C), or until a small cube of bread dropped into it begins to turn golden, about 10 seconds. Slide in 5 of the shrimp toasts, shrimp side down, and fry until golden, about 2 minutes. Using a slotted spoon, carefully flip the toasts over and fry briefly on the bread side until golden brown. Using the slotted spoon, transfer to a rack placed over paper towels to drain. Repeat until all the toasts are fried.

♨ Arrange the shrimp toasts, shrimp side up, in a single layer on a platter. Serve the toasts immediately with the sauce in small dishes for dipping.

makes 24

Northern

Jiaozi

steamed pork dumplings

You cannot travel through northeastern China without being tempted by these deliciously juicy dumplings. Each city has its own variation. In Kaifeng, cooks omit the onions. In Tianjin, the dough is thicker and puffier. In Beijing, the dumpling wraps are finer and more elaborately twisted at the top. In Shanghai, the steamer basket is lined with cabbage so its flavor mingles with the smell of the wet bamboo to give the spongy, pork-filled dumplings a unique taste.

Meat-filled dumplings and buns are one of China's most popular snack foods. Chinese New Year provides an excuse for families in the north to prepare huge trays of jiaozi to share with friends. Everyone lends a hand to fill the thin pastry with pork and cabbage, seasoned with pepper. Baozi are the large, meat-filled buns you may find stacked in steamers at street-side food markets just about anywhere in northern and western China, while in the south steamed cha shao bao—soft-textured white buns filled with sweetened red roast pork—are enjoyed.

Delicious vegetarian jiaozi are stuffed with soaked, drained, and finely chopped black fungus, grated bamboo shoot, chopped green (spring) onions, chopped cabbage, and mashed potato, taro, or diced bean curd. When seasoned with grated ginger, light soy sauce, and salt and white pepper, the result is exquisite.

DOUGH

2–2½ cups (10–12½ oz/315–390 g) all-purpose (plain) flour

1 tablespoon baking powder

⅔ cup (5 fl oz/150 ml) water

FILLING

7 oz (220 g) ground (minced) lean pork

1½ teaspoons peeled and grated fresh ginger

1½ tablespoons vegetable oil

2 tablespoons light soy sauce

about ½ cup (4 fl oz/125 ml) water

¾ cup (2 oz/60 g) finely chopped napa cabbage, plus 2 large whole leaves

¼ cup (¾ oz/20 g) finely chopped green (spring) onion, including tender green tops

1 tablespoon sesame oil

red vinegar or light soy sauce

♛ To prepare the dough, sift together 2 cups (10 oz/315 g) of the flour and the baking powder into a bowl. Make a well in the center and pour the water into the well. Using a large spoon, mix quickly to form a workable dough. It should be soft enough to work easily, but not so sticky that it will adhere to the work surface. Add additional flour if it is too moist until the correct texture is achieved. Turn it out onto a very lightly floured work surface and knead until firm and elastic, about 2 minutes. Cover with a damp kitchen towel and let rest while you make the filling.

♛ To prepare the filling, in a food processor, process the pork to a smooth paste. Add the ginger, vegetable oil, and soy sauce and mix well. Gradually add up to ½ cup (4 fl oz/125 ml) water 1 tablespoon at a time as needed to form a soft, moist filling. Add the chopped cabbage, green onion, and sesame oil and pulse until evenly mixed, but not puréed.

♛ Cut the dough into 1-inch (2.5-cm) pieces. On the floured board, lightly roll out each piece of dough into a round 3½ inches (9 cm) in diameter and ⅟₁₆ inch (2 mm) thick, making it slightly thinner at the edges. When all of the rounds are rolled out, cover them with a clean, dry cloth to keep them from drying out. You should have about 20 rounds.

♛ To form each dumpling, place a dough round in the palm of 1 hand and put a spoonful of the filling in the center of the dough round. Using 3 fingers of the other hand, gather the edge of the dough together in small pinch-pleats, bringing it together at the top so that it encloses the filling. Twist the dumpling into a point at the top. Gently tap the dumpling on the work surface so that it forms into a round shape.

♛ Bring water to a boil in the base of a steamer. Meanwhile, line bamboo steamer baskets or metal steamer racks with the whole cabbage leaves and top with the dumplings, leaving some space between them. Set the baskets or racks in the steamer, cover tightly, reduce the heat so the water continues to simmer steadily, and steam until the dumplings are slightly puffy and feel soft-firm to the touch, 7–9 minutes.

♛ Carefully remove the baskets or racks from the steamer. Serve the dumplings in the baskets, or transfer them from the metal racks to a plate. Serve at once with vinegar or soy sauce in small dishes alongside for dipping.

makes about 20

Soy Sauce

From humble beginnings as a cottage industry, to a multi-million dollar international revenue earner, the manufacture of soy sauce has spanned three millennia in the world's most populous country. Making soy sauce (*jiangyou*) is a relatively simple process. Yellow soybeans are cooked until tender, mashed, mixed with roasted wheat or barley flour, salted (and in some instances sugared), and packed into tubs to ferment, then brined and refermented with the *Lactobacillus* spp. bacteria. The first extraction, after about forty days, is a light amber brown, delicate in flavor, and pleasantly salty. Left to ferment further, the flavor and color develop in intensity, although the saltiness declines. Further processing involves the addition of sugar or caramelized sugar for dark-colored, glossy sauces in which sweet and salt flavors balance and complement, and of ingredients such as mushroom and shellfish, which further contribute to rich, complex flavors.

Use light soy sauce for flavor and saltiness in stir-fries and marinades and as a dip, and dark soy (some types of which are called mushroom soy) for richness and color in braised dishes (red cooking), spicy stir-fries, and dark sauces, and sweet thick soy where specified. Special dietary low-sodium and wheat-free soy sauces are now available.

Southern
Zheng Xiao Xia Lajiangyou
steamed shrimp with soy-chile dip

What great pleasure comes from a simple meal of cooked shellfish, salty fresh from the sea. The Chinese prefer the crustaceans to be served whole in the shell, making the eating a messy but enjoyable hands-on dining experience that calls for a plastic tablecloth and plenty of napkins. In many Chinese restaurants, a bowl of cold tea is brought to the table to serve as a finger bowl for rinsing sticky fingers once the last shrimp (prawn) is eaten.

Ask any Chinese from Hainan Island to Shanghai, and he or she will agree that soy-chile dip is the perfect partner for fresh steamed shrimp. For those who prefer extra chile zing, add chile oil rather than extra fresh chile. It increases flavor and heat, without muting the natural sea flavor of the shellfish.

18 large shrimp (prawns) in their shells, about 1½ lb (750 g) total weight

SOY-CHILE DIP
2½ tablespoons dark soy sauce

1½ tablespoons light soy sauce

2 tablespoons water

2 slices fresh ginger, each about ⅛ inch (3 mm) thick, peeled and very finely chopped

1 green (spring) onion, including tender green tops, very finely chopped

1 hot red or green chile, seeded and very thinly sliced

1½ tablespoons peanut or vegetable oil

☀ Rinse the shrimp but do not peel. Place in a bowl with ice water to cover. Leave for at least 10 minutes or for up to 1 hour to firm and crisp the flesh.

☀ To prepare the sauce, in a small bowl, lightly whisk together the dark and light soy sauces, water, ginger, green onion, chile, and oil. Pour into small serving dishes for dipping.

☀ Bring water to a boil in the base of a steamer. Place the shrimp in a steamer basket and set in the steamer. Cover tightly, reduce the heat so the water continues to simmer, and steam until pink-red and firm, 8–10 minutes. Remove from the steamer and tip onto a platter.

☀ Serve the shrimp at once with the dipping sauce.

serves 6–8

Northern

Gao Tang Yu Jiao

fish balls in soup

Traditional Chinese cooks achieve a silky texture for fish balls and meatballs by patiently grinding, kneading, and throwing the paste against the inside surface of a heavy bowl. They shape them by scooping up the mixture with a porcelain soup spoon.

FISH BALLS

7 oz (220 g) white fish fillet, cubed

1½ tablespoons finely chopped green (spring) onion, white part only

1 teaspoon peeled and grated fresh ginger

1 tablespoon water

1 teaspoon rice wine (optional)

1 egg white

¼ teaspoon baking powder

½ teaspoon salt

large pinch of ground white pepper

SOUP

4 cherry tomatoes

6 cups (48 fl oz/1.5 l) fish stock (page 250)

1 small bunch fresh cilantro (fresh coriander), trimmed to small sprigs

salt and ground white pepper to taste

☗ To prepare the fish balls, in a food processor, process the fish to a smooth paste. Add the green onion, ginger, water, rice wine, egg white, baking powder, salt, and pepper and process until very smooth and light, about 1 minute.

☗ To prepare the soup, remove the stem from each cherry tomato, cut the tomato in half, and, using a teaspoon, scoop out the seeds and soft flesh from each half and discard. Cut each half in half again.

☗ In a medium-large saucepan over high heat, bring the stock to a boil. Using a small spoon, drop spoonfuls of the fish mixture into the boiling stock and poach until they float to the surface and are cooked through, about 40 seconds. Using a slotted spoon, transfer the fish balls to warmed individual bowls, dividing them evenly. Add the prepared cherry tomatoes to the bowls, again dividing evenly, and some sprigs of cilantro.

☗ Season the stock with salt and pepper, then pour through a fine-mesh sieve into the bowls, dividing it evenly. Serve immediately.

serves 4–6

Southern

Zha Pangxie Qiu

deep-fried crab balls

When I am asked to name favorite Chinese dishes, I always include this one. Chefs in the eastern coastal province of Fujian have a knack for imparting unique flavors, due in large part to the use of the many types of citrus native to the region. They have a way of cooking goose that is incomparable, balancing its fattiness with the astringency of vinegar. In the same way, they use fresh and pickled limes to counter the richness of duck in their specialty, duckling simmered in lime juice. A sweet-tart sauce of pickled limes and sweetened soy sauce is perfect with this delicate snack.

DIPPING SAUCE

⅓ cup (2½ oz/75 g) rock sugar or firmly packed light brown sugar

½ cup (4 fl oz/125 ml) water

½ teaspoon tamarind concentrate or 2 tablespoons fresh lime juice

1½ tablespoons thick soy sauce

CRAB BALLS

7 oz (220 g) crabmeat

2½ oz (75 g) ground (minced) fat pork such as pork butt

⅓ cup (2 oz/60 g) finely chopped water chestnut

1 tablespoon chopped green (spring) onion, white part only

1 slice white bread, crusts removed and roughly chopped

1 egg white

1–2 tablespoons tapioca starch or cornstarch (cornflour)

½ teaspoon salt

½ teaspoon ground white pepper

sunflower or corn oil for deep-frying

To prepare the sauce, in a small saucepan over medium heat, combine the sugar and water, bring to a simmer, and simmer until the sugar melts and the syrup is golden brown and reduced by half, about 10 minutes. Add the tamarind or lime juice and soy sauce and stir to mix. Pour into small dishes and set aside.

To prepare the crab balls, in a food processor, combine the crabmeat and pork and process to form a smooth paste. Add the water chestnut, green onion, bread, egg white, 1 tablespoon of the tapioca starch or cornstarch, the salt, and the pepper and process until smooth. A soft, moist mixture may be difficult to roll but will result in light-textured balls. If it is too moist to form, add an extra 1 tablespoon tapioca starch or cornstarch.

Pour the oil to a depth of 2 inches (5 cm) into a wok, and heat to 375°F (190°C), or until a small cube of bread dropped into it colors within a few seconds. Using a tablespoon, scoop up balls of the crab mixture and carefully drop them into the oil. Do not crowd the pan. Fry, turning as needed to cook evenly, until golden brown, about 1½ minutes. Using a wire skimmer or slotted spoon, transfer to a rack placed over paper towels to drain. Repeat until all the crab mixture is cooked.

Arrange the crab balls on a serving plate and serve at once with the dipping sauce.

makes 18–20

Southern

Shengcai Bao

minced pork and sausage in lettuce cups

*In China, lettuce is not for salad. It is sliced
as a bed for marinated bean curd, crunchy fried
oysters and dumplings, or crispy-salty treats like
salt-and-pepper shrimp or quail. It is also crisp-fried
to serve the same purpose. It is quickly poached in
oily water to serve bathed in oyster sauce as a
vegetable, or dunked into the pot, along with noodles,
to flavor the soup in a tabletop steamboat meal.
The most common species of lettuce grown in China
is a small, sparsely leaved romaine. This dish, perhaps
more readily recognized in the West by its Cantonese
name,* sang choi bao, *literally "lettuce bun," uses
crisp iceberg lettuce to wrap a spicy filling of
minced pork or squab (pigeon).*

*To make a vegetarian version, substitute the
same amount of soft or firm bean curd or eggplant
(aubergine) for the pork, and a mixture of fried bean
curd and dried black mushrooms (first softened in
warm water to rehydrate) for the sausages.*

9 oz (280 g) ground (minced) fat pork such as
pork butt

1 tablespoon light soy sauce

3 Chinese sausages

2 tablespoons vegetable oil

½ celery stalk, finely chopped

2 teaspoons peeled and grated fresh ginger

½ teaspoon minced garlic

½ cup (2½ oz/75 g) finely chopped
bamboo shoot

½ cup (2¾ oz/80 g) finely chopped canned
straw or button (champignon) mushrooms

salt and ground white pepper to taste

1 tablespoon hoisin sauce, plus ½ cup
(4 fl oz/125 ml)

1 tablespoon dark soy sauce

3 green (spring) onions, including tender green
tops, very finely chopped

2 teaspoons cornstarch (cornflour) dissolved in
½ cup (4 fl oz/125 ml) chicken stock (page 250),
superior stock (page 251), or water

1½ tablespoons finely chopped fresh cilantro
(fresh coriander) (optional)

8 firm inner leaves iceberg lettuce, edges trimmed
to form cup shapes

In a bowl, combine the pork and light soy sauce, mixing well. Set aside to marinate while you prepare the sausages. Bring water to a simmer in a steamer base. Place the sausages on a heatproof plate in a steamer basket, place over the simmering water, cover, and steam until soft and plump, about 5 minutes. Remove from the steamer and let cool, then chop finely and set aside.

In a wok over high heat, warm the oil. Add the pork, celery, ginger, and garlic and stir-fry until the pork changes color, about 1 minute. As the pork cooks, use the wok spatula to break up any lumps. Add the sausage, bamboo shoot, and mushrooms and stir-fry until the meat and celery are cooked, about 40 seconds. Season with the salt and pepper, 1 tablespoon hoisin sauce, and the dark soy sauce and add the green onions and the cornstarch mixture. Cook, stirring constantly, until thickened, 20–30 seconds longer. Add the cilantro, mix well, and transfer to a serving bowl.

To serve, divide the ½ cup (4 fl oz/125 ml) hoisin sauce among a few small sauce dishes. Place the lettuce cups on a platter. At the table, spoon an equal amount of the hot filling into each lettuce cup. Guests add their own hoisin sauce to taste, fold the lettuce around the filling, and eat out of hand.

makes 8

*A skilled Chinese chef
can mince meat in
minutes, using a sharp
cleaver in each hand.*

Northern

Doufu Jiangyou Xiangcai

"silk" bean curd with soy sauce
and cilantro

On one of my midsummer visits to Shanghai, my
hostess served this deliciously cooling appetizer using
the freshest silk bean curd. She sometimes tops the
same dish with minced, pickled cabbage. No cooking
is needed, but careful handling of the fragile doufu is
essential. Offer your guests spoons.

Cold appetizer dishes are prominent in
Chinese cuisine and are often made with unusual
combinations of ingredients and seasonings. Crunchy
jellyfish is a good case in point, as is blanched white
fungus, which has a subdued mushroom taste and
jellylike texture. I recently discovered immature lotus
roots, and now use these in cold appetizer dishes
instead of heart of palm.

1 lb (500 g) fresh soft bean curd
1½ cups (3 oz/90 g) finely sliced
iceberg lettuce

3 tablespoons light soy sauce
1½ tablespoons water
1 teaspoon superfine (caster) sugar, or to taste
1 tablespoon sesame oil
2 teaspoons very finely chopped green (spring)
onion, including tender green tops
1½–2 tablespoons finely chopped fresh cilantro
(fresh coriander)

☙ Carefully remove the bean curd from its container, set on a flat plate, and rinse under running
cold water. Drain well. Cut the bean curd into slices
1½ inches (4 cm) square and ⅓ inch (9 mm) thick.
Spread the lettuce on a serving platter and arrange
the bean curd on top.

☙ In a small bowl, whisk together the soy sauce,
water, and sugar until the sugar is dissolved. Add the
sesame oil and green onion and mix well.

☙ Spoon the soy mixture evenly over the bean
curd, and scatter the cilantro over the top. Serve at
room temperature or lightly chilled.

serves 2–4

Babao Sucai Tang

eight treasures vegetarian soup

"Eight treasures" describes dishes featuring many (not always eight) special ingredients. In the case of sweet dishes these might include lotus seeds and gingko nuts, red dates, almonds, candied (glacé) fruits, and sweetened red beans. Savory dishes might bring together lotus root, rare special mushrooms, exotic seafoods and meats, and dried lily flowers. The latter, known as shannai, are the dried, golden flower buds of the Easter lily, with a delicate flavor and slight bitterness. Sold in packs, they should be stored in a cool, dry place. For quick-cooked dishes, lily flowers are soaked before use, and may be tied in a knot as a symbol of unity.

A winter melon looks just like a watermelon. But cut it open and in place of a juice-dripping sweet red center you will find a fine-textured, pale green, mildly flavored flesh. In the traditional Chinese yin and yang arrangement of the vegetable world, this makes the winter melon one of the coolest of all vegetables. It is especially appreciated in soups and steamed dishes where it absorbs the flavors of other ingredients. For a banquet, eight treasures soup is sometimes served in the decoratively carved shell of a large melon. Poached in chicken stock with the famed salty ham of Yunnan, the sliced melon becomes a banquet dish of distinction. Candied winter melon is a favorite sweet in the New Year gift box.

2 cups (9 oz/280 g) cubed, peeled winter melon (½-inch/12-mm cubes; about 14 oz/440 g unpeeled)

¼ cup (1½ oz/45 g) cubed carrot (½-inch/12-mm cubes)

¼ cup (1¼ oz/40 g) cubed bamboo shoot (½-inch/12-mm cubes)

¼ cup (1½ oz/45 g) raw peanuts or ginkgo nuts

⅓ cup (2 oz/60 g) cubed zucchini (courgette) (½-inch/12-mm cubes)

⅓ cup (2½ oz/75 g) canned small straw mushrooms

10 dried lily flowers, chopped (optional)

4-inch (10-cm) piece dried bean curd stick, soaked in hot water to cover for 2 minutes, drained, and cut into small pieces

1 teaspoon peeled and grated fresh ginger

1 teaspoon salt, plus salt to taste

1 tablespoon light soy sauce

6 cups (48 fl oz/1.5 l) hot water or heated chicken stock (page 250) or vegetable stock (page 251)

½ cup (3½ oz/105 g) cubed fresh soft bean curd (½-inch/12-mm cubes)

¼ cup (¾ oz/20 g) sliced green (spring) onion, including tender green tops

1 tablespoon cornstarch (cornflour) dissolved in 1 tablespoon water

ground white pepper to taste (optional)

♛ In a saucepan, combine the winter melon, carrot, bamboo shoot, peanuts or ginkgo nuts, zucchini, mushrooms, lily flowers, bean curd stick, ginger, 1 teaspoon salt, and soy sauce. Pour in the hot water or stock, place over medium–high heat, and bring slowly to a boil, stirring occasionally. Reduce the heat to medium and simmer gently, uncovered, until the vegetables are tender, about 15 minutes.

♛ Add the cubed bean curd and green onion, then taste and adjust the seasoning with salt. Stir in the cornstarch mixture and boil gently, stirring slowly, until the soup thickens only very lightly, about 1½ minutes.

♛ Tip into a deep serving bowl, season with pepper, and serve immediately.

serves 4–8

Northern

Suanni Bairou

cold sliced pork with garlic sauce

A skilled Chinese chef can make the metaphorical silk purse from a sow's ear. What could be more basic than boiled pork? Yet a spicy garlic sauce can make it taste sublime. Bean sprouts marinated in rice vinegar would be a compatible appetizer to serve with this dish, which was one of thirty cold dishes served at a banquet I attended in Beijing in the mid-1980s, in celebration of the food of the Tang dynasty (AD 618–907).

PORK

1 lb (500 g) pork rump with skin intact or rolled and tied boneless pork loin or shoulder

1 green (spring) onion, trimmed

3 slices fresh ginger, each ¼ inch (6 mm) thick

1 tablespoon salt

1 small piece cassia bark, or ½ cinnamon stick

2 or 3 points from 1 star anise

½ teaspoon white peppercorns

GARLIC SAUCE

1½ tablespoons finely chopped garlic

3 tablespoons light soy sauce

1 tablespoon black vinegar

1 tablespoon sesame oil

½–2 teaspoons chile oil

2 teaspoons superfine (caster) sugar or dark brown sugar

1–3 tablespoons pork stock (page 251)

⚜ To prepare the pork, place it in a colander in the sink. Bring a kettle filled with water to a boil, and pour the boiling water over the pork. Place the colander under running cold water until the pork is cool.

⚜ Transfer the pork to a saucepan in which it fits snugly. Add the green onion, ginger, salt, cassia bark or cinnamon, star anise, peppercorns, and water to cover. Bring to a boil over high heat, reduce the heat to medium-low, cover, and simmer, skimming the surface from time to time to remove any froth, until the pork is done, about 30 minutes. To check the pork, pierce it with a thin skewer; the juices should run clear. With 2 slotted spoons, lift the pork onto a plate, cover loosely with aluminum foil, and set aside until cooled to room temperature, 30–60 minutes.

⚜ To prepare the sauce, in a small bowl, whisk together the garlic, soy sauce, vinegar, sesame oil, chile oil to taste, and sugar until the sugar is dissolved. Adjust the intensity of the sauce by adding pork stock to taste.

⚜ Using a sharp, thin-bladed knife, very thinly slice the pork against the grain. Overlap the pork slices on a platter and spoon on the garlic sauce. Serve at room temperature.

serves 4–8

Northern

Baicai Doufu Tang

cabbage and bean curd soup

Various brine- and chile-pickled cabbages, radishes, rutabagas, leeks, and mustard greens are a mainstay of the winter diet in the remoter parts of China.

6 cups (48 fl oz/1.5 l) chicken stock (page 250), vegetable stock (page 251), or water

¼ lb (125 g) napa cabbage, white, fleshy stem portion thinly sliced and pale green tops roughly chopped

⅓ cup (2 oz/60 g) undrained, canned chopped pickled cabbage

1½ teaspoons peeled and grated fresh ginger

1½ cups (10½ oz/330 g) diced fresh soft bean curd

salt and ground white pepper to taste

⚜ In a saucepan over high heat, combine the stock or water, the napa cabbage stems, the pickled cabbage, and the ginger. Bring to a boil, reduce the heat to medium-low, and simmer, uncovered, for about 8 minutes to extract the flavor of the pickled cabbage. Add the chopped cabbage leaves and the bean curd and heat until the cabbage wilts and the bean curd is heated through, about 1 minute. Season with salt and pepper.

⚜ Ladle into warmed individual bowls and serve immediately.

serves 6–8

Western

Sucai Lengpan

vegetarian appetizer platter

Dried mushrooms to honor the guests, spicy cucumber to whet the appetite, and peanuts to absorb the wine: this is a typical appetizer for a spicy Sichuan banquet or a full vegetarian dinner.

Formal dinners call for stylized platters, symbolic of the occasion. The ingredients are artistically shaped to depict the mythical phoenix for good fortune, the peacock for business success, the pine and the crane for longevity. The five-clawed dragon of myth and legend offers congratulations, and expresses good luck and happiness.

Appetizers are served to impress the eye as well as stimulate the taste buds. So creating an appetizer platter encourages a chef's artistic flair and imagination. Strips of seaweed and black moss become miniature tree trunks, and cucumber skin is carved into fringes of pine needles. Sliced black mushrooms and sliced boiled quail eggs can emulate the elegant tail feathers of a majestic peacock, sliced melon the scales of a dragon. The expert can sculpt carrots into peonies, onions into chrysanthemums, or tomatoes into roses, to bloom beside the meticulously positioned tidbits on an appetizer plate.

MARINATED MUSHROOMS

6 large dried black mushrooms

1 teaspoon salt

1 tablespoon rice wine

1 tablespoon light soy sauce

1 teaspoon sesame oil

1 teaspoon superfine (caster) sugar

1 teaspoon peeled and grated fresh ginger

BOILED PEANUTS

1 cup (5 oz / 155 g) raw peanuts

2 teaspoons salt

SPICY CUCUMBERS

2 English (hothouse) cucumbers, about 9 oz (280 g) total weight

salt for sprinkling

1½ tablespoons rice vinegar

1½ tablespoons water

1 tablespoon superfine (caster) sugar

½ teaspoon crushed garlic

1 small, hot red chile, seeded and finely julienned (optional)

⚜ To prepare the mushrooms, place them in a saucepan with water to cover and the salt. Bring to a boil over high heat, cover, reduce the heat to low, and simmer gently until plump and soft, about 20 minutes. Remove from the heat and allow the mushrooms to cool in the water. Drain well, trim off and discard the stems if necessary, and finely slice the caps. In a small bowl, combine the rice wine, soy sauce, sesame oil, sugar, and ginger and stir until the sugar is dissolved. Add the mushrooms, mix well, and set aside to marinate while you prepare the peanuts and cucumber. Drain the mushrooms just before serving.

⚜ To prepare the peanuts, place them in a small saucepan with water to cover and the salt. Bring to a boil over high heat, reduce the heat to low, and simmer, uncovered, for 10 minutes. Remove from the heat and allow the peanuts to cool in the water. Drain well and set aside.

⚜ To prepare the cucumbers, cut each cucumber lengthwise into slices ⅓ inch (9 mm) thick, then cut the slices into sticks 2 inches (5 cm) long and ⅓ inch (9 mm) wide. Place the cucumber sticks in a colander and sprinkle generously with salt. Let stand for 15 minutes, then gently knead with your fingers to rub the salt into the sticks. Rinse lightly under running cold water.

⚜ In a bowl large enough to hold the cucumber, stir together the vinegar, water, and sugar until the sugar is dissolved. Add the garlic and cucumber, toss to mix, and marinate for 20 minutes, turning frequently. Add the chile, if using, and taste and adjust the seasoning with salt.

⚜ To serve, arrange the drained mushrooms, the peanuts, and the cucumbers in separate mounds on a platter. Serve at room temperature.

serves 4–8

The Chinese chef must be a cook, a poet, and an artist.

Northern

Beijing Kaoya Labaicai

roast duck with hot-and-sour cabbage

At home in Hong Kong I could never pass a roast meat shop without making a purchase. Perhaps just a few strips of red pork to nibble on the way home, a string of crisply roasted rice birds (tiny sparrows that feed in the fields of ripening rice) to serve with pickled leeks, or barbecued pork with bubbling crackled skin to slice into soup for a quick snack.

There is an art to roasting in the Chinese way that is irresistible. Perhaps it is the startling redness of some of the products that first captures your attention. And the smell! You can't ignore the tantalizing aromas that waft out from a roast meat shop. Why try to resist them?

When the mood took me, and it often did, I would buy a freshly roasted duck and pancakes. With some hoisin sauce and a bunch of green (spring) onions or a tender young cucumber, I had the makings of a Peking duck meal. I would warm the duck in a hot oven, and the pancakes in a steamer, then pare the amber duck skin and tender meat into fine slices.

Family and guests assembled their own pancake rolls. Leftover meat was stir-fried with bean sprouts, while the bones bubbled in a soup. The crisp-skin duck recipe (page 95) gives a simplified alternative to classic roast duck.

HOT-AND-SOUR CABBAGE

10 oz (315 g) napa cabbage

boiling water to cover, plus 2 tablespoons

2 teaspoons salt

1½ teaspoons superfine (caster) sugar

3 tablespoons rice vinegar

1 hot red chile, seeded and thinly sliced

1 tablespoon vegetable oil

1 tablespoon sesame oil

1 teaspoon chile oil (optional)

½ teaspoon Sichuan peppercorns, lightly crushed (optional)

2 green (spring) onions, white part only, for onion curls, or fresh cilantro (fresh coriander) sprigs

½ roast duck

To prepare the cabbage, cut the pale green leaves from their white stems. Cut the leaves into 1½-inch (4-cm) squares, and thinly slice the stems. Place all the cabbage in a heatproof bowl and add boiling water to cover. Let stand for 3 minutes, then drain in a colander and return to the bowl.

In a small bowl, stir together the salt, sugar, vinegar, and the 2 tablespoons boiling water until the sugar and salt are dissolved. Add the chile and pour the mixture over the cabbage. Mix well.

In a small saucepan over low heat, gently warm the vegetable and sesame oils, and the chile oil and peppercorns, if using. Pour over the cabbage and mix well. Cover and marinate for at least several hours at room temperature or for up to 4 days in the refrigerator.

If preparing onion curls, trim off the root ends from the green onions. Using a needle, a straight pin, or the tip of a small, sharp knife, shred one end of each onion, leaving a ½-inch (12-mm) base at the opposite end unshredded. Place in a bowl of ice water in the refrigerator for at least 1 hour; the shredded ends will curl.

Just before serving, remove the breast meat from the duck half and cut it into strips. Bone the remaining duck and cut or tear the meat into strips. The duck meat can be served at room temperature, or warmed in a steamer over gently simmering water for 3–4 minutes.

To serve, mound the cabbage in the center of a platter. Drape the sliced duck over the cabbage. Garnish with the onion curls or cilantro.

serves 6–8

In a sensual sixteenth-century novel, the courtesan Golden Lotus feasts on ducks' webs cured in rice wine lees.

Ducks

Barely a thirty-minute drive from the outskirts of Beijing are the huge duck farms that supply the city's famous Peking duck restaurants. Over just seventy days, thousands of ducks make the transition from fluffy golden ducklings, born and nurtured in heat-controlled indoor runs, to robust birds fast-fattened to their optimum saleable weight of 4½ Chinese katties (6 pounds/3 kg).

Over ten thousand ducks are roasted each week by a process perfected over three hundred years ago and refined in the nineteenth century for the gourmet Empress Dowager Cixi. The ducks are cleaned, plucked, and washed. Compressed air forced between skin and meat ensures crisp, dry skin, and a glaze of liquid malt sugar seals the pores, further adding to the crispness. They are then hung to dry. In some restaurants the cavity is filled with water to ensure the meat will be gently steam-cooked from the inside when the ducks are roasted over flickering fires of fruit wood.

Beijing kaoya wancan, the multicourse duck dinner, is an experience not to be missed on a visit to Beijing. The duck skin, carved separately, is served first, wrapped in soft, wheat-flour pancakes with hoisin sauce and green (spring) onions. The breast and leg meat can be served the same way or in a stir-fry. Then the carcass is cooked as a milky soup.

Western

Suan La Tang

hot-and-sour soup

This fiery soup, with its ebullient flavors, is on so many Beijing restaurant menus you'd think it was invented in the capital. But Sichuan stakes its claim to the tart and peppery dish, which can be a showcase for exotic ingredients like gelatinous sea cucumber and fish maw, tender bamboo shoots, wobbly cubes of jellied duck's blood, slippery-crunchy straw mushrooms, and various other fungi. Less esoteric family versions feature bean curd, egg shreds, chicken, and pork. Sichuan cuisine uses combinations of three or four, and as many as seven or eight, seasonings to achieve unique flavors. Here we have salty (soy), tart (vinegar), piquant (chile), aromatic (sesame), and pungent (ginger).

The Chinese regard soup as part of the main meal, not as the starter. Only a soup made from expensive and rare ingredients would be served early in the meal, as a prominent dish. But even this would usually be preceded by small plates of cold appetizers. At home, a thick soup like this one or a hearty noodle soup might be served as a one-dish meal, or perhaps accompany a simple dish of plain grilled pork chops or fried chicken served over rice or noodles. When dining in company, soups are served at intervals between main courses, to provide textural and flavor contrast, and to cleanse the palate in preparation for the main dishes still to come. Snake soup, enjoyed throughout southern China in the cooler months, is a robust and warming thick soup like this one, and snake catchers are kept busy supplying restaurants with live reptiles to satisfy demand for the popular treat. Diced bean curd and the jellied ingredients peculiar to Sichuan, star in substantial winter soups as well. Bean jellies are produced in a similar way to bean curd, using mung bean flour, sweet potatoes, and indigenous kudzu root.

¼ lb (125 g) boneless chicken breast or pork meat, very thinly sliced, then finely julienned

2 teaspoons light soy sauce

1 teaspoon ginger juice (page 246) (optional)

1 cup (7 oz/220 g) cubed soft fresh bean curd (¼-inch/6-mm cubes)

5 dried black mushrooms, soaked in hot water to cover for 25 minutes

2-inch (5-cm) square dried black fungus, soaked in hot water to cover for 25 minutes

3 cups (24 fl oz/750 ml) chicken stock (page 250) or superior stock (page 251)

¼ cup (1 oz/30 g) thinly sliced bamboo shoot

1 teaspoon peeled and finely grated fresh ginger (optional)

1 tablespoon dark soy sauce

2 tablespoons black vinegar

1 tablespoon chile oil

1 teaspoon salt

1 teaspoon ground white pepper

2 tablespoons cornstarch (cornflour) dissolved in ⅓ cup (3 fl oz/80 ml) water

2 oz (60 g) squid bodies (about 2¾ oz/85 g before cleaning, page 249), very thinly sliced

1 egg, lightly beaten

2 teaspoons sesame oil (optional)

2–3 tablespoons chopped green (spring) onion tops or fresh cilantro (fresh coriander)

❀ In a bowl, combine the chicken or pork, light soy sauce, and the ginger juice, if using, and mix well. Set aside for 10 minutes. In a bowl, combine the bean curd cubes with cold water to cover and set aside.

❀ Drain the mushrooms and fungus, reserving 1 cup (8 fl oz/250 ml) of the soaking water. Pour the water through a fine-mesh sieve into a saucepan and set aside. Remove and discard the stems from the mushrooms and the woody parts from the fungus if necessary. Finely slice the mushroom caps and fungus and place in the saucepan holding the reserved soaking water. Add the stock, bamboo shoot, chicken or pork, ginger (if using), dark soy sauce, vinegar, chile oil, salt, and pepper.

❀ Place the pan over medium-high heat and bring just to a boil. Reduce the heat to medium and simmer for 1–2 minutes. Stir in the cornstarch mixture and continue to simmer, stirring slowly, until the soup thickens slightly, about 1½ minutes.

❀ Drain the bean curd and add to the soup along with the squid. Cook gently until the bean curd is heated through, about 1 minute.

❀ Pour the egg into the soup in a thin, steady stream and immediately remove the pan from the heat. Let stand for about 20 seconds to allow the egg to set in fine strands, then stir lightly.

❀ Taste and adjust the seasoning with salt and white pepper. Transfer to a deep serving bowl and add the sesame oil, if using, and the green onion or cilantro. Serve immediately.

serves 4–8

Western

Zhang Cha Anchun

tea-smoked quail

In the poultry section of a Chinese fresh food market, twittering live quail in cages are nearly always part of the inventory. But not all are destined for the kitchen. Many of these tiny, gray-speckled birds become children's pets, ideal for the confines of inner-city living. The Chinese love for quail, on the plate or in a cage, is a blessing, as it saves much-needed crops from being consumed by the bevies of the birds that descend on the ripened fields of wheat and rice at harvesttime.

Quail have the most delicate flavor of all game birds, yet it is emphatic enough to match with strong flavors like chile and garlic (see page 135), and Chinese bean sauce. They also respond beautifully to smoking. In one Beijing dish, smoke imparts a fragrant, golden brown skin to tender, steamed chicken, and Sichuanese chefs localize that recipe for the ubiquitous quail from their rice fields, using full-flavored tea and fragrant chenpi (tangerine peel) from the region's plantations to serve as smoke fuel.

I have twice eaten a fascinating quail dish, cooked by the method of double boiling. A quail is placed in a small lidded pot with the Chinese rejuvenative herb dang gui, then slow-cooked in a steamer to infuse the quail with the potent flavor of the herb.

QUAIL

3 quail

1 teaspoon rice wine

1 teaspoon salt, plus salt to taste

1 tablespoon vegetable oil

3 tablespoons tea leaves such as black, jasmine, litchi, or Lapsang souchong

5 pieces dried tangerine peel, each about ¾ inch (2 cm) square (optional)

1½ tablespoons superfine (caster) sugar

2 teaspoons sesame oil

CHIVES

2–3 teaspoons vegetable oil

1 small bunch flowering chives or garlic chives, cut into 1½-inch (4-cm) pieces

1 tablespoon sesame oil

2 teaspoons light soy sauce

To prepare the quail, rinse and dry the birds. Cut off the necks and wing tips, then split each quail in half along the breastbone. In a large, shallow bowl, stir together the wine, 1 teaspoon salt, and vegetable oil. Add the quail halves and turn in the mixture, rubbing the birds with your fingers to coat evenly. Leave for 20 minutes, turning twice.

Bring water to a boil in the base of a steamer. Set the quail on the metal steamer rack, cover tightly, reduce the heat so the water continues to simmer, and steam for 5 minutes. Remove the quail on the rack and place the rack over a plate or bowl to drain.

Line a large, heavy saucepan or wok with a double thickness of aluminum foil. Place the tea leaves, tangerine peel (if using), and sugar on the foil in the bottom of the pan and set over medium heat. Place the quail on the rack in the pan. Cover the pan (you also may want to line the lid with aluminum foil to prevent discoloration) and smoke-cook until golden brown, about 12 minutes. Remove the quail from the rack and brush them with the sesame oil. Sprinkle lightly with salt.

To prepare the chives, in a wok, warm the vegetable oil over high heat. When hot, add the chives and stir-fry until they begin to wilt, about 20 seconds. Add the sesame oil and soy sauce and continue to stir-fry until softened, about 20 seconds longer.

Spread the chives on a platter and arrange the quail on top. Serve at once.

serves 6

Traditionally, quail are offered to the gods in the eleventh month of the lunar calendar.

The Chinese Art of Smoking

The carving of camphor-wood chests is a respected craft in China. It yields waste chips and shavings of fragrant wood that, in a smoker, impart a rich golden amber coloring and intense, yet delicate, flavor. Delectable camphor- and tea-smoked duck is now an international signature dish of Sichuan cuisine.

Smoking is an ancient cooking method and references to it are dotted throughout Chinese literature. The acclaimed Qing dynasty author Cao Xueqin (AD 1715–63) wrote on the sensuality of food, particularly citing cypress-smoked Siamese suckling pig. In that same era, pork marinated in wine and garlic was smoked over smoldering bamboo and stored, rather like a confit, in pickling jars. Tang dynasty connoisseurs raved about the black, smoked apricots of Hubei, as the Fujianese now do about silver pomfret smoked amber over black tea leaves and crushed rock sugar.

Smoking in the home kitchen is easy, with a heavy wok, a rack, and a fitted lid. Black tea leaves, fragrant green tea, and wood shavings are the smoke fuel, with extra flavor deriving from crystal sugar, tangerine peel, and whole spices. Small items cook as they smoke; large fish or poultry are steamed first. Set them on the rack, cover tightly, and let the smoke perform its magic.

Western

Siche Bai Ji Sela

hand-shredded white chicken salad

To prepare this white chicken dish is to understand the underlying philosophy of Chinese cooking. This unique method of steeping chicken, created centuries ago in the imperial kitchens, ensures supreme tenderness and accentuates its subtle, natural flavors. It is the base for numerous appetizer dishes, and in some recipes it is quickly deep-fried to brown and crisp the skin.

CHICKEN

1 chicken, about 3 lb (1.5 kg)

2 green (spring) onions, including tender green tops, finely chopped

2 tablespoons peeled and grated fresh ginger

1 tablespoon rice wine

1 tablespoon light soy sauce

1 tablespoon salt

about 5 qt (5 l) water

1 tray ice cubes

1 tablespoon chicken stock powder (optional)

4 or 5 slices fresh ginger

1 green (spring) onion, trimmed and chopped

¼ cup (2 fl oz/60 ml) rice wine

SALAD

1 cup (3 oz/90 g) finely julienned cucumber

1 cup (3 oz/90 g) finely julienned carrot

1 teaspoon salt

1 teaspoon superfine (caster) sugar

1 tablespoon rice vinegar

DRESSING

2 tablespoons sesame paste

¼ cup (2 fl oz/60 ml) water or chicken stock (page 250), or as needed

1 tablespoon light soy sauce

1 tablespoon fresh lemon juice

2 teaspoons sesame oil

salt and ground white or Sichuan pepper to taste

1–2 teaspoons peanut oil or sesame oil

3 or 4 small fresh cilantro (fresh coriander) sprigs

☙ Rinse the chicken and pat dry. Place the green onions, ginger, rice wine, soy sauce, and salt in the cavity. Cover and refrigerate the chicken for 1 hour.

☙ In a large pot over high heat, bring the water to a rolling boil. Loop a piece of kitchen string around the chicken wings and tie firmly, leaving a loop at the top large enough to provide a firm grip. Holding the loop, lower the chicken into the boiling water for 1 minute, then lift out. Repeat this dipping 4 times, then set the chicken in a colander to drain briefly. Skim the surface of the water of any froth.

☙ Fill a large bowl with water and add the ice cubes. Lower the chicken into the ice water and leave for 1 minute, then remove and drain. Reheat the water in the pot over high heat and add the stock powder, if using, the ginger slices, the chopped green onion, and the rice wine. Bring to a boil over high heat. Again lower the chicken into the hot liquid for 1 minute, and lift out. Repeat this 4 times, then submerge the chicken in the liquid and bring to a boil. Skim the surface of any froth.

☙ Remove the pot from the heat. Allow the chicken to remain in the hot liquid until the chicken feels firm, 25–30 minutes. To test for doneness, insert a thin skewer into the thickest part of the thigh; no pink juices should flow. Carefully lift out the chicken, holding a broad ladle or a wire skimmer under it for support. Drain the liquid from the cavity and place the chicken on a plate to cool. Do not attempt to shred the chicken for at least 20 minutes.

☙ Meanwhile, prepare the salad: In a bowl, combine the cucumber, carrot, salt, sugar, and vinegar. Using your fingers, knead and mash the sugar and salt into the vegetables to soften them partially, then let stand for 20 minutes. Drain just before serving.

☙ To prepare the dressing, in a small bowl, whisk together the sesame paste, ¼ cup (2 fl oz/60 ml) water or stock, soy sauce, lemon juice, sesame oil, salt, and pepper. Add additional water or stock if needed to make a creamy dressing.

☙ Remove either the whole breast or 2 whole legs (drumsticks and thighs) from the chicken. Reserve the remaining chicken for another use. Pull the chicken meat from its bones with your fingers, then tear the meat into bite-sized strips. Place the strips in a bowl, sprinkle with the peanut or sesame oil, and toss to coat evenly.

☙ To serve, mound the drained vegetables in the center of a platter. Drape the shredded chicken over the vegetables in an igloo shape. Drizzle the dressing over the chicken, scatter the cilantro over the top, and serve.

serves 4–8

MAIN COURSE DISHES

China's vast and ancient cuisine is as diverse as its people and their customs.

Preceding pages: Blue swimming crabs from the southern coast of China are eagerly desired by Hong Kong gourmets. **Top:** Temple rooftops in a village in western China display a centuries-old style. **Above:** A smiling street vendor proffers sticky rice–dough balls on skewers, a favorite snack. **Right:** A roast meat shop in Hong Kong offers red-glazed, roast suckling pig as one of its specialties.

WHEN I MOVED from a quiet bay-side village into a flat in Hong Kong's central district, smells and sounds were different— diesel taxi fumes instead of the smell of the sea, and an incessant tapping that ceased midafternoon and resumed again around five. One evening, busy preparing my own meal and chopping rapidly with my cleaver, I recognized the source of the noise— a hundred flying "choppers" in apartments all around me. When you take up Chinese cooking your cleaver becomes your most valued tool. With practice, there is practically no slicing, chopping, paring, and severing function it cannot do, and the speed of its tattoo on your chopping board tells of your growing competence.

The wok is an equally multifunctional utensil. It is a frying pan, deep-fryer, steamer, and sauté pan all in one. With a wok, rice cooker, clay pot, cleaver, and cutting board, you have a basic Chinese kitchen set up. While much cooking in China is still managed over wood fires, gas is set to become the national fuel, and it is ideally suited to wok cooking. Its readily adjustable heat gives

it the edge over electric cookers, particularly when stir-frying, which requires short bursts of intense heat.

The tradition of sharing from the communal plate is not founded on mere practicality or economy. It is sociable and extends the pleasure of eating to its fullest by giving each diner a taste of everything on the table. To be appreciated, Chinese meals must be balanced and contrasted in their various elements: in tastes and textures—sweet and sour, mild and hot, crunchy and smooth, chewy and tender—and in colors and forms. In a stir-fry, if the main ingredient is long and thin, then companion ingredients will be a similar shape. If diced chicken is the feature, other ingredients will be diced, and so on.

The concept of yin and yang originated at the beginning of the Zhou dynasty, in the 12th century BC. Yin is dark, yielding, feminine, wet, negative, and cool, while yang is bright, strong, masculine, dry, positive, and hot. This concept is applied to food, including the medicinal herbs used in cooking. Each ingredient is classified as cooling or heating: lettuce and celery are cooling, chiles are heating; fish is cool, red meat is hot. It is a fascinating precept worth further study.

Because most meals are shared affairs, it is difficult to recommend how many guests a dish will serve, or how many dishes should be prepared. At home a meal might be as simple as a single clay pot dish or stir-fry and a bowl of soup, served with rice or bread. Those same basic plates can be ordered at a neighborhood café or food stall. A restaurant meal has more scope and will depend on the budget and enthusiasm of the diners—there may be as many main dishes as there are guests at the table.

Freshness is paramount with the Chinese cook. Chefs and housewives visit their local markets daily. The marketplace is a hub of

Left: A teahouse is a popular afternoon destination for those with leisure time. **Top:** Shanghai's pavements are crowded with street cafés, busy at any time of the day or night. **Middle:** Fish heads are sold at the market for making stock and clay pot dishes. **Bottom:** The traditional mudbrick houses of Xilamuren reflect the stark colors of Inner Mongolia and the unadorned lifestyle of its people.

activity and, while the customers may appear sociable as they acknowledge familiar faces and chat with stall owners, the intent is serious: to procure the freshest fish or pork at the right price, vegetables picked that morning, not the remains of yesterday's stock, and whatever other culinary treasures their eagle eyes discover.

An estimated 70 percent of China's meat dishes contain pork. This sometimes bland, sometimes richly flavored meat is particularly revered in the south, where roast suckling pig is essential to any festive occasion. Every day, along China's snaking rail lines, trains speed cargoes of live pigs from vast piggeries to markets in Hong Kong and Guangdong, and to specialty restaurants further north.

In the north, the taste shifts. The Muslim preference for sheep and goat meat is far more evident in restaurant menus offering such enticements as mutton kabobs, tender stir-fried lamb with honey and cilantro, and the famous "rinsed lamb hot pot." This Chinese-style fondue uses lamb cut so thin it is said a good chef can produce a hundred slices from a pound (500 g) of meat. When the marauding Mongols were hungry during a campaign, they threw a battleshield over a fire, slaughtered a

sheep, and grilled the meat on the hot metal. During their dominance of the north of China (AD 1215–1368) this tradition was translated to the kitchen, using a ribbed iron grid, to become the Mongolian barbecue now enjoyed in many parts of the world.

Chicken and duck are consumed in vast quantities and with equal gusto. Chinese chefs have a way of preparing duck that accentuates its rich flavor and dense texture. The famed Peking duck is possibly one of the best-known

dishes in the world, and is a treat not to be missed on a visit to Beijing. Just a half hour's drive from the city you can visit the duck farms where the ducklings are bred under careful control. Fujian, on the east coast, also has a reputation for duck and goose dishes, and part of the secret is the use of local citrus and vinegar in the preparation. The camphor- and tea-smoked duck of Sichuan is a favorite of mine, and I borrow the smoking technique for quail and other poultry.

I could easily write a book of Chinese chicken recipes alone. It would be quite a tome, and many of the dishes would be from the southern and central regions. Sichuan cooks toss diced chicken in a hot wok with chile and peanuts, or shred it beneath a creamy sesame dressing. In Guilin I've had delicious salt-baked chicken and a challenging bowl of whole chicken steamed in stock with a spotted, red lizard! In China, chicken comes slow-simmered to gelatinous tenderness, succulent in a stir-fry, sublimely moist as "white cut," poached chicken, baked in a clay shell like the famous beggar's chicken of Hangzhou, served with rice and a salty shallot and oil sauce on Hainan Island, or crisp-skinned, roasted, or fried. Whichever way it was prepared, I cannot remember ever eating a badly cooked chicken dish in China.

All this might suggest that meat and poultry dominate Chinese cuisine. But fish and seafood are also highly regarded, perhaps

Left: Old men play a leisurely game of croquet in a square in Kunming. The British took control of nearby Burma (now Myanmar) in the mid-nineteenth century and their influence quickly spread north. **Below:** Nothing is wasted at a market; if they do not sell, fresh fish are salted and dried. **Bottom:** Carved into a horseshoe-shaped cliff face in Baoding, Sichuan, Buddhist preachers and sages surround a seated Buddha. Because Tibet and Sichuan share a border, Tibetan Buddhism is prevalent in these carvings.

even more so. The vast inland water complex of rivers, lakes, dams, and ponds provides an impressive variety of fish and shellfish, eels and turtles, and water-grown vegetables and edible mosses. Offshore, waters are abundant with deep-sea fish, shellfish, and peculiar sea creatures treasured by Chinese cooks and epicures, while estuaries supply shrimp (prawns) and crustaceans of many species. Those that are too small for the cook pot are dried and fermented into pungent shrimp paste.

Symbolism plays a significant role in the formal aspect of Chinese dining. The word for fish is *yu*, a homonym for abundance. So, to serve a whole fish is to offer guests your best wishes for abundance and prosperity. In Guangdong, a whole fish is served steamed with ginger, to highlight and intensify its fresh, natural flavor. The famous West Lake fish of Hangzhou is a dish that features a freshwater fish poached and served beneath a glossy coating, with the mild tang of rice vinegar. In Sichuan, a whole carp would be shallow-fried with a potent chile sauce, and in Beijing it would be deep-fried and bathed

in a complex, wine-based sauce. These seasoning preferences briefly show the cooking styles of the major regions of China: mild with the emphasis on natural flavors in the south; intense yet elegant for the eastern regions; fiery and pungent in Sichuan and the central west; and refined and well honed in the north.

I have never ceased to be awed by the invention of Chinese cooks when it comes to devising a palatable use for every ingredient. Nothing is too humble to be considered a potential star in the Chinese cooking pot. Even such peripheral ingredients as chicken feet, ducks' webs and tongues, pigs' ears and tails, beef tendons, and the skin and air bladders of fish are transformed into desirable dishes in the hands of these skillful innovators.

Below: China's longest river, the Changjiang (Yangtze), flows between the towering skyscrapers of Chongqing, deep in the heart of China. Ferry boats and fishermen now share the waterways. **Right:** A farmer allows his prized buffalo to graze among the rice paddies of southwest China.

Eastern

Bai Zhi Xian Bei Pang Xie

scallops and snow peas
with crabmeat sauce

I should not have been a guest at the Chinese wedding banquet in Hong Kong where I first encountered this delightful dish. As a non-Chinese-speaking journalist, I'd been invited to sample a hot pot dinner at a large restaurant. On arrival, a hostess whisked me into a private dining room and a banquet began. We were well into the dinner, with still neither sight nor mention of a hot pot, when I realized I must be in the wrong room. Mumbling apologies, I hurried out and headed for the next doorway. Inside, a flustered host had been keeping the guests and hot pot on hold. With eight courses already under my belt, to work through a ten-course hot pot banquet with enthusiasm was a serious digestive challenge. And throughout the meal, delicious as it was, my thoughts kept returning to the scallops in their creamy crabmeat sauce from the wedding banquet.

9 oz (280 g) sea scallops

½ teaspoon salt

2 teaspoons ginger wine (page 246)

CRABMEAT SAUCE

1 tablespoon vegetable oil

½ cup (2½ oz/75 g) crabmeat, flaked, or finely chopped shrimp (prawn) meat

2 green (spring) onions, white part only, chopped

2 teaspoons rice wine

1 teaspoon light soy sauce

1½ teaspoons cornstarch (cornflour) dissolved in ½ cup (4 fl oz/125 ml) fish stock (page 250), superior stock (page 251), or chicken stock (page 250)

salt and ground white pepper to taste

1 egg white, lightly beaten

2 tablespoons vegetable oil

3 oz (90 g) small snow peas (mangetouts), trimmed

2 oz (60 g) small fresh oyster mushrooms, brushed clean

5 thin fresh ginger slices, peeled and finely julienned

♛ Place the scallops in a bowl, add the salt and ginger wine, and mix gently. Let stand for 10 minutes.

♛ To prepare the sauce, in a small saucepan over high heat, warm the oil. When it is medium-hot, add the crabmeat or shrimp and green onion and stir until warmed through, about 30 seconds. Add the rice wine and soy sauce and stir briefly. Add the cornstarch mixture and stir slowly until the sauce thickens and becomes clear, about 40 seconds. Season with salt, if needed, and generously season with white pepper.

♛ Remove from the heat and slowly pour in the egg white in a fine stream. Allow to set without stirring, returning to low heat if the heat is insufficient to set the egg white.

♛ In a wok over high heat, warm the oil. Add the scallops and stir-fry for 30 seconds. Be sure the heat is as high as possible, or the juices will run from the scallops, making them tough and chewy. Add the snow peas and stir-fry briefly, then add the mushrooms and ginger and stir-fry until the scallops are firm and white, about 40 seconds longer.

♛ Add the sauce to the scallops and heat over high heat for about 20 seconds. Transfer to a serving plate and serve immediately.

serves 4

In ordinary life you must be economical, but when you are a host, your hospitality must be lavish.

Mongolia

The Mongolians are a tough, nomadic, sheep- and cattle-herding people who retain many of their old traditions. Their history of warmongering saw a Mongol emperor, Kublai Khan, installed in the imperial palace in Beijing during the thirteenth-century Yuan dynasty. The Great Wall of China was dramatically extended in the Ming dynasty, which followed, to keep the Mongols out of China. Mongolia can be credited with only one notable contribution to China's culinary traditions: the introduction of mutton and lamb. In the Yuan court, mutton was the staple food of the Mongol rulers, who had the kitchens altered to accommodate huge cauldrons for boiling sheep whole. This inelegant fare was carved at the table with the same sharp knives the Mongol warriors used on the battlefield, and was washed down with stupefying quantities of koumiss, an alcoholic beverage usually made from fermented mare's milk. Marco Polo described it as similar in color and quality to a good grape wine.

Today, Mongolian restaurants in the major northern cities feature many lamb dishes, including the famous three—*shuan yangrou*, the tabletop firepot in which thin-sliced lamb is swished to cook, the Mongolian barbecue of lamb cooked on a drum-style iron barbecue, and flaming lamb shashliks.

Northern

Mengu Zhima Yangrou

mongolian sesame lamb

In my earlier years in Hong Kong I was employed to promote New Zealand meat, and soon learned the Chinese had no great fondness for lamb. With fingers rapidly fanning beneath their noses, they pronounced it malodorous and unpalatable. Yet, during the cooler months, a potently flavored goat meat casserole was much sought after. It was originally a dish of the Hakka, an itinerant minority in the southern provinces. Goat and sheep share the same Chinese word, but obviously the association stops there. Lamb has historically found favor in China only with the nomadic people of the far north and west, and in the cuisine of resident Muslims. But times and tastes change, and lamb dishes have become an integral part of the dining experience in Beijing and other northern cities.

In the south, a lamb dish needs a gimmick, and the sizzling hot plate provides it. A cast-iron plate, of the kind used in steakhouse restaurants, is preheated in the oven. The stir-fry is half cooked, tipped onto the hot plate, and then brought to the table preceded by a theatrical crackle of sizzling sounds and wafts of enticing aromas, and followed by a drift of smoke. It is placed on a board to protect the table, and the diners swoop on it with chopsticks even before the sizzling has died down. The sizzling platter is not reserved for sesame lamb alone. Most other stir-fries could be served this way.

At a restaurant I rarely order sizzling dishes, as the taste does not always live up to the promise of the aroma. Whether you choose to serve this dish straight from the wok or on a sizzling hot plate, there is something about the combination of flavors, textures, and aromas that is irresistible.

MARINADE

¼ cup (2 fl oz / 60 ml) light soy sauce

1½ tablespoons hoisin sauce

1 tablespoon sesame oil

1 tablespoon rice wine

2 teaspoons cornstarch (cornflour)

1½ teaspoons superfine (caster) sugar or honey

½ teaspoon five-spice powder

1 lb (500 g) boneless lean lamb from leg or shoulder, sliced paper-thin, then cut into pieces 2 inches (5 cm) long by ¾ inch (2 cm) wide

1 tablespoon sesame seeds

2 tablespoons vegetable oil

1 tablespoon sesame oil

1 large yellow onion, cut into narrow wedges and the layers separated

⅓ cup (3 fl oz/80 ml) lamb stock, chicken stock (page 250), or water

1½ teaspoons cornstarch (cornflour) dissolved in 1 tablespoon water

ground Sichuan or white pepper to taste

finely julienned hot red or green chile to taste (optional)

To prepare the marinade, in a large, flat dish, stir together the soy sauce, hoisin sauce, sesame oil, rice wine, cornstarch, sugar or honey, and five-spice powder. Add the lamb and turn to coat evenly with the marinade. Cover and marinate for at least 30 minutes at room temperature or for up to overnight in the refrigerator.

Heat a dry wok over medium heat. Add the sesame seeds and toast briefly, stirring, until golden. Pour onto a small dish and set aside.

Add the vegetable and sesame oils to the wok and heat over high heat. When the oils are hot, add the onion and stir-fry until softened, about 3 minutes. Transfer to a plate.

Return the wok to high heat. When it is very hot, add the lamb and its marinade and stir-fry until cooked, about 1 minute. Using a slotted spoon, transfer the lamb to the plate holding the onion.

Pour the stock or water, and the cornstarch mixture into the wok and cook, stirring, until lightly thickened, about 1 minute. Return the lamb and onion to the pan, mix in lightly, and heat through. Season with pepper. Transfer to a warmed serving plate and sprinkle with the sesame seeds and the chile, if using.

To serve on a hot iron plate, preheat the iron pan in a 400°F (200°C) oven. Stir-fry the onion only until half cooked. Cook the lamb as directed and set aside separately from the onion. Cook the sauce as directed and return the lamb to it. To serve, remove the hot plate from the oven, spread the onion over it, and carry it to the table. Pour the lamb and sauce onto the plate at the table. Top with the sesame seeds and the chile, if using.

serves 2–4

Western

Guai Wei Ji

strange flavor chicken

The Sichuanese are expressive cooks who create ebullient flavors from robust seasoning and generous spicing. Names reflect the flavor characteristics of their dishes. "Strange flavor" denotes a dish in which sweet, sour, hot, salty, and spicy blend with no single flavor predominating.

A yu xiang sauce suggests hot and spicy, with undertones of sweet and sour, using garlic, ginger, hot bean sauce, or chile to achieve a sauce suited to the stronger-tasting meats, such as innards. Sesame products play a significant role in Sichuan cooking. The oil brings an appealing, nutty taste to sauces and marinades, and is added to frying oil as a flavor boost. Sesame paste makes a creamy contribution to dressings and dipping sauces, and is used in warm, sweet soups, while white and black sesame seeds add crunch and visual interest when used as garnishes or as coatings for fried foods and sweet pastries. Sichuan pepper, made from the tiny, red-brown berries of the prickly ash tree, is native to the central provinces of China and replaces the white or black pepper used in other parts of the country. It adds such an appealing flavor, as a condiment or seasoning, that it is easy to overlook the fact that too much can dangerously numb the lips and throat. Use with caution!

SAUCE

2 tablespoons very finely minced green (spring) onion, including tender green tops

1 tablespoon peeled and grated fresh ginger

1 tablespoon very finely chopped garlic

1 tablespoon sesame paste

2½ tablespoons light soy sauce

2 tablespoons water

5–6 teaspoons sesame oil

1 tablespoon red vinegar

1 tablespoon vegetable oil

2–3 teaspoons chile oil

2½ teaspoons superfine (caster) sugar

½ teaspoon ground Sichuan pepper (optional)

½ white-cut chicken (see Hand-Shredded White Chicken Salad, page 67) or 2 whole chicken legs

1 tablespoon light soy sauce

vegetable oil for deep-frying

First, prepare the sauce: In a bowl, using a whisk or fork, beat together the green onion, ginger, garlic, sesame paste, soy sauce, water, sesame oil, vinegar, vegetable and chile oil, sugar, and the pepper, if using, until a thin, creamy sauce forms. Set aside.

If using the white-cut chicken, brush with the soy sauce and leave uncovered, about 25 minutes, to dry.

If using the 2 uncooked whole chicken legs (drumsticks and thighs), bring water to a simmer in a steamer base. Place the chicken legs on a metal steamer rack, place over the simmering water, cover, and steam until tender, about 25 minutes. To test for doneness, insert a thin skewer into the thickest part of the thigh; no pink juices should flow. Remove from the steamer and allow to cool and dry for 5 minutes, then brush lightly with the soy sauce and leave uncovered, about 20 minutes, to dry and cool.

Pour the oil to a depth of 3 inches (7.5 cm) into a wok, and heat to 360°F (182°C), or until a small cube of bread dropped into it begins to turn golden within a few seconds. Carefully slide the chicken half or the chicken legs into the hot oil and fry until the skin is amber and glossy, about 2 minutes. Carefully lift out the chicken, using a broad ladle or a wire skimmer underneath for support and holding it over the pan for a moment to drain. Leave to cool for at least 5 minutes. The chicken is best when served just slightly warmer than room temperature.

Cut or tear the meat and the skin from the bones, and cut into bite-sized strips. Arrange in a pile on a platter. Spoon half of the sauce over the chicken, and pass the remainder in a bowl at the table.

serves 4

A good cook uses seasonings to enhance a dish. A bad cook uses them to mask incompetence.

Eastern

Xihu Yu

west lake fish

Life in the city of Hangzhou is a constant interaction with its famous scenic landmark, West Lake. In the early morning, shadowy groups arrive at the lakeside while mists still shroud its waters. On viewing platforms, ballroom dancers in high heels and dark suits swirl to Western music, while on nearby lawns shadow boxers seek inner calm through a silent routine of stylized movements. Their concentration is not interrupted by the calls of waterbirds or the shouts of fishermen on the lake in small boats as they cast nets and lines into the inky waters in hopes of snaring turtles, eels, and carp. By midmorning, visitors have claimed the lake and its shores for the day, and, as the sun sets, lovers entwine on its curved stone bridges and walkways in a courting ritual that goes back over two thousand years. Artists and poets are still inspired by the lake's beauty, and chefs by the extraordinary variety of its harvest. For perhaps Hangzhou's most famous dish, xihu yu, plump carp from the lake are seasoned with local Shaoxing rice wine, black vinegar, and lajiangyou, a thin, pungent sauce rather like Worcestershire sauce.

1 large or 2 smaller freshwater fish such as trout or carp, about 1½ lb (750 g), cleaned

2 teaspoons peeled and grated fresh ginger

1 tablespoon rice wine

2 green (spring) onions, white part only, finely chopped

large pinch of salt

SAUCE

¼ cup (2 fl oz/60 ml) light soy sauce

2 tablespoons vegetable oil

2 tablespoons Worcestershire sauce or 2 teaspoons tamarind concentrate

3–4 teaspoons black vinegar

1 tablespoon superfine (caster) sugar

large pinch of ground white pepper

2 teaspoons cornstarch (cornflour)

salt to taste

2 tablespoons peeled and finely julienned fresh ginger

2 green (spring) onions, tender green tops only, finely julienned

1 small, hot red chile, seeded and finely julienned

☗ Rinse the fish well and drain thoroughly. Using a cleaver or large, sharp knife, and working from the cavity, make a deep cut to one side of the backbone of the fish and open the fish out flat. Carefully slide the blade of the knife beneath the breastbone of the side without the backbone, releasing the bones. One side of the fish will be boneless, while the other side will retain the backbone and breastbone. Turn the fish skin side up and make several deep, diagonal slashes across the thicker side, cutting almost down to the bone.

☗ Set the fish on a plate and spread the grated ginger, rice wine, and chopped green onion evenly over the fish. Let stand for 15–20 minutes, turning once.

☗ Pour water to a depth of about ¾ inch (2 cm) into a wide, shallow frypan large enough to hold the fish flat. Add the salt and bring to a gentle boil over medium–high heat. Carefully slide in the fish and the marinade ingredients, skin side up. As soon as the water returns to a boil, remove the pan from the heat, cover, and leave the fish to poach gently in the hot liquid for about 10 minutes. Using 2 spatulas or slotted spoons, lift the fish onto a serving plate, and scrape off any remaining marinade ingredients. The fish should be opaque near the bone when pierced with a knife. Keep warm.

☗ To make the sauce, strain ⅓ cup (3 fl oz/80 ml) of the poaching liquid into a small saucepan and stir in the soy sauce, oil, Worcestershire sauce or tamarind concentrate, 3 teaspoons vinegar, sugar, pepper, and cornstarch. Place the pan over high heat and bring quickly to a boil, stirring continuously. Reduce the heat to low and simmer, stirring often, for about 2 minutes to blend the flavors. Taste and adjust the seasoning with salt and additional vinegar. It should be reasonably tart.

☗ Spread the julienned ginger, julienned green onion, and chile evenly over the fish and spoon on the hot sauce. Serve at once.

serves 4–6

To place your chopsticks on top of your rice bowl is to invite disaster at sea.

Southern

Cong Bao Niu Rou

stir-fried beef with ginger and celery

Speed, heat, and movement are the essentials of stir-frying—high heat so the food does not stew and constant turning to expose every surface briefly to the hot oil.

10 oz (315 g) well-trimmed boneless beef steak such as rump or sirloin

2 teaspoons light soy sauce

1 teaspoon cornstarch (cornflour)

¼ teaspoon baking soda (bicarbonate of soda)

1 tablespoon water

SAUCE

¼ cup (2 fl oz/60 ml) chicken or beef stock (page 250)

2 teaspoons rice wine

2 teaspoons light soy sauce

1½ teaspoons cornstarch (cornflour)

½ teaspoon superfine (caster) sugar

⅓ cup (3 fl oz/80 ml) vegetable oil

8 thin slices fresh ginger, peeled and finely julienned

3 green (spring) onions, including tender green tops, thinly sliced on the diagonal

2 celery stalks, thinly sliced on the diagonal

salt and ground white pepper to taste

☙ Cut the beef across the grain into paper-thin slices, then cut each slice into pieces about 1½ inches (4 cm) long. Place in a dish, add the soy sauce, cornstarch, baking soda, and water, and mix well. Set aside to marinate and tenderize for about 20 minutes.

☙ To prepare the sauce, in a small bowl, mix together, stirring slowly, the stock, rice wine, soy sauce, cornstarch, and sugar.

☙ In a wok over high heat, warm the oil until it shimmers and begins to smoke. Add the ginger, green onions, and celery and stir-fry until beginning to soften, about 30 seconds. Using a slotted spoon, transfer the vegetables to a plate and set aside.

☸ With the wok still over high heat, add the beef and stir-fry, keeping the meat moving and turning in the wok constantly, until barely cooked, about 1 minute. Return the vegetables to the wok and stir-fry for about 20 seconds to mix well with the beef.

☸ Pour the sauce mixture into the wok and stir until it is lightly thickened and glazes all the ingredients, about 30 seconds. Season with salt and pepper.

☸ Transfer to a serving plate and serve at once.

serves 3 or 4

Eastern

Shanghai Ganshao Daxia

shanghai braised shrimp

To accentuate the size of the jumbo shrimp he was serving at an important banquet, one noted Shanghai chef devised this way to prevent them curling during cooking. He served them on a platter "swimming in formation in a stream of scarlet sauce," to the delight of his guests.

8 large shrimp (prawns) in the shell, about
¾ lb (375 g) total weight

2 tablespoons tomato ketchup

1 tablespoon rice wine

2 teaspoons hoisin sauce

2½ tablespoons vegetable oil

1 green (spring) onion, white part only, finely chopped

1 teaspoon peeled and grated fresh ginger

¾ cup (6 fl oz/180 ml) fish stock (page 250)
or water

½ teaspoon salt

1 teaspoon sesame oil

1 teaspoon red vinegar

1 teaspoon light soy sauce, or to taste

2 teaspoons cornstarch (cornflour) dissolved in
1 tablespoon water

2 green (spring) onions, green tops only, cut into 4-inch (10-cm) lengths, finely julienned lengthwise, and placed in ice water until curled

☸ Using a small, sharp knife or kitchen scissors, trim off the shrimp legs and discard. Leaving the shrimp in their shells, cut deeply along the length of the underside of each shrimp. This will help prevent them from curling during cooking. In a small bowl, stir together the ketchup, rice wine, and hoisin sauce.

☸ In a wok over high heat, warm the oil until ripples are visible on the surface. Add the chopped green onion, ginger, and shrimp and stir-fry until the shrimp are pink and firm, about 1 minute. Stir in the wine mixture and stir-fry for 30 seconds. Add the stock and salt, stir well, cover, reduce the heat to medium-low, and simmer until the shrimp are cooked, about 2 minutes. Using tongs, transfer the shrimp to a platter and set aside.

☸ Raise the heat to high and add the sesame oil, vinegar, and soy sauce and simmer briefly. Add the cornstarch mixture and cook, stirring slowly, until lightly thickened, about 30 seconds.

☸ Return the shrimp to the wok and reheat for about 30 seconds. Using tongs, arrange the shrimp side by side, and with heads aligned, on a clean platter. Spoon the sauce over the shrimp. Drain the green onion curls and pile on top of the shrimp heads. Serve at once.

serves 2–4

Northern

Shizi Tou

"lion's head" meatballs

The four large meatballs in this Yangzhou specialty represent both the cardinal points of north, south, east, and west, and the blessings of felicity, prosperity, longevity, and happiness. As the cabbage hearts and meatballs brown in the rich broth, they come to resemble the lions' heads for which they are named.

1 lb (500 g) coarsely ground (minced) fat pork such as pork butt

½ lb (250 g) finely ground (minced) lean pork or beef

½ cup (1½ oz/45 g) finely chopped green (spring) onion, white part only

⅓ cup (2 oz/60 g) finely chopped water chestnut

1½ tablespoons peeled and grated fresh ginger

1 tablespoon finely chopped garlic

½ cup (2 oz/60 g) cornstarch (cornflour)

½ cup (4 fl oz/125 ml) light soy sauce

1 lb (500 g) napa cabbage, roughly chopped, or whole heads baby bok choy

1 cup (8 fl oz/250 ml) vegetable oil

2 cups (16 fl oz/500 ml) chicken stock (page 250) or pork stock (page 251), heated

¼ cup (2 fl oz/60 ml) rice wine

1 teaspoon salt, plus salt to taste

ground white pepper to taste

⚜ In a food processor, combine the coarsely ground pork and finely ground pork or beef and process until well mixed. Add the green onion, water chestnut, ginger, garlic, 1 tablespoon of the cornstarch, and ¼ cup (2 fl oz/60 ml) of the soy sauce. Mix thoroughly. Divide into 4 equal portions and form into 4 large meatballs.

⚜ In a bowl, whisk together 2 tablespoons of the soy sauce and the remaining cornstarch to make a creamy paste, adding a little water if needed.

⚜ In a wok over high heat, warm the oil. One at a time, coat the meatballs in the soy-cornstarch mixture and slip into the hot oil. Fry, turning as needed and handling them carefully, until the surface is lightly browned, 2½–3 minutes. Using a wire skimmer or slotted spoon, transfer the balls to a plate. Reserve the remaining soy-cornstarch mixture.

⚜ Add the cabbage or bok choy to the hot oil and fry briefly just until wilted. Using the wire skimmer or slotted spoon, lift from the wok, allow to drain briefly over the hot oil, and place in a Chinese clay pot or other flameproof dish, or in a dish suitable for placing in a steamer.

⚜ Set the meatballs over the greens, carefully pour in the heated stock, and add the rice wine, the remaining 2 tablespoons soy sauce, and the 1 teaspoon salt. Add water almost to cover the meatballs. Cover the clay pot or dish with its lid or with aluminum foil and place over medium heat, or place in a steamer over gently boiling water and cover tightly. Simmer or steam, turning the meatballs carefully halfway through cooking, until the meatballs are cooked through, about 40 minutes.

⚜ Remove from the heat or steamer, and pour off the liquid from the clay pot or dish into a wok. Place over high heat and stir in 2–3 tablespoons of the reserved soy-cornstarch mixture. Bring to a boil and stir until lightly thickened, about 2 minutes. Season to taste with salt and generously season with pepper.

⚜ Pour the sauce over the meatballs and serve directly from the pot.

serves 4–8

A person's heart is like a rice field; it is full of life but it can be stifled with disuse.

Southern

Jipurou Ningmengjiang

chicken breast with lemon sauce

Citrus fruits, which grow in the southeast, play a significant role in China's dining etiquette and gastronomy. Gold is the color of money, and therefore signifies wealth. A plate of golden oranges served at the end of a banquet is a host's symbolic wish for the guests' good fortune. Ripe mandarin oranges are offered as temple tributes to encourage wealth into the family home, and flowering kumquat trees are New Year's gifts. Many households display a ripe pomelo near the front door to invite good fortune for the coming year.

Felicitous golden-yellow citrus sauces bring a deliciously tangy taste to many popular meat and seafood dishes, like this marriage of crisp-skin chicken breasts in a lemon sauce. In the eastern coastal province of Fujian, tiny indigenous limes are pickled to use as an emphatic flavoring agent in numerous local dishes, including tender duck simmered in broth. Tangerine segments simmered in clear sugar syrup make a refreshing midsummer dessert, and the dried skins (chenpi) become a flavoring ingredient in red-cooked (soy-braised) dishes and soups and in the spicy stir-fries of Sichuan.

10–12 oz (315–375 g) skinless, boneless chicken breasts

½ teaspoon salt

2 teaspoons rice wine

2 teaspoons light soy sauce

½ cup (2 oz/60 g) cornstarch (cornflour)

2 tablespoons all-purpose (plain) flour

1 egg, lightly beaten

vegetable oil for deep-frying

SAUCE

2 lemons, 1 thinly sliced, 1 squeezed for juice

2 teaspoons rice vinegar

2 tablespoons superfine (caster) sugar

¼ cup (2 fl oz/60 ml) chicken stock (page 250) or water

3 or 4 drops yellow food coloring

1½ teaspoons sesame oil (optional)

1 teaspoon cornstarch (cornflour) dissolved in 1 tablespoon cold water

1 cup (2 oz/60 g) finely sliced iceberg lettuce (optional)

☙ Cut each chicken breast in half horizontally. Place in a dish and add the salt, rice wine, and soy sauce. Turn to coat, then let stand for 20 minutes, turning occasionally.

☙ Using about 2 tablespoons of the cornstarch, coat the chicken pieces, tapping off the excess. Place the remaining cornstarch in a bowl and whisk in the flour and egg to make a thin batter, adding a little water if needed.

☙ Pour the oil to a depth of 1½ inches (4 cm) into a wok, and heat to 360°F (182°C), or until a few drops of the batter added to the oil turn golden in seconds and float to the surface. Working in batches, dip the chicken pieces, one at a time, into the batter, allowing the excess to drip off, and slide them into the hot oil. Fry until golden brown and cooked through, about 5 minutes. Using a wire skimmer or slotted spoon, transfer to a rack placed over paper towels to drain; keep warm.

☙ When all of the chicken has been cooked, pour off the oil from the wok into a heatproof bowl, wipe out the wok, and return 2 tablespoons of the oil to the wok. Place the wok over high heat. To make the lemon sauce, add the lemon slices and juice, rice vinegar, sugar, stock or water, food coloring, and sesame oil to the wok and bring to a boil. Reduce the heat to medium and simmer for about 30 seconds to blend the flavors. Add the cornstarch mixture and stir until lightly thickened, about 30 seconds.

☙ Line a platter with the lettuce, if using. Cut the chicken into thick slices and arrange over the lettuce, or arrange directly on the platter. Pour the sauce, including the lemon slices, over the chicken and serve at once.

serves 4–6

Every farmhouse in Guangdong keeps a few chickens to graze on fallen rice grains.

Chinese Wine

When the Chinese accidentally discovered a palatable wine made from fermented rice some four thousand years ago, they embraced the new beverage with such gusto that the emperor of the day had to introduce hastily four decrees that are still followed today: wine must only be drunk from small cups; "wine-accompanying dishes" (hot and cold hors d'oeuvres) must be eaten to absorb the alcohol; wine should not be served during the main part of the banquet menu; and, lastly, drinkers must indulge in mild forms of physical and mental exercise. The "drinking games" devised in those far-off days—scissors-paper-stone and the fingers game—are still played with noisy enthusiasm in Chinese restaurants around the world. Toasts usually accompany drinks. At a signal from the toast maker, the tiny cups are filled and raised and the wine is tossed back in one gulp with shouts of *gan bai* (bottoms up).

Shaoxing, southwest of Shanghai, in Zhejiang province, is where China's finest amber rice wines are made and marketed under that name. The best rice wines, which are mild in taste, have an alcohol content of around 20 percent, and sometimes flowers are steeped in them to make elegant dessert

and aperitif beverages. However, as the wines are usually served warm, their effect can be immediate and invigorating. Flavors range from mellow and slightly sweet to sharp and scorching, depending on the quality and alcohol content. Unwary travelers should accept a glass of "white wine" with caution—it may be local millet brew as potent as vodka, or fiery *maotai*, eighty to one hundred proof rice wine. Chinese-distilled rice wines are different and far more potent than the sakes brewed in Japan.

Rice wine is used in stir-fries and marinades, and is a primary seasoning ingredient in hot and cold wine sauces, particularly in seafood and chicken dishes. It imparts a distinct flavor and aroma reminiscent of dry sherry, which can be used if rice wine is not available. Japanese *mirin* may be substituted if the dish demands a sweet flavor.

Sweet fruit wines from plums and grapes have been made on a small scale in China since early times, but the grape wine industry began in the nineteenth century when Germans resident in Shandong decided their Alsace-style wines were perfect with Chinese food. Grape wine production continues today in the Yangtai and Tianjin wineries in the north.

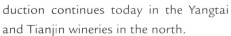

Northern

Jiu Suan La Jiao Xiaren

shrimp with chile and garlic
in wine sauce

Rice wine and some unique and interesting by-products of the wine industry are used in many Chinese recipes. As flavoring ingredients, they impart a yeasty aroma and taste that ranges from subtle to overt. The red mash residue (wine lees) left in the fermentation vats after the rice wine has been drawn off for filtering is called hongzao *(red rice). It is used in northern cuisine as a colorful flavor base in sauces for strong-tasting meats, such as pork liver and duck. Dried red rice mash is sold in small packs, and is also available in jars in liquid form mixed with rice wine.*

Sweetened, fermented rice is an ingredient in delicately flavored desserts with fresh fruit. This can be easily made in a week by mixing soaked glutinous rice and sugar with brewing yeast. Perfumed wines like Guilin's prized guihuajiu *(cassia blossom wine) and Tianjin's* meigui liu jiu *(rose petal liqueur) are aromatic sweet wines that serve as aperitifs and have interesting applications in cooking. Sauces featuring flower-perfumed rice wines are an integral part of Beijing cuisine. In one popular dish from the northern province of Hebei, three types of wine are used in the marinade, seasoning, and sauce to make a popular dish of chicken with sweet wine sauce. Chinese wines, including the mellow Shaoxing rice wine, are becoming more readily available outside of China. In a sauce, such as this Beijing classic, the real thing is best, but Japanese* mirin *is a worthy substitute.*

12 peeled shrimp (prawns), about 7 oz (220 g) total weight (about 1 lb/500 g unpeeled)

1 tablespoon salt, plus salt to taste

2 egg whites

⅓ cup (1½ oz/45 g) cornstarch (cornflour)

2½ cups (20 fl oz/625 ml) vegetable oil

1 large, hot red chile, seeded and sliced

3 cloves garlic, sliced

¾ cup (6 fl oz/180 ml) rice wine

2 teaspoons light soy sauce

1½ teaspoons superfine (caster) sugar

2 teaspoons cornstarch (cornflour) dissolved in ½ cup (4 fl oz/125 ml) fish or chicken stock (page 250)

few drops of chile oil

1½ tablespoons chopped green (spring) onion tops

❈ Cut each shrimp in half lengthwise and remove and discard the dark vein. Sprinkle the shrimp with the 1 tablespoon salt and let stand for 10 minutes. Rinse under running cold water and drain well. Pat dry with paper towels.

❈ In a bowl, beat the egg whites until blended. Whisk in the cornstarch to make a thin batter.

❈ In a wok over high heat, warm the vegetable oil. When it is hot, dip about half of the shrimp in the batter, and slip into the oil. Fry until lightly golden, about 1 minute. Using a slotted spoon, transfer to a rack placed over paper towels to drain. Repeat with the remaining shrimp.

❈ Pour off the oil into a small, heatproof bowl, wipe out the wok, and return 1 tablespoon of the oil to the wok. Place the wok over high heat. When it is hot, add the chile and garlic and stir-fry for 20 seconds. Add the rice wine, soy sauce, and sugar and simmer until partially reduced, about 40 seconds. Add the cornstarch mixture and cook, stirring slowly, until lightly thickened, about 1½ minutes. Season with salt.

❈ Return the shrimp to the wok and heat through, turning to coat evenly with the sauce. Transfer to a serving dish, sprinkle with the chile oil and green onion tops, and serve immediately.

serves 4

Southern

Xiang Su Ya

crisp-skin duck

This duck is the southern equivalent of northern Beijing's famous roast duck. It is deliciously full-flavored and, although its skin might not acquire quite the same dramatic amber translucence and wafer crispness, it can replace roast duck in any recipe.

1 duck, about 4 lb (2 kg)

2 tablespoons dark soy sauce

1 tablespoon hoisin sauce

1 tablespoon honey

1¼ teaspoons five-spice powder

½ teaspoon salt

2 tablespoons thinly sliced fresh ginger

1 green (spring) onion, trimmed

hoisin sauce or pepper-salt (page 33)

❧ Place the duck in a colander in the sink. Bring a kettle filled with water to a boil, and pour the boiling water evenly over the entire surface of the duck. This will tighten the skin, making it crispier when the duck is cooked. Let drain for 15 minutes.

❧ In a bowl, stir together the soy sauce, 1 tablespoon hoisin sauce, honey, five-spice powder, and salt. Brush the mixture thickly over the duck, and pour the remainder into the cavity. Push the ginger and whole green onion into the cavity. Place the duck on a rack in a roasting pan and let stand for about 2 hours.

❧ Preheat the oven to 360°F (182°C).

❧ Set the pan in the center of the oven and roast the duck for about 40 minutes. With a fine, sharp skewer, prick the duck all over to release the fat and help crisp the skin. Continue to roast until the duck is tender and the skin is crisp and golden brown, 20–30 minutes longer. If the duck is almost done, and the skin has not crisped, raise the oven temperature to 375°–400°F (190°–200°C) for the last 10 minutes of roasting. Test by pushing the skewer into the thickest part of the thigh; if no pink juices flow, the duck is done.

❧ Remove from the oven and let rest for at least 10 minutes. Debone the duck, cut into thin slices, and arrange on a plate. Serve with hoisin sauce or pepper-salt.

serves 8

Northern

Shandong Xianggu Ji

shandong chicken and mushrooms

The rich, mellow flavors of this dish typify the cuisine of this northern province.

4 large dried black mushrooms, soaked in hot water to cover for 25 minutes

9 oz (280 g) boneless, skinless chicken breast, cut into ½-inch (12-mm) cubes

1 small egg white, beaten until frothy

1½ tablespoons tapioca starch or cornstarch (cornflour)

1 tablespoon peeled and grated fresh ginger

1 teaspoon rice wine

1 cup (8 fl oz/250 ml) melted rendered chicken or pork fat or vegetable oil

1½ tablespoons hoisin sauce

1½ teaspoons yellow bean paste

salt to taste

❧ Remove the mushrooms from their soaking water and remove and discard the stems if necessary. Quarter each cap and return the pieces to the water. Set aside and drain when ready for use.

❧ In a bowl, combine the chicken, egg white, and tapioca starch or cornstarch and mix well. Let stand for 10 minutes.

❧ Place the grated ginger on a piece of clean cloth, gather up the cloth, and squeeze to release the ginger juice into the rice wine. Add 1 teaspoon of the grated ginger flesh to the wine, and discard the remainder.

❧ In a wok over medium-high heat, warm the fat or oil. When it begins to smoke slightly, add the chicken and stir-fry until almost cooked, about 1½ minutes. Using a slotted spoon, transfer to a plate. Pour off the fat or oil and reserve for another use.

❧ Return the wok to medium-high heat, add the chicken and mushrooms, and stir-fry for 20 seconds. Add the rice wine mixture, the hoisin sauce, and the bean paste. Stir-fry until the seasoning ingredients coat the chicken evenly, the chicken is cooked, and the dish is very aromatic, about 40 seconds.

❧ Season with salt, then transfer to a serving plate and serve immediately.

serves 3 or 4

Southern

Hongshao Zhurou

pork simmered in soy and spices

*Simmering or braising food in a sealed pot is called
men in China, but when soy sauce is the dominant
ingredient in the cooking liquid it becomes hongshao,
literally "red cooking." It is a popular cooking method
for large cuts of meat, tough cuts like pig's feet, and
whole poultry, particularly game birds, which require
slow, gentle cooking to achieve gelatinous, melt-in-the-
mouth tenderness. Certain dishes cooked by this
method have a special symbolism and are served
on festive occasions, such as New Year or wedding
banquets. The Chinese name of a dish of pork
shoulder or pig's feet red-cooked with black moss
for longevity and lettuce for prosperity translates
as "windfall everywhere," while hongshao zhurou
earns the poetic Chinese title "peace and harmony."
Brown-sauce cooking is the less evocative description
of the richly flavored Shanghai dishes cooked in
hongshao style. Popular favorites include freshwater
and saltwater eels braised in rich brown sauce, and
served liberally dusted with white pepper. Wonderfully
fragrant dried black mushrooms, fleshy amber abalone
mushrooms, and eggplant (aubergine) are frequent
additives in hongshao dishes. They absorb the rich
flavors of the sauce, returning their own intense flavor
and textural contributions, as do ginger, crunchy
bamboo shoots, and chestnuts.*

1½ lb (750 g) pork leg or pork shoulder, with
skin intact

2½ tablespoons hoisin sauce

8 dried black mushrooms, soaked in boiling water
to cover for 5–10 minutes and drained

¾ cup (6 fl oz/180 ml) light soy sauce

2 tablespoons rice wine

1 star anise

1 small cinnamon stick

1 teaspoon Sichuan peppercorns

1 green (spring) onion, trimmed

1 tablespoon peeled and julienned ginger

2 cups water (optional)

salt to taste

1 lb (500 g) baby bok choy, halved lengthwise, or
other Chinese greens, leaves separated (optional)

2 teaspoons cornstarch (cornflour) dissolved in
2 tablespoons water

♛ Score the skin of the pork with a sharp knife.
Using a brush, paint the skin with the hoisin sauce.
Let stand for 1 hour.

♛ Place the pork in a saucepan in which it fits reasonably snugly. Add the mushrooms, soy sauce, rice
wine, star anise, cinnamon stick, Sichuan peppercorns, green onion, ginger, and water just to cover.
Place over medium-high heat, bring to a boil, cover
tightly, reduce the heat to low, and simmer gently
until the pork is tender when pierced, about 1 hour.

♛ Transfer the pork to a plate and cover loosely with
aluminum foil to keep warm. Pick out the mushrooms from the sauce and, using a small, sharp knife,
trim off and discard their hard stems if necessary.
Return the mushrooms to the sauce.

♛ Bring the sauce to a boil over high heat. Reduce
the heat to medium and boil gently until reduced to
about ½ cup (4 fl oz/125 ml), about 10 minutes.

♛ Meanwhile, to serve the pork with the bok choy
or other Chinese greens, in a wok or another
saucepan, bring the water to a boil and salt lightly.
Add the greens and remove immediately from the
heat. Leave in the hot liquid for 5 minutes, then drain
well and arrange around the edge of a serving platter.

♛ Slice the pork and place in the center of the platter. Add the cornstarch mixture to the reduced sauce
and stir over medium heat until it is lightly thickened
and becomes clear, about 1 minute. Spoon the sauce
and mushrooms over the pork, and serve at once.

serves 4–6

When a child is born,
the new mother eats
chicken or pork braised
with ginger to restore
her energy.

Clay Pot Cooking

Clay pot cooking is widespread in China. For everyday cooking, unglazed "sand pots" made of sand and clay are designed to be used directly on top of the wood, charcoal, and gas ovens in most homes. The pots have a shiny interior glaze to make cleaning easier, and to hold in moisture and conduct heat. They come with a tight-fitting lid that makes them perfect for cooking rice, simmering soups, and long, slow braising and poaching.

Clay pots are lightweight, inexpensive, and hard-wearing. However, to avoid cracking, they should never be heated without liquid inside, used directly on electric rings or hot-plates, or placed when hot on a cold surface. The wire cage on some clay pots makes them more resistant to breakage.

Yunnan clay steam pots have a unique function. Made from the same hard, dark clay that makes a perfect Chinese teapot, these pots have a tapering funnel inside. They are used in a steamer, and the funnel directs a flow of steam into the closed pot so the contents are at once steamed from inside and outside, producing an unsurpassed tenderness.

Eastern

Hai Xian Geng

seafood clay pot

The diverse cuisines of the coastal provinces, from Hainan Island in the south to Jiangsu and Shandong in the northeast, employ a plentitude of seafood year-round. A dish using six different varieties of fish and shellfish might not be considered an extravagance in those coastal areas, while inland this indulgent compilation would be reserved for the banquet table. Seafood soups and stews cooked in clay pots are a welcome dish in a home-cooked Chinese meal, particularly in the cooler months. With steamed rice and a plate of steamed greens, a seafood clay pot is a meal in itself. Timing is everything when cooking fresh seafood, and even more so when cooking several different varieties together. Shrimp (prawns) should retain a palatable crunch and fish should be tender enough to separate in moist flakes without crumbling dryly. Oysters and crabmeat require no more than a gentle warming.

½ lb (250 g) large shrimp (prawns) in the shell

2½ oz (75 g) cleaned squid bodies
(about ¼ lb/125 g before cleaning, page 249)

½ lb (250 g) firm white fish fillet

2-inch (5-cm) piece carrot

2 tablespoons vegetable oil

1 celery stalk, thinly sliced on the diagonal

½ yellow onion, cut into narrow wedges and layers separated

8 very thin slices fresh ginger, peeled

1¼ cups (10 fl oz/310 ml) fish stock (page 250)

2 teaspoons rice wine

2 tablespoons oyster sauce

¼ cup (1¼ oz/40 g) thinly sliced bamboo shoot

¼ cup (1¼ oz/40 g) canned small straw mushrooms

1½ tablespoons cornstarch (cornflour) dissolved in 2 tablespoons water

2–3 oz (60–90 g) shucked oysters (optional)

3 oz (90 g) peeled small shrimp (prawns)

3 oz (90 g) crabmeat or 2 egg whites, lightly beaten

salt and ground white pepper to taste

2 tablespoons thinly sliced green (spring) onion tops

If you have a large, flameproof Chinese clay pot, fill it with hot water and set it aside to warm up. If not, have ready a heavy saucepan.

To prepare the large shrimp, peel each shrimp, leaving the last segment of the shell and the tail in place. Cut deeply down the back, devein, and rinse in cold water. Pat dry with paper towels. To prepare the squid, using a sharp knife, slit each body lengthwise to open it flat. Using the knife, score a ⅛-inch (3-mm) crosshatch pattern over the inside surface. Cut into ¾-inch (2-cm) squares and set aside. Cut the fish into 1-inch (2.5-cm) cubes.

Peel the carrot and, using a carving tool or sharp knife, remove 5 or 6 V-shaped strips along the length. Slice the carrot crosswise to create flower-shaped pieces. Set aside.

Drain the water from the clay pot, if using. In the clay pot or saucepan over high heat, warm the oil. When it is hot, add the carrot, celery, yellow onion, and ginger and stir-fry until beginning to soften, about 1 minute. Pour in the stock and bring to a boil. Add the rice wine and oyster sauce and simmer for about 30 seconds to blend the flavors.

Add the large shrimp, squid, fish, bamboo shoot, and mushrooms and cook until the stock returns to a boil, about 2 minutes. Stir in the cornstarch mixture and cook, stirring, until the mixture returns to a boil, about 40 seconds.

Stir in the oysters, if using, the small shrimp, and the crabmeat, if using. If using the egg whites, pour them through a fine-mesh sieve held above the clay pot or saucepan, so that they fall in fine streams. Remove from the heat and do not stir the dish for at least 2 minutes.

Season with salt and pepper and stir to distribute the seafood evenly. Leave in the clay pot, or tip into a deep serving dish. Scatter on the green onion tops and serve at once.

serves 4–8

Northern

Dun Ya Meijiang

braised plum sauce duck

*The richness of duck is superbly balanced
by a tart-sweet plum sauce.*

1½ lb (750 g) mixed duck pieces such as
legs, wings, and thighs

about ½ cup (2 oz/60 g) cornstarch (cornflour)
or tapioca starch

vegetable oil for frying

1 tablespoon sesame oil

¾ cup (6 fl oz/180 ml) bottled plum sauce

1 cup (8 fl oz/250 ml) water

salt and ground black pepper to taste

❀ If the duck pieces are large, cut them in half.
Rinse under running cold water, drain well, and pat
dry with paper towels. Place the cornstarch or tapioca starch in a plastic or sturdy paper bag, add the
duck pieces, hold the bag top firmly closed, and
shake gently to coat the duck evenly. Tip into a
colander and shake off the excess cornstarch or tapioca starch.

❀ Preheat the oven to 360°F (182°C).

❀ Pour the vegetable oil to a depth of 1 inch (2.5 cm)
into a large frying pan or wok, and heat over high
heat until the oil shimmers and begins to smoke. Add
the sesame oil, then carefully slide half the duck
pieces into the hot oil. Fry for 1 minute, reduce the
heat to medium-high, and continue to fry until the
duck is well browned, 5–8 minutes. Using a slotted
spoon, transfer the duck pieces to a Chinese clay pot
or covered baking dish. Fry the remaining duck in
the same way and add to the clay pot or dish. (This
step adds rich brown color to the duck and draws off
excess fat.)

❀ In a small bowl, stir together the plum sauce,
water, and a big pinch each of salt and pepper. Pour
evenly over the duck. Cover, place in the center of
the oven, and oven-braise for 30 minutes. Uncover,
turn the duck pieces over, re-cover, and cook until
the duck is tender, about 30 minutes longer.

❀ Taste and adjust the seasoning with salt and pepper. Serve directly from the clay pot or dish, or use
tongs to transfer the duck pieces to a serving plate,
then spoon the sauce over the top.

serves 4–6

Southern

Zheng Cong Jiang Yu

steamed fish with ginger
and green onions

*To make the carrot flowers, using the point of a small,
sharp knife, make 5 or 6 deep angled incisions into
the narrow end of a carrot, about ¾ inch from the tip.
The cuts should meet in the center of the carrot. Twist
off the tip of the carrot to give a flower-bud shape.*

1 whole fish such as snapper, porgy, or sea bass,
1¾–2 lb (750 g–1 kg), cleaned

2-inch (5-cm) piece fresh ginger, peeled, thinly
sliced, and then finely julienned

3 green (spring) onions, white part only, cut
into 2-inch (5-cm) lengths and finely julienned
lengthwise

3 tablespoons light soy sauce

2 tablespoons rice wine

1 tablespoon vegetable oil

fresh cilantro (fresh coriander) sprigs

carrot flowers (see note)

❀ Hold the fish under running cold water to rinse
the cavity thoroughly. Drain and pat dry with paper
towels. Place on a cutting board and, using a sharp
knife, cut deep slashes on the diagonal across both
sides, spacing them about 1¼ inches (3 cm) apart.

❀ Place the fish on a large, heatproof plate. Place
about one-third of the ginger and green onions inside
the cavity of the fish, and spread the remainder over
the top. Pour the soy sauce, rice wine, and vegetable
oil evenly over the fish.

❀ Bring water to a boil in the base of a steamer. (If
you do not have a large steamer or a covered wok, a
double thickness of aluminum foil to cover the wok
will work as well.) Set the plate in the steamer, cover
tightly, reduce the heat so the water continues to
simmer, and steam, for 15–18 minutes. To test for
doneness, insert the tip of a knife into the thickest
part of the fish below the head. If it penetrates easily
and no pink shows, the fish is done.

❀ Using oven gloves to protect your hands from the
steam, carefully remove the plate from the steamer.
Garnish the plate with the cilantro and carrot flowers and serve at once.

serves 4–6

Eastern

Dou Shi Pai Gu

pork ribs with black beans and chile

My nostrils twitch in appreciation when I smell salted black beans frying in a hot pan with garlic and ginger. However, while I know that fish and chicken dishes with black bean sauce are hugely popular Cantonese dishes, I am not a fan. To me the earthy, leguminous saltiness of black beans is a better balance with strongly flavored ingredients. I happily home in on a food vendor's wok full of black bean mussels or sea snails, and at a dim sum restaurant or outdoor market café rarely pass up the opportunity to enjoy tripe in what I consider is its best treatment—slow-braised with black beans and loads of garlic and chile. But it is with meaty, fat-layered pork ribs that I think this salty seasoning has the best opportunity to showcase its distinctive flavor. A large amount of fat is drawn off the pork ribs. It may be skimmed off and kept in the refrigerator to use when stir-frying.

In many of China's food markets soft, black, wrinkled, salt-fermented soybeans can be purchased by the handful. But it is not essential they be bought in small quantities, as they will keep fresh for easily a year in a sealed container. I prefer to wash and dry them before use, to decrease their saltiness. But if you don't, taste first before adding the full quantity of soy sauce or salt in a recipe.

2 lb (1 kg) belly pork on the bone or thickly sliced meaty pork ribs, cut into 2-by-3-by-1-inch (5-by-7.5-by-2.5-cm) pieces

1 cup (3 oz/90 g) chopped green (spring) onion, including half the tender green tops, plus remaining chopped green tops for garnish

2 tablespoons peeled and chopped fresh ginger

1½ tablespoons chopped garlic

1 tablespoon seeded and chopped fresh or dried red chile

2 tablespoons thick black bean sauce or ⅓ cup (1½ oz/45 g) salted black beans, rinsed, drained, and chopped

1 tablespoon light brown sugar

¾ cup (6 fl oz/180 ml) water

⅓ cup (3 fl oz/80 ml) rice wine

¼ cup (2 fl oz/60 ml) light soy sauce

chopped fresh cilantro (fresh coriander)

1 tablespoon cornstarch (cornflour) dissolved in 1½ tablespoons water (optional)

♛ Spread the pork pieces in a single layer in a baking dish, scatter the 1 cup (3 oz/90 g) green onion, ginger, garlic, and chile evenly over the top. In a bowl, stir together the black bean sauce or chopped beans with the sugar, water, rice wine, and soy sauce. Pour over the pork. Cover with a lid or aluminum foil and refrigerate for at least 1 hour or for up to 4 hours, turning the pork pieces several times.

♛ Preheat an oven to 325°F (165°C). Place the covered dish in the preheated oven and braise, turning the pork occasionally, for 1¼ hours. Uncover, raise the heat to 375°F (190°C), and cook until the pork has crisped in places and the liquid is partially reduced, about 20 minutes longer.

♛ Alternatively, steam the pork: Bring water to a rapid boil in the base of a steamer. Reduce the heat slightly, uncover the dish holding the pork, and place in the steamer. Cover the pork loosely with a piece of parchment (baking) paper and cover the steamer tightly. Steam over simmering water until the pork is tender, 1–1¼ hours.

♛ Remove the dish from the oven or steamer, uncover, and skim off the excess fat from the surface. Garnish with the green onion tops and cilantro and serve directly from the dish.

♛ If a thicker sauce is preferred, use tongs to transfer the ribs to a serving dish. Pour the skimmed pan juices into a wok or small saucepan, place over high heat, add half of the cornstarch mixture, bring to a boil, and cook, stirring and adding the remaining cornstarch mixture if the sauce is not thickening sufficiently, until the sauce turns clear and glossy, about 2 minutes. Spoon over the pork, garnish with the green onion tops and cilantro, and serve at once.

serves 4–6

Introduced to China by Portuguese traders in the sixteenth century, chiles soon replaced peppercorns in many dishes.

Qingsun Xiangcai Yangrou

fried lamb fillet with cilantro

Fresh cilantro is one of the few herbs regularly used in Chinese cooking. Introduced from the Mediterranean centuries ago, it flourishes in the south as a ubiquitous garnish and in soups and noodle dishes, and is chopped into fillings for buns and dumplings. On occasion it is treated as a vegetable, stir-fried with strips of meat or bean sprouts, but mostly it plays a supporting role, as in this stir-fry.

10 oz (315 g) lamb tenderloin or boneless lamb steak cut from leg, sliced paper-thin across the grain

1 tablespoon hoisin sauce

½ teaspoon black vinegar

¼ teaspoon superfine (caster) sugar

1 tablespoon sesame oil

1 clove garlic, sliced

¾ cup (3¼ oz/100 g) sliced bamboo shoot

2 green (spring) onions, including tender green tops, sliced

1½ tablespoons light soy sauce

2 teaspoons cornstarch (cornflour) dissolved in ⅓ cup (3 fl oz/80 ml) chicken or beef stock (page 250)

salt and ground white pepper to taste

½ cup (½ oz/15 g) fresh cilantro (fresh coriander) leaves

☗ In a bowl, combine the lamb slices, hoisin sauce, vinegar, and sugar and mix well. Set aside to marinate for 20 minutes.

☗ In a wok over high heat, warm the sesame oil until it begins to smoke. Add the garlic and stir-fry for about 10 seconds until fragrant. Using a slotted spoon, transfer to a small dish and set aside.

☗ With the wok still over high heat, add the lamb and stir-fry just until it changes color and is barely cooked, about 1½ minutes. Add the bamboo shoot and green onions and return the garlic to the wok. Cook, stirring constantly, until the lamb is lightly browned, about 30 seconds.

✤ Pour the soy sauce down along the inside surface of the wok, and stir it in as it sizzles and flows onto the meat. Pour in the cornstarch mixture and stir slowly until the sauce is lightly thickened and becomes clear, about 30 seconds. Season with salt and pepper.

✤ Stir in the cilantro leaves, and tip the mixture onto a serving plate. Serve at once.

serves 2–4

Eastern

Gong Bao Bang

clams with garlic and chile

On one trip to Taipei, I was delighted to discover a popular street-side café where people lined up to order bowls of the tiniest clams imaginable, redolent with garlic and fiercely hot red chile. The potent flavors and use of garlic echo the cuisines of mainland Jiangxi, the ancestral home of many Taiwanese.

14 oz (440 g) frozen shelled clams, thawed, or 1½ lb (750 g) clams in the shell

½ cup (4 fl oz / 125 ml) water

2 tablespoons vegetable oil

½ cup (2 oz / 60 g) diced yellow onion

½ cup (2½ oz / 75 g) diced celery

1½ tablespoons salted black beans, rinsed, drained, and chopped

1½ tablespoons finely chopped garlic

1½ tablespoons finely chopped hot red chile

1½ tablespoons peeled and grated fresh ginger

1 tablespoon light soy sauce

2 teaspoons cornstarch (cornflour) dissolved in ⅓ cup (3 fl oz / 80 ml) fish stock (page 250) or water

½ teaspoon superfine (caster) sugar

large pinch of ground white pepper

salt to taste

¼ cup (⅓ oz / 10 g) chopped fresh cilantro (fresh coriander)

✤ If using shelled clams, reserve. If using clams in the shell and you think they may be sandy, soak them for several hours in cold water to cover so that they will expel any sand. If not, simply rinse them under running cold water and scrub the shells clean. Discard any clams that do not close to the touch, then tip the remainder into a saucepan and add the water. Cover tightly, place over high heat, bring to a boil, and cook just until the shells open, about 3 minutes. Drain well and discard any clams that failed to open. Remove the clams from their shells, discarding the shells. Set the clams aside.

✤ In a wok over medium-high heat, warm the oil. When it is hot, add the onion and celery and stir-fry until beginning to soften, about 1 minute. Add the black beans, garlic, chile, and ginger and stir-fry until aromatic, about 30 seconds. Add the shelled clams and soy sauce and stir-fry until the ingredients are evenly mixed with the clams, about 40 seconds.

✤ Pour in the cornstarch mixture and season with the sugar and pepper. Reduce the heat to medium-low and simmer, stirring occasionally, until the clams are cooked and the sauce is lightly thickened, about 2 minutes. Season with salt.

✤ Stir in the cilantro leaves, tip the clams into a serving bowl, and serve immediately.

serves 4

Dong Jiang Yan Jiu Ji

salt-baked chicken

A savory, gray-tinged salt from Sichuan is traditionally used for this showpiece dish. Despite its thick blanket of salt, the chicken absorbs just enough to flavor it subtly, and its skin dries as crisp as paper.

1 chicken, about 3 lb (1.5 kg)

2 tablespoons peeled and grated fresh ginger

1 tablespoon rice wine

1 green (spring) onion, including tender green tops, chopped

3 lb (1.5 kg) rock salt or other very coarse salt

1½ teaspoons fennel seed, lightly crushed

1 teaspoon Sichuan peppercorns, lightly crushed

Rinse the chicken under running cold water and place in a bowl. In a small bowl, stir together the ginger and rice wine, then strain the mixture through a fine-mesh sieve held over the chicken. Place the contents of the sieve in the cavity with the green onion. Marinate at room temperature for 1 hour.

Spread the salt in an ovenproof dish a little larger than the chicken and place in the oven. Turn the oven to 375°F (190°C) to heat for about 20 minutes.

Remove the dish from the oven and leave the oven on. Scoop out half the salt. Sprinkle half of the fennel seed and Sichuan peppercorns over the salt remaining in the dish. Nestle the chicken, breast side up, in the salt. Sprinkle the remaining fennel seed and peppercorns over the chicken, and cover the chicken with the removed salt. Cover the dish with its lid or with aluminum foil and return to the oven.

Bake the chicken for 45 minutes. Uncover the dish and continue baking until the skin is crisp and golden, about 15–20 minutes. No pink juices should flow when the thickest part of the thigh is pierced with a thin skewer.

Transfer the chicken to a cutting board, brushing off any salt clinging to the skin. Using a cleaver, cut the chicken into bite-sized pieces, cutting straight through the bones.

Arrange the cut chicken on a platter and serve immediately.

serves 4–6

Southern

Cuipi Wakuai Yu

"broken tile" fish
with sweet-and-sour sauce

A fanciful chef named the result "broken tiles" after an apprentice's unskillful slicing of a fish. The apprentice improved, but the name stayed.

FISH "TILES"

10 oz (315 g) firm white fish fillets

½ teaspoon salt

1½ teaspoons rice wine

SWEET-AND-SOUR SAUCE

¼ cup (2 fl oz/60 ml) chicken stock (page 250) or water

⅓ cup (3 fl oz/80 ml) rice vinegar

1 tablespoon light soy sauce

⅓ cup (1½ oz/45 g) superfine (caster) sugar

½ teaspoon salt

2 tablespoons vegetable oil

1–3 teaspoons peeled and finely julienned fresh ginger

½ teaspoon crushed garlic (optional)

½ cup (2 oz/60 g) diced red bell pepper (capsicum)

½ cup (2 oz/60 g) diced, unpeeled English (hothouse) cucumber

2 green (spring) onions, including tender green tops, chopped

3 or 4 drops red food coloring (optional)

1 tablespoon cornstarch (cornflour) dissolved in 1 tablespoon water

⅔ cup (2½ oz/75 g) cornstarch (cornflour) or tapioca starch

vegetable oil for deep-frying

1 tablespoon sesame oil (optional)

❦ To prepare the fish "tiles," working from the tail end of a fillet, and holding a sharp knife or cleaver at a 45-degree angle, cut the fillet crosswise into slices ⅓ inch (9 mm) thick. Sprinkle with the salt and rice wine and set aside.

❦ To prepare the sauce, in a small bowl, combine the stock or water, vinegar, soy sauce, sugar, and salt and stir until the sugar dissolves. In a saucepan over medium heat, warm the vegetable oil until the surface shimmers. Add the ginger to taste, garlic (if using), bell pepper, cucumber, and green onions and stir-fry until slightly softened, about 1 minute. Raise the heat to medium-high, pour in the vinegar mixture, bring quickly to a boil, and simmer for 1 minute, stirring constantly. If using the food coloring, first stir it into the cornstarch mixture and then stir the mixture into the sauce. Simmer over medium-high heat, stirring slowly, until the sauce is lightly thickened and becomes clear, about 1 minute. Remove from the heat and set aside.

❦ Place the cornstarch or tapioca starch in a plastic or sturdy paper bag. Add the fish slices to the bag, hold the bag top firmly closed, and shake vigorously to coat the fish slices thickly. Tip into a colander and shake off the excess cornstarch or tapioca starch.

❦ Pour the vegetable oil to a depth of 1¾ inches (4 cm) into a wok, and heat to 360°F (182°C), or until a small cube of bread dropped into it begins to turn golden within a few seconds. Add the sesame oil, if using, then carefully slide half the fish into the hot oil. Fry until lightly browned, about 1½ minutes. Using a wire skimmer or slotted spoon, lift out the fish, holding it over the oil for a few moments to drain, and spread on a large serving plate. Cook and drain the remaining fish slices.

❦ If the sauce has cooled, return it to high heat and reheat, stirring constantly. Pour the sauce evenly over the fish. Serve at once.

serves 4–6

Fresh from the Water

The Chinese word for fish is *yu*. When pronounced with a different inflection it means abundance, so the presence of seafood at a banquet carries great symbolic importance. The Chinese are so fastidious about the freshness of their seafood that, whenever possible, they purchase fish still live and flapping. From gargantuan fresh food markets to the tiniest shopfront, fish sellers display their wares in tubs of bubbling fresh water, to be carried home wriggling in a plastic bag. Garoupa, rock cod, silver and black pomfret, dory, golden thread, hairtail, dace, and red snapper are the favored saltwater fish, while China's wide rivers and lotus-covered lakes yield eels, turtles, bearded catfish, many varieties of carp, and freshwater shrimp. Good seafood restaurants stock their fish and shellfish in giant aquariums. Your choice is brought live to your table for inspection, and the restaurateur offers advice on how it should be cooked.

Huge, oceangoing junks head away from the coast to ply the far reaches of the sea. They pursue the exotics so prized in Chinese cuisine: shark's fins, jellyfish, sea slugs, and drifts of sea laver, a type of seaweed, to compress into papery sheets. In river estuaries from rocky shorelines, fishermen harvest shellfish, including scallops, mussels, oysters, winkles, clams and cockles, shrimp (prawns) and crayfish, and the now scarce abalone.

Hundreds of thousands of Chinese who work on the water seldom leave it. Generations of junk- and sampan-dwelling ethnic Hoklo fishermen rarely step on land, and the cormorant fisherman and his birds have a partnership that may span a lifetime.

Not everyone relies on the fish markets. Give him a fishing pole and a pond of water and you have a very contented man, and not just in rural China. The pensive fisherman watching for the tug on his line has been the subject of paintings for thousands of years, and an artist today in the heart of any major city can still easily find a subject on a bridge over a river, on a wooden boat on a lake, or on a rock beside a stream.

Southern

Zhulijirou Boluo

crisp-fried pork with pineapple sauce

Many different fruits are grown in China—incomparably sweet melons on the far western plateaus; crisp, red-skinned apples and hawthorn fruits in the north; pears so large and white that Marco Polo, in the thirteenth century, was inspired to describe them as "so large they weigh ten pounds [5 kg] apiece!" Citrus and stone fruits grow in the lush Sichuan river basin and the Fujian hinterlands. Litchis, bananas, and other tropical species thrive beside stands of swaying ginger and sugarcane in Guangdong and on Hainan Island. Exotic fruit juices, such as soursop and longan, are popular iced beverages, and are sometimes also used in cooking to make sweet sauces for dessert and savory dishes. Perhaps the most universally popular use of fruit in a sauce is golden chunks of pineapple in a sweet-and-sour sauce. The sauce here is a variation on that theme, with the added zing of black pepper, ginger, and chile.

¾ lb (375 g) pork tenderloin or lean boneless pork leg steaks, thinly sliced across the grain

2 teaspoons peeled and grated fresh ginger

1 teaspoon salt

2 eggs

¼ cup (1½ oz/45 g) all-purpose (plain) flour

¼ cup (1 oz/30 g) cornstarch (cornflour) or tapioca starch

3 tablespoons water

SAUCE

⅓ cup (3 fl oz/80 ml) water

¼ cup (2 fl oz/60 ml) rice vinegar

2 tablespoons sweet chile sauce

3½ teaspoons cornstarch (cornflour)

2½ tablespoons superfine (caster) sugar

½ teaspoon salt

½ teaspoon cracked black pepper

2 tablespoons vegetable or peanut oil

2 teaspoons finely chopped green (spring) onion, including tender green tops

2 teaspoons peeled and finely chopped fresh ginger

1½ teaspoons finely chopped garlic

½ cup (3½ oz/105 g) finely diced pineapple

vegetable or peanut oil for deep-frying

☗ Cut the pork into pieces about 2 inches (5 cm) square and place in a bowl. Add the ginger and salt and mix well. Set aside to marinate for 10 minutes.

☗ In another bowl, lightly beat the eggs, then add the flour, cornstarch, and water to make a thin batter.

☗ To prepare the sauce, in a small bowl, stir together the water, vinegar, chile sauce, cornstarch, sugar, salt, and pepper. In a small saucepan over medium heat, warm the oil. Add the green onion, ginger, and garlic and fry, stirring constantly, until aromatic, about 30 seconds. Add the vinegar mixture and, still over medium heat, bring to a boil, stirring slowly. When the sauce is lightly thickened and has become clear, add the pineapple and simmer until heated through, about 30 seconds. Remove from the heat and keep hot.

☗ Pour the oil to a depth of 1½ inches (4 cm) into a wok, and heat to 375°F (190°C), or until a bit of batter dropped into it turns golden within 2 seconds. Add the pork to the batter and stir to coat each piece. Add one-third of the pork, a piece at a time, to the oil and fry until golden and crisp, about 4 minutes. Using a wire skimmer, transfer to a plate. Allow the oil to return to temperature before cooking the remaining pork in 2 batches. When all the pork has been fried, return it all to the wok at the same time and fry, stirring, until hot and crisp, about 1 minute. Using the wire skimmer, lift it out of the pan, holding it over the oil for a moment to drain, and then spread it on a serving plate.

☗ Pour the sauce evenly over the pork. Serve at once.

serves 4–6

For contentment and productivity, hurry men at work, not at meals.

Western

Chongqing Huoguo

chongqing hot pot

*Sichuan, in China's west, is a basin of silt-rich, fertile
river valleys. It is one of my favorite destinations,
as much for its spectacular scenery as for its food.
Chongqing is a city with a reputation for outstanding
gastronomy, and the hometown of one of China's
most important chef-training institutes. On my first
Sichuan trip, I was longing to try one of the local
hot pots. They feature tripe and other innards
among the meats, all sliced paper-thin in preparation
for the pot. At the table, diners use wooden
chopsticks or small wire baskets to suspend their
choice of ingredients in the bubbling moat of soup.
In this province, which reveres strong flavors,
the soup is redolent of hot bean sauce, pepper,
garlic, and chile.*

*But I visited Chengdu en route, and while there was
introduced to the yin-yang hot pot. Our party gathered
around a tabletop cooker, fitted with a wok segmented
into a yin-yang, two-part configuration by an internal
baffle. In one segment was a mildly seasoned stock,
in the other a potent liquid, scarlet with mashed chiles.
The skewered ingredients were exotic. Tiny, slippery
catfish, baby eels, chunks of turtle and python,
curling fungi, a frog's (or perhaps a quail's) leg.
Two hours later, after we had dunked and eaten
the last skewer, we sat back sweating, drip-splattered,
replete. Chongqing's hot pot would have
to await another visit.*

6 oz (185 g) boneless, skinless chicken breast,
very thinly sliced

6 oz (185 g) beef tenderloin, very thinly sliced

6 oz (185 g) honeycomb tripe, parboiled and
cut into strips 2 inches (5 cm) long by ½ inch
(12 mm) wide, or additional 6 oz (185 g)
uncooked chicken or beef, very thinly sliced

¼ lb (125 g) pork or calf's liver, very thinly
sliced and blanched in boiling water for
20 seconds (optional)

12 large freshwater shrimp or 6 small freshwater
crayfish, about 1¼ lb (625 g) total weight

12 shrimp balls (see page 249)

¼ small head napa cabbage, sliced
(about 2½ cups/7½ oz/235 g)

6 small pieces dried black fungus, soaked in
hot water to cover for 25 minutes

6 dried black mushrooms, soaked in hot water
to cover for 25 minutes

1 oz (30 g) bean thread noodles, soaked in cold
water to cover for 10 minutes, drained, and cut
into 4-inch (10-cm) lengths

2 cups (4 oz / 125 g) bean sprouts, blanched in
boiling water for 10 seconds and drained

chile oil

ground Sichuan pepper

HOT POT

2–2½ qt (2–2.5 l) water

2 tablespoons rice wine

2 tablespoons garlic-chile sauce

2 tablespoons hot bean sauce

2 tablespoons light soy sauce

2 teaspoons salt

❦ Arrange chicken, beef, tripe (if using), and liver (if
using) on a serving platter. Peel the shrimp or crayfish, cut in half lengthwise, and remove the dark vein.
Place the shellfish and shrimp balls on another serving platter, together with the cabbage. Drain the fungus and mushrooms and remove and discard the
stems from the mushrooms and the woody parts
from the fungus if necessary. Squeeze out the excess
water and place on a platter with the noodles and
bean sprouts.

❦ Fill small sauce dishes with the chile oil and
Sichuan pepper for dipping.

❦ To prepare the hot pot, on the table, set up a traditional Chinese fire pot, an electric wok, or a flameproof pot over a portable gas or electric burner. Pour
in the water and bring to a boil over high heat.
Reduce the heat slightly and add the rice wine,
garlic–chile and hot bean sauces, soy sauce, and salt.
Simmer, for 4–5 minutes, skimming off any froth that
accumulates on the surface.

❦ Each guest will cook his or her own selection of
meats and shellfish in the hot stock, 1 or 2 pieces at
a time, retrieving them with wooden chopsticks or
small wire baskets and dipping them in the chile oil
or Sichuan pepper before eating. When all the meats
and shellfish have been cooked and eaten, add the
noodles and cabbage to the simmering stock to heat
through, then ladle into bowls and eat as soup.
Alternatively, place noodles and cabbage in the bowl
and ladle the stock over the top.

serves 6

Western

Dong'an Ji

braised spicy ginger chicken

Ginger, garlic, chiles, vinegar, and Sichuan pepper are the typically exuberant flavors of the landlocked province of Hunan. The city of Dong'an, the reputed birthplace of this dish, is on its southern border.

SAUCE

½ cup (4 fl oz/125 ml) chicken stock (page 250) or water

1½ tablespoons light soy sauce

1 tablespoon black vinegar

2 teaspoons chile oil

1 tablespoon superfine (caster) sugar

14 oz (440 g) boneless chicken thighs, cut into ¾-inch (2-cm) cubes

1 tablespoon dark soy sauce

1 tablespoon cornstarch (cornflour)

peanut or vegetable oil for deep-frying

¾ cup (2½ oz/75 g) chopped green (spring) onion, including tender green tops

1 hot red chile, seeded and sliced

1 tablespoon peeled and grated fresh ginger

1 tablespoon crushed garlic

salt to taste

large pinch of ground white or Sichuan pepper

☙ To prepare the sauce, in a small bowl, stir together the stock or water, light soy sauce, vinegar, chile oil, and sugar. Set aside.

☙ In a bowl, combine the chicken, dark soy sauce, and cornstarch and mix well. Let stand for at least 15 minutes.

☙ Pour the oil to a depth of 1 inch (2.5 cm) into a wok, and heat to 360°F (182°C), or until a small cube of bread dropped into it begins to turn golden within a few seconds. Carefully slide the chicken into the oil, and stir with wooden chopsticks or a slotted spoon to separate the pieces. Fry until golden brown, about 1½ minutes. Using a slotted spoon, transfer to a rack placed over a plate to drain.

Pour off all but 2 tablespoons of the oil, and return the wok to high heat. Add the green onion, chile, ginger, and garlic and stir-fry until partially wilted, about 30 seconds. Return the chicken to the wok and stir-fry over high heat until the ingredients are evenly mixed, about 30 seconds.

Pour in the sauce and stir over high heat until well mixed, about 10 seconds. Reduce the heat to medium-low, cover, and simmer gently until the chicken is tender and the flavors are well blended, about 4 minutes. Season with salt and the pepper.

Transfer to a serving plate and serve at once.

serves 4

Southern

Cha Shao Rou

red roast pork

The red-glazed meats hanging in a Chinese barbecue shop are an irresistible lure. I can never pass by without stopping to shop. Roast pork is a versatile ingredient for which Chinese cooks find many uses: tossed in a stir-fry, diced into fried rice, fanned over steamed rice, chopped into noodles or soups, rolled in steamed rice sheets, or minced into dumpling fillings.

Most roast meat shops are run by families over generations. Sons learn roasting skills from their fathers, mothers teach daughters to wield the cleaver.

1 or 2 pork tenderloins, ¾–1 lb (375–500 g) total weight

MARINADE

2 tablespoons light soy sauce

1½ teaspoons dark soy sauce

1½ tablespoons superfine (caster) sugar

1½ teaspoons five-spice powder

¾ teaspoon baking soda (bicarbonate of soda)

1 teaspoon crushed garlic

1½ tablespoons vegetable oil

3 or 4 drops red food coloring (optional)

1 cup (8 fl oz/250 ml) water

Trim the pork tenderloin(s) to remove any sinew, skin, and fat. Cut in half lengthwise, and then cut the halves crosswise into 6-inch (15-cm) pieces.

To prepare the marinade, in a wide, flat dish, combine the light and dark soy sauces, sugar, five-spice powder, baking soda, garlic, and oil, mixing well. If you want the pork to have its typical red hue, mix in the food coloring. One by one, dunk the pork strips into the marinade, turning to coat evenly, then arrange them in a single layer in the dish. Cover and refrigerate for at least 1½ hours, turning every 20 minutes, or for up to overnight, turning occasionally.

Position a rack in the second highest level in the oven. Pour the water into a drip pan and place it on a rack below. Preheat the oven to 400°F (200°C).

Arrange the marinated pork on the rack, allowing space between the strips, and roast for 12 minutes. Turn and roast for 5 minutes longer. The surface should be glazed and slightly charred at the edges, and the meat inside still pink and tender.

Remove from the oven and allow the pork to rest for 6 minutes before slicing. If cooking in advance, let cool completely on the rack, wrap loosely in waxed (greaseproof) paper, and refrigerate until needed or for up to 4 days.

serves 4–8

Southern

Qing Chao Xiaren

shrimp with cashew nuts

*In Chinese cuisine, no other seafood ingredient
enjoys as much popularity as shrimp (prawns). The
best and freshest go into the stir-fries of the south, the
plumpest into the casseroles of the center and west, and
others, sometimes shell and all, into the "drunken"
dishes of the north. The tiniest of the haul are dried
to become an important flavor additive for soups, rice
dishes, and casseroles. Occasionally, shrimp trawlers
harvest giant shrimp as thick as a broom handle and
as long as a ruler. I cook these in their shells directly
over hot coals, or on a hot iron plate thickly encrusted
with coarse salt. The sweet taste of shrimp offers a
perfect background for myriad Chinese flavors—salty
black beans, tangy sweet-and-sour, and pungent* kung
pao *sauces redolent of chile and Sichuan pepper.
Shrimp are superb simmered in sweet wines, or with*
Longjing *tea leaves and rich, deep soy seasonings.
And what can compare with a pile of the freshest
shrimp straight from the steamer?*

*18 shrimp (prawns) in the shells, about
7 oz (220 g) total weight*

½ cup (4 fl oz/125 ml) vegetable oil

½ cup (2½ oz/75 g) raw cashew nuts

6 thin carrot slices, halved

*1 small yellow onion, cut into wedges
⅓ inch (9 mm) thick and layers separated*

*8 pieces red bell pepper (capsicum), each
¾ inch (2 cm) square*

pinch of salt, plus salt to taste

6 small, very thin fresh ginger slices

*2 asparagus, tough ends removed and sliced
on the diagonal ½ inch (12 mm) thick, or
8 small snow peas (mangetouts)*

2 heads baby bok choy, quartered lengthwise

2 tablespoons water

2 teaspoons rice wine

1 tablespoon light soy sauce

*6 canned straw mushrooms or button mushrooms
(champignons), halved*

*1 tablespoon cornstarch (cornflour) dissolved in
¾ cup (6 fl oz/180 ml) chicken stock (page 250)*

ground white pepper to taste

2 tablespoons chopped green (spring) onion tops

❦ Peel each shrimp, leaving the last segment of the
shell and the tail in place. Using a sharp knife, cut
deeply down the back, devein, and rinse in cold
water. Pat dry with paper towels.

❦ In a wok over high heat, warm the oil. When it is
hot, add the cashews and fry until golden, 45–90 seconds. Using a slotted spoon, transfer to paper towels
to drain.

❦ Add the shrimp to the hot oil and stir-fry until
they curl, turn pink, and are firm, about 1 minute.
Using the slotted spoon, transfer the shrimp to a
plate and set aside.

❦ Pour off the oil into a small, heatproof bowl, wipe
out the wok, and return 2 tablespoons of the oil to
the wok. Place the wok over high heat. When it is
hot, add the carrot, yellow onion, bell pepper, and a
pinch of salt and stir-fry for 40 seconds until the vegetables begin to soften. Add the ginger, asparagus or
snow peas, and bok choy and stir-fry for 20 seconds.
Add the water and stir-fry until the water has evaporated, about 1 minute. Season with the rice wine
and soy sauce, add the mushrooms, and toss and stir
to mix.

❦ Reduce the heat to medium, add the cornstarch
mixture, and cook, stirring slowly, until lightly thickened, about 1½ minutes. Season with salt and pepper.

❦ Return the shrimp to the wok and heat through,
turning to coat evenly with the sauce. Fold in the
cashews and the green onion tops, then transfer to a
serving plate. Serve at once.

serves 2–4

Chinese junks still sail
the South China Sea,
trawling the waters
for their daily catch.

Western

Chenpi Niurou

tangerine peel beef

Peel a tangerine and your nose will tell you why dried tangerine peel (chenpi) makes an interesting seasoning ingredient. In the central provinces of Sichuan and Hunan, it is a common ingredient in dishes from stir-fries to casseroles. Dried peels look like speckled wood chips, but scrape them with a fingernail and they release their wonderful aroma. Juzi is the generic term for the fruit of the orange family. It is a word associated with good fortune, and so oranges are symbolically offered in tribute to the gods, served to guests, and cultivated in gardens.

The use of tangerine or mandarin orange peel in a dish also invites good fortune upon those who eat it. As an ingredient in "red-cooked" dishes, slow-simmered in a soy-based sauce, this aromatic ingredient is often accompanied by the fragrant, dried spice star anise to bring deliciously complex flavors and aromas. Next time you peel a mandarin, scrape the white pith from the underside and place the peeling in a sunny place or low oven. Some Chinese markets sell or give away peels to take home and dry. Dried peel should be kept in a small airtight jar away from heat and damp, or in the freezer to prevent it becoming mildewed; for stir-fries it should be hydrated by soaking in water before use.

10 oz (315 g) trimmed, boneless beef steak such as rump or sirloin

2 teaspoons peeled and grated fresh ginger

1 teaspoon superfine (caster) sugar, plus sugar to taste

2 tablespoons dark soy sauce

3 tablespoons vegetable oil

½ yellow onion, cut into narrow wedges and layers separated

1 hot red chile, seeded and sliced

6 pieces dried tangerine peel, each about ¾ inch (2 cm) square, soaked in hot water for 20 minutes and drained

½ teaspoon Sichuan peppercorns

2½ teaspoons hoisin sauce

1–2 teaspoons hot bean sauce or garlic-chile sauce

salt to taste

❦ Cut the beef across the grain into paper-thin slices, then cut the slices into pieces about 1½ inches (4 cm) long. Place in a dish and add the ginger, 1 teaspoon sugar, and 1 tablespoon of the soy sauce and mix well. Set aside to marinate for about 20 minutes.

❦ In a wok over high heat, warm 2 tablespoons of the oil until it shimmers and begins to smoke. Add the onion and stir-fry until it begins to soften and color, about 40 seconds. Push to the side of the wok or, using a slotted spoon, transfer to a plate.

❦ With the wok still over high heat, add the beef and stir-fry, keeping the meat moving and turning in the wok constantly, until lightly cooked, about 1½ minutes. Using the slotted spoon, transfer to a plate (with the onion, if it has been removed) and set aside.

❦ Add the remaining 1 tablespoon oil to the wok, reduce the heat to medium-high, and add the chile, tangerine peel, and Sichuan peppercorns. Stir-fry until the chiles and tangerine peel are crisp and the peppercorns are very fragrant, about 1½ minutes. Transfer to a separate plate and set aside.

❦ Raise the heat to high and return the beef and onion to the wok. Add the remaining 1 tablespoon soy sauce, the hoisin sauce, and the hot bean or garlic-chile sauce to taste, reduce the heat to medium-high, and stir-fry until the meat and onion are cooked and glazed with the sauce, about 40 seconds. Raise the heat to high again, return the chile, tangerine peel, and peppercorns to the wok, and mix with the beef and onion for 20 seconds. Season to taste with salt and sugar.

❦ Transfer to a serving plate and serve at once.

serves 3 or 4

Vegetables from the market gardens of Sichuan are transported along the Yangtze River to cities in the east.

Western

Hui Guo Rou

twice-cooked pork

During the time I worked in a Hong Kong newspaper office, the editors and journalists in our section ordered in lunch every day from a small food-vending operation nearby. From a minuscule kitchen the cook turned out surprisingly delicious food. He proudly boasted that he'd learned to cook from his mother in a small rural town in Sichuan province. I never did find out how he'd managed to make his way to Hong Kong, and set up his own small establishment in North Point near the newspaper offices. No doubt his story would have been one of courage and fortuitous timing. We ordered this dish several times a week. Hui guo rou translates as "return to the pot," giving the dish its name: twice cooked or double cooked.

"Twice-cooked" dishes began as a kitchen practicality, in the days before refrigeration. Boiled meat keeps better than fresh, so large cuts were cooked, and then carved as needed to make subsequent dishes. Thinly sliced boiled pork, with a pungent garlic sauce, is one of China's most popular appetizer dishes (page 56).

For stir-fries, thinly sliced preboiled pork cooks quickly and is usually more tender than unmarinated fresh pork. Sichuan stir-fries are much more robust and flavorful than their Guangdong counterparts. Garlic, ginger, and hot sauces are used lavishly, and in this region where sweet bell peppers (capsicums) and hot chiles grow profusely, these ingredients also turn up regularly in local dishes.

PORK

1½ lb (750 g) pork belly or pork loin with thick fat layer, in one piece

2 teaspoons salt

¾-inch (2-cm) piece fresh ginger, peeled and thickly sliced

1 green (spring) onion, trimmed

2½ tablespoons vegetable oil

½ red bell pepper (capsicum), about 2½ oz (75 g), seeded and cut into 1-inch (2.5-cm) diamonds

½ green bell pepper (capsicum), about 2½ oz (75 g), seeded and cut into 1-inch (2.5-cm) diamonds

pinch of salt, plus salt to taste

1½ teaspoons chopped garlic

1½–3 teaspoons hot bean sauce

2 tablespoons hoisin sauce

¼ cup (1¼ oz/40 g) sliced bamboo shoot

1 green (spring) onion, including tender green tops, cut into 1-inch (2.5-cm) lengths

1 small, hot red chile, seeded and sliced

¾ cup (1½ oz/45 g) bean sprouts

1 tablespoon light soy sauce

2 teaspoons rice wine

ground white pepper to taste

To prepare the pork, bring a saucepan three-fourths full of water to a boil. Add the pork, blanch for 10 seconds, and pour into a colander in the sink to drain. Place the pork under gently running cold water until cool.

Return the pork to the saucepan, add fresh water to cover, and add the salt, ginger, and green onion. Bring to a boil over high heat, reduce the heat to medium, and simmer, uncovered, skimming the surface occasionally to remove froth, until the pork is barely cooked, about 25 minutes. It will be a pink-gray and a hint of blood will seep if the meat is pierced with a thin skewer.

Leave the pork in the liquid to cool partially, about 15 minutes, then transfer to a plate and let air-dry for 20 minutes. Using a sharp knife or cleaver, thinly slice the pork. Cut the slices into 2-by-1-inch (5-by-2.5-cm) pieces. (If desired, strain the stock and freeze for use in soups or other dishes.)

In a wok over high heat, warm half of the oil. When the oil is hot, add the red and green bell peppers and the pinch of salt and stir-fry until barely softened, about 40 seconds. Transfer to a plate.

Add the remaining oil to the wok and return to high heat. Add the pork and stir-fry for 20 seconds. Add the garlic, hot bean sauce to taste, and hoisin sauce and stir-fry until the pork is well coated, about 20 seconds longer. Return the bell peppers to the wok and add the bamboo shoot, green onion, and chile and stir-fry for 20 seconds. Add the bean sprouts, soy sauce, and rice wine and stir-fry just until well mixed. Season with salt and white pepper.

Transfer to a warmed serving plate and serve immediately.

serves 4

Roast Suckling Pig

Ru zhu (roast suckling pig) has been called the Peking duck of the south. It, too, has glassy amber-red skin, featherlight and crisp as a wafer, over meat that is pink-tender and as soft as butter. These attributes make it the star of banquet menus in Guangdong, Hong Kong, and nearby southern regions. Suckling pig is regarded as one of the ultimate symbols of good fortune, and is served at all celebratory occasions.

A young pig, slaughtered at two months of age and weighing around twelve pounds (6 kg), is considered ideal for a banquet, yet pigs of all sizes are selected for the occasion. The skills of roasting have been handed down from father to son over generations. The pigs, suspended on chains over glowing wood embers, are roasted in tall brick ovens. Alternatively, they are slowly turned on a spit over a pit of coals, to produce a crisp, bubbled crackling over sweetly succulent meat.

The Chinese of the far west also enjoy pork when they can. Eating houses in remote Lanzhou in Gansu province, once a strategic town on the ancient Silk Road, offer a succulent specialty meal of baby roast suckling pig, even though mutton is the favored meat of the region.

Northern

Hongshao Ya Qingsun Xianggu

braised duck with bamboo shoots and mushrooms

"When eating bamboo shoots, remember the men who planted them." So says a Chinese proverb about this uniquely Chinese food product. Only the young shoots are eaten, being harvested just after they break through the earth. Within days they can grow from a tender protruding tip to a lengthy twenty inches (50 cm) of thick shoot that is too fibrous to eat. Fresh bamboo shoots have a layered husk that is removed to reveal a ridged ochre tip. Boiling softens them and removes some of their resinous flavor. Bamboo shoots have a distinct but delicate taste; they lend some of their characteristics to a dish, yet readily absorb other flavors. This makes them perfect accessories to braised dishes featuring soy and strong spices and excellent accompaniments to duck and game meats. Bamboo shoots are sold salted, ready to use in cans, and fresh in plastic bags packed in water. They come sliced and julienned, in chunks and whole tips. Salted dried bamboo shoots should be rinsed and blanched before use.

½ large duck, about 1¾ lb (875 g), chopped into 2-inch (5-cm) pieces

½ cup (2 oz/60 g) cornstarch (cornflour)

1 cup (8 fl oz/250 ml) vegetable or peanut oil

6 oz (185 g) bamboo shoot, cut into 1-inch (2.5-cm) chunks

2 green (spring) onions, white part only, cut into ½-inch (12-mm) pieces, plus tender green tops of 1 green onion, thinly sliced

12 large dried black mushrooms, soaked in hot water to cover for 25 minutes

2½-inch (6-cm) piece fresh ginger, cut into chunks

½ cup (4 fl oz/125 ml) dark soy sauce

¼ cup (2 fl oz/60 ml) oyster sauce

1 tablespoon rice wine

3–4 teaspoons superfine (caster) sugar

1¾ oz (50 g) bean thread noodles, soaked in hot water for 15 minutes, drained, and cut into 4-inch (10-cm) lengths

salt and ground black pepper to taste

1 tablespoon chopped fresh cilantro (fresh coriander) (optional)

❈ Rinse the duck under running cold water and pat dry. Spread the cornstarch in a shallow dish, then dip the duck into the cornstarch, coating lightly and evenly and tapping off the excess.

❈ In a wok or frying pan over high heat, warm the oil until smoking. Add half of the duck pieces and fry, turning once or twice, until the surface is lightly browned, about 5 minutes. Using tongs or a wire skimmer, transfer to a flameproof Chinese clay pot or heavy saucepan. Fry the remaining duck pieces in the same way and add to the clay pot or saucepan.

❈ Add the bamboo shoot and white part of the green onions to the oil and stir-fry until glazed with the oil, about 30 seconds. Add to the duck.

❈ Drain the mushrooms, reserving ¾ cup (6 fl oz/180 ml) of the soaking water. Remove and discard the stems from the mushrooms if necessary, and add the whole caps to the duck. Add the ginger, soy sauce, oyster sauce, rice wine, 2 teaspoons of the sugar, and the reserved mushroom water. Bring to a boil over medium heat, cover the clay pot or saucepan tightly, and simmer, turning the duck pieces occasionally, until the duck is almost tender, about 1 hour.

❈ Add the noodles and simmer briefly to soften and absorb the flavors of the sauce. Taste and season with salt and pepper and with 1–2 teaspoons sugar. Add the green onion tops and the cilantro, if using, and mix briefly. Serve directly from the clay pot or saucepan, or transfer to a serving bowl.

serves 4–6

The Chinese passion for the exotic can surprise the most adventurous gourmet.

Western

Sichuan Douban Yu

sichuan chile and garlic fish

The landlocked province of Sichuan has never wanted for fresh fish and shellfish in its cuisine. Its many lakes, rivers, ponds, and streams are the habitat of an impressive variety of freshwater fish, from carp, perch, and catfish to eels, frogs, turtles, and deliciously sweet freshwater shellfish. It is the Sichuanese penchant for vibrant flavors and powerful, peppery seasoning, rather than the need to disguise inferior quality, that has resulted in some of their most delicious fish and shellfish dishes.

Several species of carp are fished in Chinese waters. Crucian or silver carp is small, meaty, and tender. Grass carp is longer, with a rounded body thick right down to its tail. Rock carp is sweet-fleshed, with a small head and squat, thick body. Chub is the variegated carp, the largest of the species, with a head that can weigh up to half that of its body. These meaty fish heads star in rich and milky fish stews and soups that can be a highlight of a banquet menu during a visit to this fascinating province, or the one-pot meal of a local family. Eels and catfish are meaty and full of flavor, amply making up for the extra effort required to pull off the strong, thick skin that protects them as efficiently as scales. Turtle meat is tender, with a texture more akin to liver than fish. Frogs are considered beneficial and are often recommended during convalescence. Whole frogs are steamed or braised with nutritious herbs, and plump, meaty frog legs are stir-fried or otherwise cooked in the same ways as chicken.

Not every dish cooked in Sichuan is fiery hot. Ginger grows prolifically in this humid subtropical food basin, as do garlic, chile, and sweet bell peppers (capsicums). Together with the local pepper and pungent vinegars, the Sichuanese have a flavor base for their cuisine that is generally not for the faint-hearted, but is definitely addictive.

10 oz (315 g) white fish fillets

1 tablespoon rice wine

2 tablespoons light soy sauce

1–4 teaspoons hot bean sauce

1 teaspoon superfine (caster) sugar

1 cup (8 fl oz/250 ml) vegetable oil

1 celery stalk, thinly sliced on the diagonal

5 thin slices fresh ginger, peeled and finely julienned

2 large cloves garlic, very thinly sliced

½–1 hot red chile, seeded and finely sliced

⅓ cup (1½ oz/45 g) thinly sliced bamboo shoot

2 teaspoons cornstarch (cornflour) dissolved in ½ cup (4 fl oz/125 ml) fish stock (page 250) or water

salt to taste

1 green (spring) onion, including tender green tops, chopped

❧ To prepare the fish, working from the tail end of a fillet, and holding a sharp knife or cleaver at a 45-degree angle, cut the fillet crosswise into slices ½ inch (12 mm) thick. Cut each slice into 2 or 3 pieces. Place the fish in a bowl, and season with 1½ teaspoons of the rice wine and 1 tablespoon of the soy sauce. Set aside for 10 minutes.

❧ In a small bowl, stir together the remaining 1 tablespoon soy sauce, the hot bean sauce to taste, and the sugar. Set aside.

❧ Drain the marinade from the fish into the bowl holding the soy mixture, and pat the fish dry with paper towels. Pour the oil into a wok or large frying pan and place over high heat until the oil begins to shimmer and is nearly smoking. Carefully slide half the fish into the hot oil and fry until lightly cooked, 1½–2 minutes. Using a slotted spoon, transfer the fish to paper towels to drain. Fry the remaining fish in the same way. Pour the oil through a fine-mesh sieve into a heatproof container and reserve.

❧ Wipe out the wok or frying pan and place over high heat. Add 2 tablespoons of the strained oil and heat over high heat until smoking. Add the celery, ginger, garlic, and chile and stir-fry until slightly softened, about 40 seconds. Still on high heat, add the bamboo shoot and the soy–bean sauce mixture and cook for about 30 seconds, stirring slowly. Pour in the cornstarch mixture and stir over high heat until the sauce is lightly thickened, about 40 seconds. Season with salt.

❧ Reduce the heat to low, return the fish to the sauce, and add the green onion. Allow the fish to reheat gently, without stirring, for about 1 minute. Carefully transfer the fish and sauce to a serving dish and serve at once.

serves 4–6

Western

Hongshao Niurou

braised brisket

*Hongshao, the technique of "red braising" in
soy sauce, cooks meats to melting tenderness.*

1 beef brisket, about 2 lb (1 kg), trimmed of fat

2-inch (5-cm) piece fresh ginger, thickly sliced

2 tablespoons vegetable oil

6 cloves garlic, thickly sliced

*2 green (spring) onions, including tender green
tops, thickly sliced*

3 whole star anise

1 teaspoon Sichuan peppercorns

*2 pieces dried tangerine peel, each about
¾ inch (2 cm) square*

¾ cup (6 fl oz/180 ml) dark soy sauce

½ cup (4 fl oz/125 ml) rice wine

¼ cup (2 fl oz/60 ml) hoisin sauce

1–2 teaspoons superfine (caster) sugar

salt and ground black pepper to taste

*⅓ cup (1½ oz/45 g) sliced bamboo shoot or
1½ cups (7 oz/220 g) peeled and cubed daikon
(optional)*

☗ Place the brisket and ginger in a flameproof
Chinese clay pot or heavy saucepan and add water to
cover. Place over low heat and bring slowly to a boil.
Simmer for 20 minutes. Lift out the meat and set
aside on a plate until cool enough to handle, then cut
into 1½-inch (4-cm) cubes. Pour the cooking liquid
through a fine-mesh sieve and measure out 5 cups
(40 fl oz/1.25 l); set aside. Rinse the clay pot or
saucepan and return the cubed meat to it.

☗ In a wok over medium-high heat, warm the oil.
Add the garlic, green onions, star anise, and Sichuan
peppercorns and stir-fry until fragrant, about 40 seconds. Add the tangerine peel, 1 cup (8 fl oz/250 ml)
of the reserved cooking liquid, the soy sauce, and the
rice wine and bring to a boil. Pour the mixture over
the meat and add the remaining 4 cups (32 fl oz/1 l)
cooking liquid. Bring to a boil over medium-high
heat, cover, reduce the heat to low, and simmer until
the meat is almost tender, about 1½ hours.

⚜ Uncover the pot and add the hoisin sauce and the sugar, salt, and pepper to taste. If using the bamboo shoot or daikon, stir in now as well. Simmer, uncovered, over low heat until the meat is very tender and the sauce is reduced, about 30 minutes longer.

⚜ Serve directly from the clay pot, or transfer to a deep serving dish.

serves 6–8

Northern

Muxu Rou

pork with eggs and mushrooms

The character xu *can mean cassia, the Chinese cinnamon, and the eggs in this dish resemble yellow cassia blossoms.*

PORK

½ lb (250 g) lean pork, cut into very thin slices 1½ inches (4 cm) long by ½ inch (12 mm) wide

2 teaspoons light soy sauce

1 teaspoon rice wine

1 teaspoon cornstarch (cornflour)

SAUCE

¼ cup (2 fl oz/60 ml) chicken stock (page 250)

1½ teaspoons sesame oil

1 teaspoon rice wine

¾ teaspoon cornstarch (cornflour)

4 dried black mushrooms, soaked in hot water to cover for 25 minutes and drained

4-inch (10-cm) square dried black fungus, soaked in hot water to cover for 25 minutes and drained

3 tablespoons vegetable oil

3 eggs beaten with ½ teaspoon light soy sauce

¼ cup (1½ oz/45 g) canned straw mushrooms, sliced

⅓ cup (2 oz/60 g) sliced bamboo shoot

2 green (spring) onions, white part only, sliced on the diagonal

1 tablespoon peeled and finely julienned fresh ginger

1 tablespoon light soy sauce

salt and ground white pepper to taste

⚜ To prepare the pork, in a bowl, stir together the pork, soy sauce, rice wine, and cornstarch. Let stand for 20 minutes, stirring occasionally.

⚜ To prepare the sauce, in a bowl, stir together the stock, sesame oil, rice wine, and cornstarch. Set aside.

⚜ Remove and discard the stems from the mushrooms and the woody parts from the fungus if necessary. Thinly slice the mushroom caps and fungus. Set aside.

⚜ In a wok over medium-high heat, warm 1½ tablespoons of the vegetable oil. Pour in the eggs and allow to set softly before breaking up with a spatula into chunks. Turn and cook until firm but still soft, about 2 minutes' total cooking time. Transfer the eggs to a plate and rinse the wok.

⚜ Place the wok over high heat and add the remaining 1½ tablespoons vegetable oil. Add the pork and stir-fry for 30 seconds. Add the black mushrooms, fungus, straw mushrooms, bamboo shoot, green onions, and ginger and stir-fry until thoroughly heated, about 1 minute. Add the soy sauce and stir-fry for 20 seconds. Then add the reserved sauce and stir slowly until lightly thickened, about 1 minute.

⚜ Return the egg to the wok and reheat gently. Season with salt and pepper. Transfer to a serving dish and serve at once.

serves 4

Western

Chengdu Ji

chicken with chiles and peanuts

Harmony and balance are important principles in Chinese cooking. To achieve them, the ingredients in a dish should all be cut into similar sizes and shapes. Peanuts are used frequently in the food of Sichuan, and in this recipe they dictate the size of the diced main ingredients—the chicken, bell peppers (capsicums), and bamboo shoots—which are cut into small cubes. Similarly, in a dish featuring strips of meat, conformity of shape in the accompanying vegetables would call for ingredients like bean sprouts and julienne of carrot and bell pepper.

La is the Chinese word applied to all things hot, and refers not only to hot red chiles and black and Sichuan pepper, but also to spicy bean pastes and crushed chile pastes. Douban lajiang is hot bean sauce, an ingredient that finds favor with most Sichuanese cooks and diners, who appreciate its fiery-salty taste. In Chengdu ji, one of the most popular dishes of this western gastronomic capital city, red chile, Sichuan pepper, and hot bean sauce all contribute their unique taste and heat characteristics.

Using the oil in which the peanuts were fried to cook the chicken further adds to the distinctive Sichuan flavor of this dish. Peanuts grow abundantly in the rich Sichuan basin, where excellent peanut oil is produced for the world market. Boiled and fried peanuts are enjoyed as an appetizer, and are often served as an accompaniment to sliced meats. It is a delightful discovery to find salty boiled peanuts beneath chunky slices of roast suckling pig or crisp-skin chicken.

¾ lb (375 g) boneless, skinless chicken thighs, cut into ½-inch (12-mm) cubes

2 teaspoons cornstarch (cornflour)

1 teaspoon rice wine

2 tablespoons light soy sauce

1 cup (8 fl oz/250 ml) peanut or vegetable oil

⅓ cup (1½ oz/45 g) raw peanuts

½ cup (2½ oz/75 g) cubed bamboo shoot (⅓-inch/9-mm cubes)

⅓ cup (1½ oz/45 g) diced green bell pepper (capsicum)

2 green (spring) onions, including tender green tops, thickly sliced

1 large, hot red chile, seeded and sliced

2 teaspoons peeled and finely chopped fresh ginger

2 teaspoons finely chopped garlic

1 teaspoon hot bean sauce or garlic-chile sauce

½ teaspoon superfine (caster) sugar

2 teaspoons cornstarch (cornflour) dissolved in ¼ cup (2 fl oz/60 ml) chicken stock (page 250)

¼ teaspoon ground Sichuan pepper (optional)

❧ In a bowl, combine the chicken, cornstarch, rice wine, and 1 tablespoon of the soy sauce and mix well. Let stand for 15 minutes.

❧ In a wok over high heat, warm the oil. When hot, add the peanuts and fry until golden, about 1 minute. Using a slotted spoon, transfer to paper towels to drain. Set aside.

❧ Return the wok to high heat. When the oil is smoking, add the chicken and stir-fry, keeping the chicken pieces constantly moving and turning so they cook quickly and evenly, until lightly colored and almost cooked, about 1½ minutes. Using a slotted spoon, transfer to a plate.

❧ Pour off all but 2 tablespoons of the oil from the wok and reheat over high heat until smoking. Add the bamboo shoot, bell pepper, green onions, chile, ginger, and garlic and stir-fry until beginning to soften, about 40 seconds. Add the hot bean or garlic-chile sauce, the remaining 1 tablespoon soy sauce, and the sugar and stir-fry for 10 seconds until well mixed and aromatic. Return the chicken to the wok and continue to stir-fry until cooked, about 30 seconds.

❧ Add the cornstarch mixture and stir until the sauce is lightly thickened and glazes the ingredients, about 30 seconds. Stir in the peanuts and transfer to a serving dish. Sprinkle on the pepper, if using, and serve at once.

serves 4–6

One need not devour a whole chicken to know the flavor of the bird.

Southern

Chao Pangxie Heidou

stir-fried crab with black beans

Crabs are best during the Chinese first, fifth, and ninth lunar months, which means some are at their optimum in flavor and plumpness in October, when orange trees and chrysanthemums bloom, while river crabs are heavy with orange roe in June. Swimmer crabs and green crabs with rounded bodies and long legs are netted out at sea, while freshwater crabs breed abundantly in silt-laden river estuaries. Crab cooked with black bean has international appeal, as does crab wok-tossed with chunky slices of ginger and green onions, or with loads of fresh red chile.

China's most prized crab is the small, box-shaped hairy crab. The most delicious of these freshwater crustaceans are harvested from the lakes around Shanghai, and have become popularly known as Shanghai hairy crabs. Enthusiasts from all over the country flock eastward during the season to enjoy this treat, while Hong Kong gourmets anxiously await the first air shipments. To balance the succulence and sublime sweetness of the roe and pincer meat, tiny cups of ginger tea are served with a crab feast.

1 live hard-shelled saltwater crab, about 1½ lb (750 g)

1 tablespoon rice wine

1 tablespoon cornstarch (cornflour)

1½-inch (4-cm) piece fresh ginger, peeled

SAUCE

½ cup (4 fl oz/125 ml) water or chicken stock (page 250)

1½ tablespoons light soy sauce

2 teaspoons cornstarch (cornflour)

¾ teaspoon superfine (caster) sugar

2 cups (16 fl oz/500 ml) vegetable or peanut oil

1 green bell pepper (capsicum), seeded and cut into ¾-inch (2-cm) squares

pinch of salt dissolved in 1 tablespoon water

1 green (spring) onion, including tender green tops, sliced on the diagonal

1½ tablespoons salted black beans, rinsed, drained, and chopped

1½ teaspoons finely chopped garlic

♛ Bring a large pot three-fourths full of water to a boil. Rinse the crab well under running cold water, then slip the crab into the boiling water and leave for 20 to 30 seconds. Lift the crab from the boiling water and immediately place under running cold water to halt the cooking. Drain well.

♛ Place the crab upside down on a cutting board. Using a cleaver or heavy knife, cut the body into 4 pieces, cutting straight through the shell. Pull off the carapace (top shell) and scrape out the inedible parts, including the dark gray intestines, the liver, and the spongy, feathery gills. Rinse under gently running cold water and drain well. Break off the claws, and crack the hard shells with a meat mallet or heavy pestle.

♛ In a large, shallow dish, stir together the rice wine and cornstarch. Grate the ginger onto a clean cloth, gather up the cloth, and squeeze to release the ginger juice into the wine mixture. Dip the cut edges of the crab pieces into this mixture to coat, and let stand for 5 minutes. Reserve the squeezed ginger flesh.

♛ To prepare the sauce, in a small bowl, stir together the water or stock, soy sauce, cornstarch, and sugar. Set aside.

♛ In a wok over high heat, warm the oil to about 360°F (182°C), or until it begins to shimmer and is smoky. Add the crab pieces and fry, stirring and turning frequently, until the shells are bright red and the cut edges are lightly browned, about 1½ minutes. Lift out with tongs and set on a plate. Pour the oil into a heatproof container.

♛ Return 1 tablespoon of the oil to the wok and reheat over high heat. Add the bell pepper and stir-fry until beginning to soften, about 30 seconds. Add the salted water and stir over high heat until the pepper is almost softened, about 1 minute. Transfer to a plate.

♛ Return the pan to the heat and add 1 tablespoon of the reserved oil. Warm over high heat until it shimmers and is smoky, then add the crab pieces. Stir-fry until warmed through and coated with the oil, about 40 seconds. Return the bell pepper to the wok and add the green onion, black beans, reserved ginger pulp, and garlic. Stir-fry until aromatic and the ingredients are well mixed, about 40 seconds.

♛ Pour the sauce into the wok and cook over high heat, stirring and turning, until the sauce thickens and clings to the crab and bell pepper, about 30 seconds.

♛ Transfer to a serving platter and serve at once.

serves 2–6

Food for an Empress

Because the Qing dynasty Dowager Empress Cixi enjoyed a gourmet reputation, to remain in her favor the imperial chefs had to constantly please her with innovative creations. Lavish meals were served, even when she dined alone. Much went untasted, and when she found something special, her praise was usually veiled behind a demand for the name of the new dish. Lamb was not highly regarded at court. One daring dish of lamb tenderloin in a sweet glaze might have cost the chef his head, had he not invited the empress to suggest a name. Her response—"it's like honey"—became the name of the dish still served today in Beijing.

The empress loved sweet and savory snacks—bite-sized corn breads, sesame-flavored buns, and lotus-filled pastries. On a trip to Guangzhou, she proclaimed *xia jiao* (shrimp dumplings) the "food of heaven." Cixi's fondness for sweet flavors was appeased by countless variations on the sweet-and-sour theme, including a dish of fish served over noodles cooked for her in the ancient capital of China, Kaifeng, in Henan province. Chef Fang Shi was something of an alchemist in the kitchen, devising ways to turn simple food into gold for the empress by embellishing his dishes with egg yolks.

Eastern

Guifei Ji

empress chicken wings

In the exuberant 1920s, Shanghai was a city of wealth, culture, and flamboyance. Chefs flocked from all parts of China, and its restaurants strove to delight an international clientele with the most creative dishes imaginable. Yang Kueifei had been a celebrated imperial concubine in the Tang dynasty (AD 618–907). In tribute to her legendary beauty and desirability, a Sichuanese chef in Shanghai created this dish, in which he bathed the tenderest of chicken wings in a subtly sweet, ruby red sauce made from imported port wine. It became an instant hit with Shanghai society, and an intrinsic part of the repertoire of many of the city's elite restaurants.

Shadows of the opulent lifestyle of the day and fragments of the distinctive architecture of Shanghai's international settlements can be glimpsed amid the densely packed recent developments of China's most populous city. A drift of jazz from the legendary Long Bar of the Peace Hotel wafts through thronged streets, competing with the burr of bicycle bells and the thump of pile drivers. Nearby, the Bund, the riverside walkway of yesteryear, has been transformed into a slick marble-clad pedestrian walkway, where students accost passing tourists to try out their English, and lovers still entwine at night.

Most Chinese have a fondness for textural contrast, the blending of smooth with crunchy or soft with crisp. Some foods are enjoyed even more for their texture than their taste. Beef tendons, tripe, birds' nests and jellyfish come to mind here. Chicken feet and ducks' webs have a texture that many enjoy, as you can witness at a dim sum restaurant any day of the week. I am a fan, myself, as I am of the tips of chicken wings, which have little meat to speak of, but offer a pleasing toothsome experience.

5 large chicken wings, 1–1¼ lb (500–625 g) total weight

⅓ cup (1½ oz / 45 g) sliced bamboo shoot

2 large dried black mushrooms, soaked in hot water to cover for 25 minutes and drained

½ cup (4 fl oz / 125 ml) plus 2 tablespoons vegetable oil

1¾ teaspoons superfine (caster) sugar

1 thin slice fresh ginger, peeled and finely julienned

1 tablespoon rice wine

1 tablespoon light soy sauce

1½ cups (12 fl oz/375 ml) chicken stock
(page 250)

scant ½ teaspoon salt, plus salt to taste

¼ cup (2 fl oz/60 ml) port wine

1 green (spring) onion, including tender green
tops, cut into 1½-inch (4-cm) lengths and
finely julienned

2 teaspoons cornstarch (cornflour) dissolved in
1 tablespoon water

fresh cilantro (fresh coriander) sprigs

❀ Using a cleaver or heavy knife, separate the
wings at the joints. Rinse and drain well. Cut the
sliced bamboo shoots into julienne. Remove and
discard the stems from the mushrooms and thinly
slice the caps.

❀ In a wok over high heat, warm the ½ cup (4 fl oz/
125 ml) oil until smoking. Add 1 teaspoon of the
sugar and, using a wok spatula or wooden chopsticks, stir it in the hot oil for about 10 seconds; it
will bubble and brown. Add the wings and stir-fry

until lightly browned, about 1½ minutes. Using
a slotted spoon, transfer the wings to a rack placed
over a plate to drain. Pour off the oil from the wok
and discard.

❀ Rinse the wok, wipe dry, and replace over high
heat. Add the remaining 2 tablespoons oil and heat
until smoking. Add the bamboo shoot and mushrooms and stir-fry until glazed with the oil, about
20 seconds. Return the chicken wings to the wok
and add the ginger, rice wine, and soy sauce. Heat
briefly, then pour in the stock and add the salt. Bring
to a gentle boil, reduce the heat to low, and simmer
until the wings are just tender, about 15 minutes.

❀ Add the port and the remaining ¾ teaspoon sugar
to the wok and bring to a boil. Reduce the heat to
medium, stir in the green onion, and then the cornstarch mixture. Simmer, stirring continuously, until
the sauce is lightly thickened and becomes clear,
about 20 seconds. Season to taste with salt.

❀ Using tongs, lift the chicken wings onto a serving
plate. Spoon the sauce evenly over the wings and
garnish with cilantro sprigs.

serves 4

Western

Zha Ganlajiao Anchun

crisp-fried chile-and-garlic quail

In cooking this dish, a technique the Chinese call peng is used. The main ingredient is first fried in oil until cooked, then the oil is drained off and additional ingredients and seasonings are stir-fried in the same pan. In this instance only seasoning ingredients are added, while in other applications the second part of the cooking involves the addition of an unthickened sauce, which coats the ingredients in a velvety glaze.

When the first chill winds of winter begin to sweep the north, wild quail assemble for their mass migration to the warmer climes of Guangdong. They are smaller and less tender than the plump-breasted birds bred for the table, but quail trappers and their catch are always welcome at the poultry markets. Guangzhou restaurants and dim sum houses have many recipes for quail and their tiny eggs. Of particular delight is a clear soup in which float tiny poached quail eggs, and shrimp (prawn) toasts or tender meat dumplings in fine wrappers as thin as a scarf, each portion containing a whole hard-boiled quail egg.

3 large quail

1 teaspoon chile oil

2 teaspoons dark soy sauce

vegetable or peanut oil for frying

1 tablespoon sesame oil (optional)

2 teaspoons peeled and finely chopped fresh ginger

2 teaspoons finely chopped garlic

2 teaspoons finely chopped hot red chile

2 teaspoons light soy sauce

pepper-salt (page 33)

1 tablespoon finely chopped green (spring) onion tops

To prepare the quail, cut each quail in half along the breastbone. Trim off and discard the necks and wing tips. Rinse under running cold water, drain well, and pat dry with paper towels. In a small dish, stir together the chile oil and soy sauce, and brush evenly over the quail. Set aside for 10 minutes.

Pour the vegetable oil to a depth of ½ inch (12 mm) into a large frying pan or wok, and heat over high heat until the oil shimmers and begins to smoke. Add the sesame oil, if using. Pat the quail dry again with paper towels, and carefully slide them into the oil. Fry for 1 minute, reduce the heat to medium-high, and continue to fry until golden brown and cooked through, 7–8 minutes. Test by pushing a fine skewer into the thigh or breast of a quail half; if no pink juices flow, the quail are done. Lift them out with a wire skimmer or 2 slotted spoons and set aside on a plate.

Pour off all but 1 tablespoon of the oil, and return the pan to medium-high heat. Add the ginger, garlic, and chile and stir-fry until very fragrant and beginning to brown, about 30 seconds. Return the quail to the pan and add the soy sauce. Shake the pan over high heat, about 10–20 seconds, so the quail tumble and turn until evenly coated with the seasonings. Add 1 teaspoon of the pepper-salt and the green onion tops and repeat the shaking, tossing action, about 10–20 seconds.

Tip the quail onto a serving plate and serve at once with the remaining pepper-salt.

serves 3–6

In some of China's more fanciful dishes, whole hard-boiled quail's eggs symbolize pearls.

Northern

Fengmi Niulijirou Hetaoren

honey-glazed beef and walnuts

Chinese chefs have a great fondness for introducing sweet flavors into meat dishes. In the south, sugar is melted in a hot wok as the base for sweet-and-sour sauces for seafood, chicken, and pork. Chunks of rock sugar melt into soy sauce as the cooking liquid for endless red-braised dishes. In Sichuan, sweetness is balanced with several kinds of pepper, chiles, and vinegar to deliciously pungent effect. Some of the best honey in China comes from the far west. In the days of trading along the legendary Silk Route, it was brought east and north to the imperial courts where chefs used it in sauces for deep-fried foods. The challenge was to ensure the food remained crisp beneath its sweet glaze. Honey-glazed tenderloin is the signature dish of Xining, the capital of outlying Qinghai province, where rare birds and animals feature in many unique dishes.

This version of honey-glazed beef may have derived from a famous dish created in the fall of 1772. Emperor Qianlong, on a tour of the northern reaches outside the Great Wall, indulged in a spot of hunting and bagged three deer. Back in the imperial kitchens, he entrusted them to his head chef with the order to create something worthy of the imperial hunt. The tenderest meat was sliced finely, dipped into egg, and quick fried, then tossed with a sauce of sugar, vinegar, soy, and rice wine. The delighted emperor declared it "sweeter than honey."

10 oz (315 g) lean beef round, partially frozen

3 tablespoons cornstarch (cornflour) or tapioca starch

1 tablespoon water

1 small egg

1 tablespoon light soy sauce

2 teaspoons five-spice powder

vegetable or peanut oil for deep-frying

¾ cup (3 oz/90 g) walnut halves

¼ cup (3 oz/90 g) honey

1 tablespoon rice wine

1 tablespoon light soy sauce

1 tablespoon ginger juice (page 246)

¾ teaspoon black vinegar

½ teaspoon salt

1½ teaspoons sesame seeds (optional)

♕ Using a very sharp knife, cut the meat across the grain into paper-thin slices, then stack the slices and cut into long strips no wider than a matchstick.

♕ In a bowl, stir together 2½ tablespoons of the cornstarch or tapioca starch, the water, egg, soy sauce, and five-spice powder. Add the meat strips and, using chopsticks to separate the strips, mix thoroughly.

♕ Pour the oil to a depth of 1¾ inches (4 cm) into a wok, and heat to 360°F (182°C), or until a small cube of bread dropped into it begins to turn golden within a few seconds. Carefully add the marinated meat and, using long wooden or metal chopsticks, quickly stir the meat to separate the strips. Stir-fry until lightly browned, about 2 minutes. Using a wire skimmer or slotted spoon, lift out the beef, holding it over the oil for a few moments to drain, then tip onto a plate.

♕ Add the walnuts to the hot oil and fry until lightly crisped, about 1 minute. Using the skimmer or spoon, transfer to the plate with the beef.

♕ Pour the oil into a heatproof container. Rinse out the wok and dry carefully. In a small bowl, stir together the honey, rice wine, soy sauce, ginger juice, vinegar, and salt.

♕ Return the wok to high heat and add 2 tablespoons of the reserved oil. When it is hot, add the wine mixture and simmer for 15–20 seconds to make a glaze. Add the meat and walnuts, reduce the heat to medium–high, and stir until each piece is evenly glazed and dry enough on the surface so that the pieces do not stick together, 3–5 minutes.

♕ Pile the beef and walnuts on a serving plate, sprinkle with the sesame seeds, if using, and serve at once.

serves 4–6

A paste of ground walnut and white lead was an ancient Chinese "cure" for baldness.

VEGETABLES, EGGS, AND BEAN CURD

Blocks of fresh bean curd, a variety of vegetables, and a basket of eggs are kitchen staples.

CHINA'S FOOD IS UNMATCHED in its scope and diversity. It is inventive and healthful, and much of it is economical and easy to prepare and cook. This is especially true of the vegetable and vegetarian aspects of the cuisine, where creativity and freshness shine. Chinese greens, in particular, are an abundant source of health-promoting antioxidants; onions, garlic, ginger, and chile bring myriad benefits; and steaming and stir-frying cooking methods ensure natural flavor and vitamins are retained.

One of the cuisine's greatest assets is bean curd. The soybean is a superstar and its health benefits are legendary. What other legume provides such a valuable range of food products? Among its forms are the palatable and easily digested soy milk, pungent seasoning pastes and salty-earthy sauces, skins for wrapping and shredding into noodles, and protein-rich bean curd products that offer a gamut of textures from butter soft to the pleasing firmness of a well-done steak.

Soy products extend the limits of vegetarian food into the infinite. With bean curd as its prime inspiration, China's vegetarian cooks, many of them practicing Buddhists, have

Preceding pages: Chinese cabbage is a staple of the northern winter diet. It is a common sight to see a household's winter stock of cabbages lining hallways or entrances.
Left: Handmade bean curd sheets and noodles laid out ready for sale. **Top:** Charcoal destined for household braziers lines this vendor's cart. Charcoal is the traditional fuel for heating and cooking in China, and is still widely used despite the gradual introduction of gas to the cities.
Above: Lunchtime at a market in Yunnan. This southern province is home to a third of China's ethnic minorities. On market day, village women trek down from the hills to shop and sell their handmade wares.

devised a unique cuisine that is well worth investigating on a visit to China. The menus at two renowned Chinese vegetarian restaurants, Chengdu's Wen Shu Yuan and Beijing's Zhen Su Zhai, are testament to the creativity of their chefs and this fascinating element of Chinese cuisine: eight treasure "duck," "yellow croaker" in spicy sauce, "chicken" or "pork" in stir-fries with peppers and peanuts, and crisp-fried "eel." The vegetarian mock meats and seafoods are made from dried mushrooms and other fungi, mashed taro and other root vegetables, pressed bean curd, and layer upon layer of moistened bean curd skins, molded into the shape of the meats they emulate.

I have the fondest memories of one small vegetarian restaurant in Wanchai, Hong Kong. For years I visited it almost once a week, to eat in or take out. Dishes I ordered often were mock chicken drumsticks glazed with a salty-sweet hot sauce, tiny dumplings with pastry so fine you could see the chopped mushroom and marinated bean curd filling inside, and a thin, diced bean curd and vegetable soup with flavors so alive they all but jumped from the bowl.

China's natural harvest of unique fungi adds variety to the cuisine. Many species are gathered wild in the mountains to the north and west of Sichuan, and some are grown under

Left: During the Cultural Revolution, teahouses were thought to be gathering places for those in opposition and many were forced to close. Today, this teahouse in Chengdu is once again a meeting place for young and old. **Below:** Stone and clay braziers are the portable kitchens of the street vendor. **Below middle:** A woman patiently peels garlic cloves for market. **Bottom:** Eggplants (aubergines) originated in India, but varieties peculiar to China have developed since. Eggplants were first mentioned in a Chinese book written in the fifth century BC.

controlled conditions. The dried food section of the Guangzhou Qing Ping Market is one of the best places to see just how many types there are—lacy bamboo fungi, elegant puffs of white fungi, great curling ears of black wood fungi, and black mushrooms in upwards of twenty sizes, qualities, and prices. In the fresh food area you'll find more: clumped golden mushrooms with heads smaller than a fingernail, round button-like straw mushrooms, fleshy abalone mushrooms, and their pearly cousin, the oyster mushroom. Mushrooms and other edible fungi lend both flavor and texture to vegetable dishes and vegetarian cooking.

Top: The Buddhist Goddess of Mercy dominates this brightly colored shrine in the Dazhao Lamasery, a wooden temple in Hohhot, the capital of Inner Mongolia. Built in 1580, the temple was a center for the city's wealthy citizens. **Above:** Individually labeled, freshly laid eggs are stacked in a basket ready for sale in a Beijing stall. **Right:** A village woman preparing for market selects fresh greens from her terraced garden in a scene played out across China by millions daily. Most vegetables are still grown on small plots and tended by hand.

Fresh vegetables are hugely important in the cooking of the central and southern provinces, but less so in the north where harsh winters limit growing seasons to all but the hardiest of varieties. Cucumbers, cabbages, and cool-climate crops like kohlrabi and turnips prevail in the north, but the south can paint from a far more colorful palette. Sichuan is the vegetable bowl of China, with Guangdong its near rival.

I lived for a time in a little cottage on Cheung Chau island, near Hong Kong. Twenty-five years ago it was one of the main vegetable gardens for the markets and restaurants of Hong Kong, but is now so urbanized it is practically a suburb of the city. There was access by public ferry, but begging a ride on a vegetable delivery boat was often quicker and more interesting, if rather uncomfortable. En route to the markets of Wanchai and Central, perched on a three-legged wooden stool wedged between mountainous stacks of *gai lan* and bok choy, I had time to chat with the farmers about vegetable growing. Organic

farming prevailed on the island, with manure the only fertilizer. With good management they could harvest a crop every two to three months.

The harvests were largely made up of the many varieties of dark green, leafy cabbages for which China and its cuisine is renowned. They picked them small—bok choy often no longer than a finger so it could be cooked whole, *gai lan* and *choi sum* a little larger so flavor had time to develop in the stems. "Bigger is better" is definitely not a principle that applies to Chinese vegetables, with a few exceptions. A large winter melon has the best taste and texture, stem lettuce and white radish should be at least eighteen inches (45 cm) long, and, in the case of the napa cabbage and common round head cabbage so important to the diet of northerners, big means value without loss of quality.

Indigenous vegetables introduce unique tastes and textures. There is nothing to compare to the resinous woodiness of bamboo shoot. Water chestnuts have a sweet, crisp texture reminiscent of the local variety of yam bean, which is almost identical to the jicama of South America. Sprouts from mung beans and soybeans have gained worldwide appeal.

Ginkgo and lotus roots and seeds are useful ingredients in vegetarian cooking, and, on home ground, stem lettuce and West Lake's slippery, textured water shield are available. The mashed flesh of sweet potato and the starchy kudzu root, harvested in mountainous regions from China to Japan, is gelled in a technique similar to that used for bean curd to make firm-soft jellies that cooks use in much the same way as they use soft bean curd.

Along with cultivating vegetables, farmers and housewives have raised chickens and ducks since the beginning of China's recorded history. Eggs have long been part of the cuisine, although the thousand-year egg requires, in reality, only a couple of months to mature. Chefs appreciate the rich flavor of duck eggs, the versatility of chicken eggs, and the elegance of tiny quail and pigeon eggs, and use them all creatively and practically. Cooks in the south embellish soups and clear sauces for vegetables with beaten egg, drizzling it into the hot liquid so it cooks into fine gold and white threads. Hard-boiled or poached quail eggs garnish dim sum, fried toasts, and soups. Chicken eggs are simmered in black tea, or preserved by age-old methods that turn the whites gray-green and make the yolks firm and pungent, to serve as appetizers, and to dice into rice breakfast soup. Eggs broken over a stir-fry result in an effect called "cassia blossom" after the yellow flower of that spice tree. The satiny texture of the *mu xu* pork of Sichuan is the most famed example of this concept.

There is one dish I often use to judge the standard of a restaurant—an omelet. The top should be golden and smooth, the inside trembling-tender. My favorite will contain small chunks of fresh crabmeat or diced shrimp (prawns), with, perhaps, finely sliced asparagus. Its viscous dressing sauce would be redolent of oyster flavors, a mirror-smooth glaze that adds just enough salt to balance the delicacy of the egg. In the hands of a top-notch Guangdong chef, an omelet can be sheer perfection.

Left: The Li River wends its way through the limestone pinnacles near the village of Yangshuo in Guangxi. The pinnacles are riddled with caves that were used by locals to hide from Japanese invaders during the Second World War. These vistas, which have inspired artists and poets for centuries, today delight thousands of visitors to this southern province. **Right:** Bean shoots in vast quantities are needed to satisfy demand at Beijing's Big Bell produce market. **Below:** When temperatures rise, a shady teahouse is the place to gather with friends for tea and a chat.

Southern

Sushijin

spring vegetable stir-fry

Crisp textures, bright colors, and distinct flavors epitomize a good stir-fry. This quick-cook technique is perfect for fresh spring vegetables, as it also retains all of their natural nutrients. For successful stir-frying you need a good nonstick wok and high heat, preferably gas. Heat the wok before adding the oil, and make sure the oil is smoky-hot before adding the ingredients. Once in the pan, keep the ingredients moving and turning so they sear and seal on the hot surface, rather than gather at the bottom to stew.

Many of China's indigenous vegetables are ideal candidates for a stir-fry, especially bamboo shoots, bean sprouts, water chestnuts, and stem lettuce, which has long, thick stems with the taste and texture of asparagus and few leaves. All the Chinese cabbages, of course, and their common relatives broccoli and cauliflower work well in the wok but, like carrot and jicama, may need to be partially steamed before frying.

4 dried black mushrooms, soaked in 1 cup
(8 fl oz/250 ml) hot water for 25 minutes

2-inch (5-cm) piece carrot

2 tablespoons vegetable oil

1 cup (2 oz/60 g) small broccoli florets

1 cup (2 oz/60 g) small cauliflower florets

1½ tablespoons water

4 asparagus, tough ends removed and sliced
on the diagonal ½ inch (12 mm) thick

1 celery stalk, sliced on the diagonal

1 small zucchini (courgette) or other summer
squash, trimmed and sliced

3 oz (90 g) baby bok choy or other small
Chinese cabbages, leaves separated

6–8 small snow peas (mangetouts)

½ cup (2½ oz/75 g) sliced bamboo shoot

1 tablespoon light soy sauce

⅓ cup (3 fl oz/80 ml) chicken stock (page 250)
or reserved mushroom water

½ teaspoon superfine (caster) sugar

1½ teaspoons cornstarch (cornflour) dissolved
in 2 tablespoons water

salt and ground white pepper to taste

☸ Remove the mushrooms from the soaking water, reserving the water. Remove and discard the tough stems from the mushrooms if necessary. Place the mushrooms and their soaking water in a small saucepan and bring to a boil over high heat. Reduce the heat to medium and simmer until tender, 5–6 minutes. When the mushrooms are cool enough to handle, drain, reserving the water for using later if desired; strain through a fine-mesh sieve before use. Cut the mushrooms into quarters and set aside.

☸ Peel the carrot and, using a carving tool or sharp knife, remove 5 or 6 V-shaped strips along the length. Slice the carrot crosswise to create flower-shaped pieces. Set aside.

☸ In a wok over high heat, warm 1 tablespoon of the oil. When it is hot, add the carrot slices, broccoli, and cauliflower and stir-fry for 20 seconds. Add the water, cover the wok, and cook over high heat until the liquid has almost evaporated, about 1 minute.

☸ Add the asparagus, celery, zucchini or squash, and bok choy or cabbage, cover, and cook, splashing in a little more water if needed to prevent scorching, until the bok choy or cabbage is wilted, about 30 seconds.

☸ Uncover, add the remaining 1 tablespoon oil, the snow peas, bamboo shoot, and mushrooms, and stir-fry until the snow peas are bright green, about 20 seconds. Add the soy sauce, stock or mushroom water, sugar, and cornstarch mixture and boil briskly, stirring, as the sauce thickens and becomes clear, 20–30 seconds. Season with salt and pepper.

☸ Transfer to a warmed serving plate and serve immediately.

serves 4–6

New shoots and spring vegetables inspire southern cooks.

Northern

Luohan Cai

buddhist vegetable clay pot

*Buddhism has inspired a creative vegetarian cuisine
that is served daily in temples and is eaten by
the devout throughout China. This dish, which
incorporates black fungus and hair vegetable among
other indigenous ingredients, is served on Chinese
New Year's Day to remind Buddhists of their vow
to respect life in all its forms.*

1 cup (8 fl oz/250 ml) water or vegetable stock
(page 251)

⅓ cup (3 fl oz/80 ml) light soy sauce

2–3 teaspoons yellow bean paste or
1½ tablespoons drained yellow bean sauce

1 teaspoon superfine (caster) sugar

1½ oz (45 g) bean thread noodles, soaked in
cold water to cover for 10 minutes, drained, and
cut into 4-inch (10-cm) lengths if desired, or
1 dried bean curd stick, soaked in hot water
to cover for 2 minutes, drained, and cut into
1½-inch (4-cm) lengths

5-oz (155-g) piece peeled winter melon or
daikon, cut into 1½-inch (4-cm) cubes

1 small carrot, peeled and sliced

½ lb (250 g) napa cabbage, roughly chopped

¼ oz (7 g) hair vegetable, soaked in cold water
to cover for 10 minutes and drained (optional;
see page 246)

½ cup (2½ oz/75 g) sliced bamboo shoot

⅓ cup (2 oz/60 g) canned golden, button
(champignon), or straw mushrooms

⅓ cup (2 oz/60 g) drained, canned abalone
mushrooms; 2-inch (5-cm) square dried black
fungus, soaked in cold water for 10 minutes,
drained, woody parts removed, and chopped; or
1 oz (30 g) fresh oyster mushrooms, brushed clean

7 oz (220 g) fried bean curd, cut into
1½-inch (4-cm) squares, soaked in hot water
to cover for 10 minutes, and drained

2 green (spring) onions, including tender green
tops, roughly chopped

salt and ground white pepper to taste

☼ In a bowl, stir together the water or stock, soy
sauce, bean paste or sauce, and sugar.

☼ Spread the noodles or bean curd stick in the bottom of a Chinese clay pot or a heavy saucepan. Top
with the winter melon or daikon, carrot, and cabbage.

Arrange the hair vegetable (if using); bamboo shoot;
golden or other mushrooms; abalone mushrooms,
fungus, or oyster mushrooms; and the fried bean
curd over the top. Pour in the sauce mixture.

☼ Place over medium heat and bring to a boil.
Cover, reduce the heat to low, and simmer gently,
turning the vegetables occasionally, until all the
ingredients are tender, about 20 minutes.

☼ Stir in the green onions, and season with salt and
pepper. Serve directly from the clay pot or saucepan.

serves 4–8

Northern

Shengbai Bocai

quick-fried spinach with garlic

*Chinese vegetable markets offer several leaf vegetables
akin to spinach. Qingcai is tender winter rape.
Een choi is summer spinach, said to reduce body
heat. Ong choi is a water vegetable with hollow
stems and pointed leaves, and "red in snow" is
a northern variety with red-tipped leaves.*

1½ tablespoons vegetable oil

1 teaspoon sesame oil

3 large cloves garlic, chopped

¾ lb (375 g) young, tender spinach, stems
removed

1 tablespoon oyster sauce

1 tablespoon light soy sauce

½ teaspoon superfine (caster) sugar

☼ In a wok over medium–high heat, warm the vegetable and sesame oils. When the oils are hot, add the
garlic and stir-fry for 10 seconds until fragrant. Add
the spinach and stir-fry, stirring constantly, until
every leaf has wilted, about 1 minute. Add the oyster
and soy sauces and the sugar and stir-fry for 30 seconds to blend the flavors.

☼ Transfer to a warmed serving plate and serve
immediately.

serves 4

Northern

Ganshao Dongsun
Meifenyu Toufa

"mermaid's tresses"

Everything about this dish is a delight, from its romantic name, which equates the crisp green vegetable with the seaweed mane of a mermaid, to its unique combination of textures and tastes. It has been a favorite all my life. As a young girl, I was enraptured by the wafer lightness of the greens, and loved the sweet, dry-fried walnuts that often replace the pungent ganbei (dried scallops). It was a feature at my wedding banquet in Hong Kong, and at a banquet to celebrate my daughter's birth.

Crisp-fried Chinese broccoli (gai lan) leaves make a festive garnish for fried chicken, grilled pork chops, and purchased roast duck or suckling pig. I also mound them high on thick soups as a dramatic garnish.

Ganbei are a type of deep-sea scallop harvested off the China coast. They are cut into slices and dried into rock-hard, amber disks with a flavor and aroma so superb the Chinese will gladly pay exorbitant prices for them. They can be bought more economically as small chips or floss.

1 rounded tablespoon dried scallops (about ½ oz/15 g), soaked for 25 minutes in ½ cup (4 fl oz/125 ml) warm water (optional)

6 oz (185 g) bamboo shoot, quartered lengthwise

1 tablespoon light soy sauce

1 tablespoon cornstarch (cornflour) or tapioca starch

3½ teaspoons superfine (caster) sugar

vegetable oil for deep-frying

3 cups (9 oz/280 g) sliced Chinese broccoli leaves (from 2 bunches, about 1½ lb/750 g total weight)

vegetable oil for deep-frying

1½ teaspoons salt

♛ Put the soaked scallops and their soaking liquid in a heatproof bowl and place in a steamer basket. Bring water to a simmer in a steamer base. Place the steamer basket over the simmering water, cover, and steam until soft enough to crumble, about 20 minutes. Remove the scallops from the steamer, let cool to room temperature, then shred the scallops by rubbing the pieces between your finger and thumb. Drain well and set aside on a paper towel to dry.

♛ In a shallow dish, combine the bamboo shoot, soy sauce, cornstarch or tapioca starch, and 1 teaspoon of the sugar. Set aside for 10 minutes, then drain and dry on paper towels.

♛ Pour the oil to a depth of 1¾ inches (4.5 cm) into a wok, and heat to 375°F (190°C), or until a small cube of bread dropped into the oil colors within a few seconds. Add the sliced broccoli leaves and fry until crisp, bright green, and you hear a rustling sound, 1½–2 minutes. Be careful that the oil does not spatter you. Using a wire skimmer, lift the leaves from the oil, holding them over the oil for a few moments to drain, then place in a colander lined with paper towels.

♛ Carefully add the dried scallop shreds to the same hot oil and fry until crisp, about 30 seconds. Using the wire skimmer, transfer to paper towels to drain.

♛ Reduce the heat to medium and add the bamboo shoot. Fry, turning occasionally, until well colored and partially crisped on the surface, about 2 minutes. Using the wire skimmer, transfer to paper towels to drain.

♛ To assemble the dish, sprinkle ¾ teaspoon of the salt and 1¼ teaspoons of the remaining sugar over the crisp vegetable leaves, then toss to mix. Pile onto a serving platter. Season the bamboo shoot with the remaining ¾ teaspoon salt and 1¼ teaspoons sugar and arrange over the leaves. Scatter the crisp scallop shreds on top. Serve at once.

serves 6

The Chinese hold green vegetables in high regard, associating their color with jade, a much-revered gemstone.

Gong Bao Doufu

stir-fried bean curd and bell pepper

Sichuan dishes stir-fried over high heat with chiles and hot oil are often called gong bao.

2½ tablespoons vegetable oil

⅔ cup (3 oz/90 g) diced red bell pepper (capsicum)

½ cup (2½ oz/75 g) diced green bell pepper (capsicum)

½ cup (2½ oz/75 g) diced yellow bell pepper (capsicum)

½ cup (2½ oz/75 g) chopped green beans or peeled and diced broccoli stems

salt to taste

5 oz (155 g) fresh firm bean curd, cut into ⅓-inch (9-mm) cubes

½ cup (2½ oz/75 g) canned button (champignon) or straw mushrooms, halved

¼ cup (1¼ oz/40 g) diced bamboo shoot or water chestnut

1 teaspoon peeled and grated fresh ginger

2 tablespoons light soy sauce

1½ tablespoons hoisin sauce

2 teaspoons cornstarch dissolved in ½ cup (4 fl oz/125 ml) cold water

4 green (spring) onions, white part only, chopped

1–2 teaspoons chile oil or 1 hot red chile, seeded and chopped (optional)

ground Sichuan or white pepper to taste

In a wok over high heat, warm the oil. When the oil is hot, add the bell peppers and beans or broccoli stems and stir-fry, adding a little salt, until beginning to soften, about 1 minute. Add the bean curd, mushrooms, and bamboo or water chestnuts and stir-fry briefly. Season with the ginger, soy sauce, and hoisin sauce, stir in the cornstarch mixture, and cook, stirring slowly, until lightly thickened, about 1½ minutes.

Add the green onions and the chile oil or chopped chile to taste and heat gently, stirring carefully and turning the bean curd until heated through. Taste and adjust the seasoning with salt.

Transfer to a warmed serving plate and sprinkle with the Sichuan or white pepper. Serve at once.

serves 4–6

Southern

Hao Zhi Jie Lan Cai

greens in oyster sauce

Apart from the obvious health benefits derived from eating antioxidant-rich, dark green, leafy vegetables, I think Chinese greens are addictively delicious. Even at a dim sum restaurant, faced with carts loaded with dumplings, buns, rolls, and tempting crisp-fried tidbits, I always make room for a plate of Chinese greens. In several of my favorite haunts, they are cooked to order on a mobile cart right beside the table, and served redolent of salty oyster sauce, a perfect flavor companion.

Chinese greens are unique varieties belonging to the Brassica genus of green vegetables. In general, their flavor and appealing bitterness is more pronounced than in common cabbages, although they can be compared to Italian varieties such as broccoli rabe.

1 bunch Chinese greens such as Chinese broccoli or bok choy, about 10 oz (315 g)

2 cups (16 fl oz / 500 ml) chicken stock (page 250) or water

1 teaspoon salt

1 tablespoon vegetable oil

3½ tablespoons oyster sauce

☙ If using Chinese broccoli, cut off the hard stems and discard any large, tough leaves. Cut the stems in half crosswise. If using bok choy, and they are no more than 6 inches (15 cm) long, trim the ends and slit the whole head in half lengthwise. If the bok choy are larger, trim the ends, separate the leaves, cut the stems into 4-inch (10-cm) lengths, and keep the leaves and stems separate.

☙ In a wok or saucepan over high heat, bring the stock or water to a boil. Add the salt and oil. If using Chinese broccoli, add and boil, uncovered, until crisp-tender, about 2½ minutes. If using bok choy, cook halved small bok choy for 1½ minutes. If using large bok choy, cook the stems first for 2 minutes, then add the leaves and cook for 20 seconds. Using tongs, lift out the greens and arrange on a serving plate. Pour off the cooking liquid, reserving 1½ tablespoons.

☙ Reheat the wok over medium heat and add the reserved cooking liquid and the oyster sauce. Warm gently until almost boiling. Pour evenly over the greens and serve at once.

serves 4

Eastern

Xierou Danguan

crabmeat omelet

Fujian chefs are known for the lightness and delicacy of their dishes. Seafood features prominently in the coastal provinces, and this crabmeat omelet is a triumph of texture and flavor.

OMELET

6 eggs

2 tablespoons water

1 teaspoon rice wine

1 teaspoon light soy sauce

½ teaspoon salt

SAUCE

¼ cup (2 fl oz / 60 ml) chicken stock (page 250) or water

1½ tablespoons oyster sauce

½ teaspoon cornstarch (cornflour)

¼ teaspoon superfine (caster) sugar

2 tablespoons vegetable oil

½ teaspoon sesame oil (optional)

2 green (spring) onions, including tender green tops, thinly sliced, plus 1 tablespoon very thinly sliced green onion tops for garnish

5 oz (155 g) crabmeat, flaked

½ cup (¾ oz/20 g) chopped fresh cilantro (fresh coriander)

To prepare the omelet, in a bowl, whisk the eggs until barely blended, then quickly whisk in the water, rice wine, soy sauce, and salt.

To prepare the sauce, in a small bowl, stir together the stock or water, oyster sauce, cornstarch, and sugar. Set aside.

Heat an 8½-inch (21.5-cm) omelet pan over medium heat. When it is hot, add 1 tablespoon of the vegetable oil and the sesame oil, if using. Heat until the oil begins to shimmer, then add the green onions and fry until partially wilted, about 30 seconds. Using a slotted spoon, transfer to a plate.

Reheat the pan over high heat. When very hot, pour in the egg mixture and cook for 10 seconds. Spread the fried green onions, crabmeat, and cilantro evenly over the eggs. Cook over high heat for another 30 seconds, until the egg has set underneath, then reduce the heat to medium. Cook until the underside is firm and brown and the top is softly set, about 5 minutes.

Using a wide spatula, flip the omelet. Raise the heat to medium-high and cook on the second side until golden, about 40 seconds. Remove from the heat and slice into squares with the spatula. Carefully slide the omelet pieces onto a warmed plate.

In a small saucepan over medium heat, warm the remaining 1 tablespoon vegetable oil. Pour in the sauce mixture and bring to a boil. Cook, stirring, until the sauce is lightly thickened, about 30 seconds.

Pour the sauce over the omelet pieces and garnish with the green onion tops. Serve at once.

serves 2–4

Zhi Jie Lancai Dan Xian Jiang

broccoli with egg thread sauce

Balance achieved through contrast is an admired characteristic in Chinese cooking. This simple vegetable dish is a perfect example of the precept, with tender ribbons of white egg draped over crisp, jade green broccoli. "Egg threads" appear in many southern Chinese dishes to supplement more expensive ingredients, such as shark's fin and crabmeat, and provide an extra boost of nourishing protein.

2 tablespoons vegetable oil

3½ cups (7 oz/220 g) broccoli florets

1 teaspoon peeled and grated fresh ginger

1 cup (8 fl oz/250 ml) water

1 teaspoon salt

EGG THREAD SAUCE

½ cup (4 fl oz/125 ml) chicken stock (page 250) or reserved broccoli water

1 tablespoon light soy sauce

1½ teaspoons cornstarch

2 teaspoons vegetable oil

2 egg whites, well beaten

salt and ground white pepper to taste (optional)

☗ In a wok over high heat, warm the oil. When the oil is hot, add the broccoli florets and ginger and stir-fry for 20 seconds. Pour in the water, add the salt, cover, and cook until the broccoli is crisp-tender, about 2 minutes. Uncover and, using a slotted spoon, transfer the broccoli to a warmed serving plate; keep warm. Pour the water out of the wok, reserving ½ cup (4 fl oz/125 ml) for the sauce, if desired.

☗ To prepare the sauce, in a small bowl, stir together the stock or reserved broccoli water, soy sauce, and cornstarch. In the wok over high heat, briefly warm the oil. Pour in the stock mixture and stir until lightly thickened, about 1 minute. Remove from the heat. Holding a fine sieve high above the wok, strain the egg whites into the sauce. They should fall in fine streams. Do not stir the sauce for at least 30 seconds, allowing the egg to set in fine ribbons. Then stir gently, and season with salt and white pepper, if needed.

☗ Pour the hot sauce over the broccoli and serve at once.

serves 4–6

Nimble Fingers

The Chinese have never found the need for table cutlery. Instead, two slender sticks called *kuaizi*, which translates as "quick little boys," became indispensable tools at the table and in the kitchen. Chopsticks come in all manner of materials and decoration, from the elegant solid silver and jade chopsticks reserved for the grandest occasions and durable ebony pairs from Guangxi to functional plastic, plain bamboo, and the artistically lacquered chopsticks of Fujian province. An archeological dig in southern China unearthed chopsticks dating back to the Qin dynasty (221–207 BC) showing that earlier styles were much longer than the standard ten-inch (25-cm) chopsticks commonly used today.

Children begin to use chopsticks as soon as they are old enough to hold them, and quickly learn that speed and dexterity mean they can beat others to the choicest pieces from the communal dish. Etiquette dictates chopsticks should not be waved about or used as pointers, and after a meal should be left neatly on the table beside the rice bowl. A popular old saying advised, "If you rattle your chopsticks against the bowl, you and your descendants will always be poor."

Southern

Chao Niunai Xiaren Mifen

stir-fried milk with shrimp
on crisp rice noodles

I could not believe I had heard correctly when I was first invited to share a dish of stir-fried milk. Milk is almost never used in Chinese cooking, except in a limited way in Muslim cuisine. Stabilized with mashed shrimp (prawns), beaten egg whites, and cornstarch (cornflour), the fried milk forms a sublime, velvety scramble with textural highlights from the fragments of ham and nuts. It's irresistible.

The concept of using milk in cooking may have its origins in Portuguese Macao, the coastal neighbor of Guangdong, where beef cattle and milk were plentiful. The Tibetans, Muslims, and other minority groups in southwestern Yunnan and in the western parts of China traditionally include milk in their diets, whether from cows, goats, yaks, or buffalo. The cheeses are salty and crumbly like feta, or mild and firm like haloumi. Yak milk and butter are important dietary supplements in the far west, where a potent alcoholic drink, a type of koumiss, is made from fermented yak milk. Processed and fresh dairy products are becoming more readily available, at least in the major cities. Milk can now be used in dishes such as Cabbage with Creamy Sauce and Bacon (page 169); traditionally the creamy effect was achieved by whisking stock and fat with cornstarch.

SHRIMP

¾ cup (4½ oz/140 g) diced shrimp (prawn) meat

1 teaspoon cornstarch (cornflour)

¼ teaspoon baking soda (bicarbonate of soda)

¼ teaspoon salt

1 tablespoon water

1¼ oz (40 g) rice vermicelli

vegetable oil for deep-frying

6 egg whites

1 tablespoon tapioca starch or cornstarch (cornflour)

1¼ cups (10 fl oz/310 ml) milk

½ teaspoon salt

1 tablespoon finely minced ham (optional)

2 teaspoons pine nuts or cashews, toasted and chopped

fresh cilantro (fresh coriander) sprigs or finely chopped green (spring) onion tops

♕ To prepare the shrimp, in a small bowl, mix together the shrimp, cornstarch, baking soda, salt, and water. Let stand for 10 minutes.

♕ Lightly break up the bundle of rice vermicelli. Pour the oil to a depth of 1½ inches (4 cm) into a wok, and heat to 375°F (190°C), or until a length of noodle dropped into the oil puffs up and floats immediately. Add half of the rice vermicelli and fry, turning once, until crisp and white, about 3 seconds on each side. Using a wire skimmer, lift the noodles from the oil, drain briefly over the wok, and then place on a flat plate lined with paper towels to drain. Fry the remaining rice vermicelli in the same way. Set aside. Pour off the oil into a heatproof bowl. Wipe out the wok.

♕ In a bowl, beat the egg whites until light and fluffy and fold in the tapioca starch or cornstarch, milk, and salt. Return 1 tablespoon of the hot oil to the wok and heat over high heat. When the surface of the oil is rippling, add the shrimp and stir-fry until white and firm, 40–50 seconds. Using a slotted spoon, transfer to a plate.

♕ Rinse and dry the wok and add 3 tablespoons of the reserved oil. Place over medium–high heat and heat until the oil is warm. Gradually pour in the milk-egg mixture and cook, stirring it slowly in one direction, until softly set, about 1½ minutes. Add the shrimp and the ham, if using, and mix in evenly.

♕ Gently crumble the fried vermicelli and spread over a platter. Spoon the egg scramble over the top, then scatter on the nuts. Garnish with the cilantro or green onion tops and serve at once.

serves 2–4

The Chinese meal observes a sequence that alternates heavy- and light-flavored dishes, and serves salty dishes before sweet.

Food Markets

A market tour is an enlightening, heady experience, with its urgent press of humanity, its evocative aromas, its cacophonous noise. I came to understand many aspects of Hong Kong through my daily trek to the Central Market or the markets in Wanchai, where I watched in fascination as butchers expertly dissected carcasses, poultry was plucked and gutted, and scurrying crabs were restrained with skillfully knotted strings. Every day, crouched on a stool in the corner of the onion seller's stall, an elderly woman patiently peeled garlic cloves. I remember one instance of a stall holder shrieking abuse as a shopper tripped over a cage of live frogs, and his merchandise instantly scattered.

China's markets crackle with action and noise from daybreak, with the arrival of vegetable-laden trucks and merchandise in cages, boxes, and bags—live snakes, cats, dogs, frogs, pigs, quail, chickens, and ducks. There's a frenzy of activity and lively banter while stalls are set up and merchandise displayed—herbs and fruit in mounds, pristine vegetables stacked in precise rows. Then the public and the restaurateurs surge in, and the noise level cranks up several notches as vendors raucously announce their merchandise and prices.

Just about every village in China has a market and, even if you don't plan to shop, visiting them is one of the best ways to discover the specialties of the area, to listen to the different dialects and accents, to observe the dress and mannerisms of the stall holders and their customers. I am always spellbound by three of China's largest markets: Guangzhou's Qing Ping, for its dried foods in particular—you could walk for hours in this section alone; Chengdu's Free Market, for its vegetables and freshwater fish products—you could not find fresher anywhere in the country; and Chongqing's Central Market, for its mounds of bean jelly and bean curd wobbling in trays beside piles of strangely shaped mushrooms, scarlet bell peppers (capsicums), and fat, pink garlic.

Western

Sichuan Yu Xiang Qui Zi

sichuan spicy eggplant

The Sichuanese say that, to be at its best, this popular dish should be made with unpeeled eggplant, to give it a purple color, and be loaded with garlic. Surprisingly, the taste is strong but not overpowering. Several species of garlic-flavored plants grow in Sichuan, and local cooks use them all without restraint. The common garlic has small, tightly packed pink heads containing small cloves. Slender, pungent garlic chives proliferate, as does a mild-flavored variety of garlic with a large, round bulb.

4 slender (Asian) eggplants (aubergines) or
1 or 2 round eggplants, about 1 lb (500 g)
total weight

1 tablespoon salt

¼ lb (125 g) coarsely ground (minced) pork

1 tablespoon hot bean sauce

1 cup (8 fl oz/250 ml) vegetable oil

¼ cup (1 oz/30 g) chopped garlic

2 tablespoons peeled and grated fresh ginger

2 tablespoons light soy sauce

1 tablespoon hoisin sauce

1 teaspoon black vinegar

¾ teaspoon superfine (caster) sugar

2 teaspoons cornstarch (cornflour) dissolved in
⅓ cup (3 fl oz/80 ml) chicken stock (page 250)
or water

½ cup (1½ oz/45 g) chopped green (spring)
onion, including tender green tops

2 teaspoons sesame oil

½ teaspoon Sichuan peppercorns, crushed
(optional)

1–2 tablespoons chopped fresh cilantro
(fresh coriander)

If using slender eggplants, trim and cut into strips 2 inches (5 cm) long by ¾ inch (2 cm) wide by ¼ inch (6 mm) thick. If using round eggplants, trim and cut into slices ⅓ inch (9 mm) thick, then cut the slices in half. Place the eggplant pieces in a colander and sprinkle with the salt. Let stand for 30 minutes to draw off the bitter juices. Rinse thoroughly in cold water, drain, and pat dry with paper towels.

In a bowl, combine the pork and hot bean sauce, mixing well. Set aside.

In a wok over high heat, warm the vegetable oil until the surface ripples. Add the eggplant pieces and cook for 1 minute. Reduce the heat slightly and continue to cook until the eggplant pieces are browned but still retain their shape, 5–6 minutes. Place the colander over a bowl. Tip the eggplant and oil from the pan into the colander and leave to drain for at least 30 minutes or for up to 4 hours.

Return the wok to high heat and add 1 tablespoon of the strained oil. Add the pork, garlic, and ginger and stir-fry until the pork is cooked and lightly colored, 1½–2 minutes. Return the drained eggplant to the wok and add the soy sauce, hoisin sauce, black vinegar, and sugar. Cook, stirring carefully, for about 30 seconds. The eggplant will begin to break up at this stage. Add the cornstarch mixture and simmer, stirring slowly, until lightly thickened, about 40 seconds.

Stir in the green onion and sesame oil. Taste and adjust the seasoning with salt. Transfer to a warmed serving plate, sprinkle with the Sichuan peppercorns (if using) and cilantro, and serve at once.

serves 4–6

Mapo Doufu

"old pock-marked mother's" bean curd

Her scarred face immortalized in the name of Sichuan's most famous dish, the old woman was the wife of Ch'en Fuchih, a chef who operated a small restaurant in Chengdu in the late 1800s.

2-inch (5-cm) square dried black fungus, soaked in hot water to cover for 25 minutes and drained (optional)

2 tablespoons vegetable oil

½ lb (250 g) lean ground (minced) beef or fat pork such as pork butt

1 tablespoon peeled and grated fresh ginger

1 teaspoon chopped garlic

2–4 teaspoons hot bean sauce

2–4 teaspoons thick black bean sauce or additional hot bean sauce

1 tablespoon rice wine

1 cup (8 fl oz/250 ml) chicken stock (page 250) or pork stock (page 251)

1½ tablespoons cornstarch (cornflour) dissolved in ¼ cup (2 fl oz/60 ml) water

1 lb (500 g) fresh soft bean curd, cut into ½-inch (12-mm) cubes (2½ cups)

½ cup (1½ oz/45 g) chopped green (spring) onion, including half of tender green tops

salt and ground Sichuan pepper to taste

❦ If using the black fungus, remove and discard the woody parts from the fungus if necessary. Chop the fungus very finely.

❦ In a wok over high heat, warm the oil. When it is hot, add the fungus and meat and stir-fry until the meat is lightly browned, 1½–2 minutes. Add the ginger, garlic, hot bean sauce and black bean sauce (or more hot bean sauce) to taste, and the rice wine and stir-fry for 20 seconds. Pour in the stock, bring to a boil, and simmer, stirring frequently, for 3–4 minutes to blend the flavors. Add the cornstarch mixture and cook, stirring slowly, until lightly thickened, about 1 minute. Carefully fold in the bean curd and green onion and heat through gently. Season with salt.

❦ Transfer to a warmed bowl, and sprinkle generously with Sichuan pepper. Serve immediately.

serves 4–6

Northern

Chao Ludouya Ji

bean sprouts stir-fried with chicken

Fastidious cooks like to transform bean sprouts into elegant "silver sprouts." All that is required is to snap off the seedpod and slender tapering root from each sprout, leaving just the crisp, translucent stem. This step not only makes it more attractive, but gives the dish a more delicate flavor.

4 cups (8 oz/250 g) bean sprouts

3 oz (90 g) boneless, skinless chicken breast, cut into fine strips

4 teaspoons light soy sauce, plus soy sauce to taste

2 tablespoons vegetable or peanut oil

1 green (spring) onion, including tender green tops, cut into 1½-inch (4-cm) lengths and finely julienned

½ teaspoon peeled and grated fresh ginger

1½ teaspoons cornstarch (cornflour) dissolved in ⅓ cup (3 fl oz/80 ml) chicken stock (page 250) or water

☗ Place the bean sprouts in a colander in the sink. Bring a teakettle filled with water to a boil, and pour the boiling water evenly over the bean sprouts. Drain well, tip the bean sprouts into a bowl, and cover with cold water for 1 minute to cool and crisp. Drain well again and set aside.

☗ In a bowl, stir together the chicken, 2 teaspoons of the soy sauce, and 2 teaspoons of the oil. Set aside for 10 minutes.

☗ In a wok over high heat, warm the remaining oil until it shimmers and begins to smoke. Add the chicken shreds and stir-fry, using long wooden or metal chopsticks to separate the shreds, until the chicken is almost cooked and has turned white, about 40 seconds. Add the bean sprouts, green onion, ginger, and the remaining 2 teaspoons soy sauce and stir-fry over high heat until the bean sprouts are soft and the chicken is firm, about 30 seconds longer.

☗ Stir in the cornstarch mixture and simmer, stirring, until the sauce is lightly thickened and becomes clear, 30–40 seconds. Taste and adjust the seasoning with soy sauce, then tip onto a serving plate and serve at once.

serves 4–6

Western

Ji Youcai Xin

cabbage with creamy sauce and bacon

Yunnan province, on China's southwestern border, is famed for its spectacular scenery, the diverse ethnic mix of its population, and its ham—said to equal the finest in the world. The use of dairy milk in cooking is rare, but this dish is a symphony of compatible flavors and textures.

1 small head napa cabbage (¾ lb/375 g)

2 tablespoons vegetable oil

1½ oz (45 g) bacon, very finely diced

1 cup (8 fl oz/250 ml) chicken stock (page 250)

½ teaspoon chicken stock powder

CREAM SAUCE

¼ cup (2 fl oz/60 ml) milk

1 egg yolk (optional)

1½ teaspoons cornstarch (cornflour)

salt and ground white pepper to taste

☗ Trim the base of the cabbage. Cut the head lengthwise into strips 1⅓ inches (3.5 cm) thick. Set aside.

☗ In a wok over medium-high heat, warm the oil. Add the bacon and fry until crisp, about 1½ minutes. Using a slotted spoon, transfer the bacon to a plate and set aside.

☗ Pour the chicken stock into the fat remaining in the wok and add the stock powder. Stir well and add the cabbage. Cover and cook over high heat, turning the cabbage once or twice, until it is barely tender, 1½–2½ minutes. Using tongs, transfer the cabbage to a serving plate, leaving the liquid behind in the wok.

☗ To prepare the sauce, in a bowl, stir together the milk, egg yolk (if using), cornstarch, salt, and pepper. Pour the mixture into the wok over medium heat and stir slowly until lightly thickened, about 30 seconds. If using the egg yolk, do not allow the mixture to begin to boil or the yolk will curdle. Drain off any liquid from the cabbage into the sauce and cook briefly to combine. Taste and adjust the seasoning with salt and pepper.

☗ Pour the sauce over the cabbage, and scatter the bacon evenly over the top. Serve at once.

serves 4–6

Vegetable Carving

Early in an apprenticeship, a Chinese chef is taught the art of carving garnishes. Initial lessons are undemanding—simple leaf shapes carved from slices of cucumber skin, brushes and curls made from the root ends of green (spring) onions, small flower buds shaped from the tips of carrots, or roses formed from the folded skin of a plump red tomato. If an instructor detects the budding of an artistic talent for this most specialized of culinary skills, a young chef may be encouraged to undergo training in the art of vegetable and fruit carving. This may involve an apprenticeship of up to ten years, but the skills will ensure a lifetime's employment in a five-star restaurant or hotel kitchen.

"Excite the eye to stimulate the stomach," instructs an old Chinese saying. Chefs and diners alike consider the eye appeal of a dish as the next most important factor to taste. Even a simple stir-fry does not go to the table without a wisp of fresh cilantro (fresh coriander), a border of shapes stamped from cucumber or carrot, a bouquet of carved radish or tomato flowers nestled in parsley, or a scattering of green onion curls.

Western
Rang Zhurou Doufu
stuffed bean curd

Bean curd is not considered an ingredient too humble to feature on a banquet menu. Surrounded by poached Chinese greens, stuffed bean curd earns the title "enriched millionaire" in the Chinese culinary repertoire. Bland-flavored bean curd has many qualities that please the Chinese, apart from its valuable contribution of vegetable protein. At its finest, it has an appealing, delicate, velvety texture, and it happily absorbs seasonings and flavorings from sweet to tart, hot to salty.

The pork in this stuffing can be replaced by chicken, shrimp (prawn), or fish, and for a vegetarian version you could use a mixture of ¾ cup (6 oz/185 g) mashed, boiled taro with 2 or 3 dried black mushrooms, soaked to soften and finely chopped. Other versions of stuffed bean curd use bean curd sheets to wrap a selection of vegetables or meats into thumb-sized rolls, which are steamed in bamboo baskets or braised in a rich chicken broth.

¼ lb (125 g) coarsely ground (minced) lean pork, lean beef, or chicken

1½ tablespoons chopped water chestnut or jicama

2 teaspoons chopped green (spring) onion, white part only

1 teaspoon light soy sauce

½ teaspoon salt

¼ teaspoon ground white pepper (optional)

1 lb (500 g) fresh soft bean curd

2 tablespoons tapioca starch or cornstarch (cornflour)

vegetable oil for frying

SAUCE

1 tablespoon vegetable or peanut oil

2 teaspoons salted black beans, rinsed and drained

1 teaspoon minced garlic

1–2 teaspoons seeded, finely chopped hot red chile

1½ tablespoons light soy sauce

1 teaspoon superfine (caster) sugar

2 teaspoons tapioca starch or cornstarch (cornflour) dissolved in ¾ cup (6 fl oz/180 ml) chicken stock (page 250) or water

1 tablespoon finely chopped green (spring) onion tops or fresh cilantro (fresh coriander)

In a food processor, process the meat to a smooth paste. Add the water chestnut or jicama and green onion and pulse briefly to combine. Add the soy sauce, salt, and the pepper, if using, and pulse until a relatively smooth paste is formed.

Cut the bean curd into 12 equal pieces, each about 1⅓ inches (3.5 cm) square. Using a teaspoon, scoop out a shallow, round cavity from the top of each square, making it no more than one-third the depth of the square. Lightly dust the cavities with some of the tapioca starch or cornstarch.

Gently press an equal amount of the filling into each cavity and dust the top with tapioca starch or cornstarch. If time allows, cover and refrigerate for 1 hour to help the filling set and prevent it from dislodging during cooking.

Pour the oil to a depth of ½ inch (12 mm) into a large, wide, shallow pan, and place over medium-high heat. When the oil is hot, place the bean curd, stuffing side down, in the pan and fry until golden brown, about 5 minutes. Turn and fry on the second side until golden brown, about 2½ minutes longer.

Meanwhile, prepare the sauce: In a wok or small saucepan over medium-high heat, warm the oil.

When it is hot, add the black beans, garlic, and chile and fry until very aromatic, about 40 seconds. Add the soy sauce and sugar and cook very briefly, then stir in the tapioca starch or cornstarch mixture and simmer, stirring slowly, until lightly thickened, about 40 seconds. Set aside.

When the bean curd is ready, carefully transfer to a warmed platter, arranging in a single layer filling side up. Reheat the sauce, if necessary, and spoon over the bean curd. Sprinkle with the green onion tops or cilantro and serve immediately.

serves 4–6

At lunchtime the ringing of bicycle bells announces the arrival of itinerant food vendors.

Northern

Mogu Youcai

mushrooms and green vegetable platter

*From my first heady sniff of black mushrooms
poaching in a clear soup, I was hooked on pursuing
a career involving Chinese cooking.*

MUSHROOMS

*12 dried black mushrooms, soaked in hot water
to cover for 25 minutes*

1 cup (8 fl oz/250 ml) water

1 tablespoon light soy sauce

½ teaspoon superfine (caster) sugar

*1 teaspoon cornstarch (cornflour) dissolved in
1 tablespoon water or chicken stock (page 250)*

1 tablespoon oyster sauce

GREENS

*10 oz (315 g) small, tender Chinese greens
such as baby bok choy or Shanghai cabbage*

3 tablespoons vegetable or peanut oil

1 teaspoon salt

⚜ To prepare the mushrooms, drain them and trim
off and discard the stems if necessary. In a saucepan
over medium-low heat, combine the mushroom
caps, water, soy sauce, and sugar. Bring to a simmer
and simmer, uncovered, until very tender and the liquid is well reduced, about 20 minutes.

⚜ Stir in the cornstarch mixture and the oyster
sauce and cook, stirring slowly, until the sauce is
lightly thickened and becomes clear, about 1 minute.
Remove from the heat and set aside; keep hot.

⚜ To prepare the greens, pour water to a depth of
about 2 inches (5 cm) into a wok and bring to a boil
over high heat. Add the greens and simmer until tender, about 2½ minutes. Drain well, tip the greens into
a bowl, and cover with cold water for 1 minute to
retain crispness and color. Drain again.

⚜ Wipe out the wok, return it to high heat, and add
the oil and salt. When hot, add the greens and toss
and stir until warmed through and glossy with oil,
about 30 seconds.

⚜ Using tongs, lift the greens from the wok and
arrange around the edge of a serving dish. Tip the
mushrooms and their sauce into the middle and
serve at once.

serves 4–6

Southern

Feicui La Doufu

spicy bean curd and eggs

*I like to surprise breakfast guests with this delicious,
spicy scramble that can be served with toast, although
it is even better with Green Onion Pastries (page 203).
In China, this dish would not be served for breakfast:
a bowl of millet or rice soup with a fried doughnut
stick is the first meal of the day for millions.*

4 whole eggs, plus 3 egg whites

1 tablespoon cornstarch (cornflour)

1½ tablespoons vegetable oil

½ cup (2½ oz/75 g) finely chopped yellow onion

*½ cup (2½ oz/75 g) finely chopped red bell
pepper (capsicum)*

*¼ cup (1¼ oz/40 g) finely chopped celery or
zucchini (courgette)*

½ teaspoon salt, plus salt to taste

*2 teaspoons finely minced hot green chile
(optional)*

½ teaspoon minced garlic

2 teaspoons light soy sauce

½ teaspoon hot bean sauce

*10 oz (315 g) fresh soft bean curd, finely
diced*

*2 tablespoons chopped fresh cilantro
(fresh coriander)*

ground white pepper to taste (optional)

⚜ In a bowl, whisk together the whole eggs, egg
whites, and cornstarch. Set aside.

⚜ In a wok over medium-high heat, warm the oil.
When it is hot, add the onion, bell pepper, celery or
zucchini, and ½ teaspoon salt and stir-fry until crisp-
tender, 1½–2 minutes. Add the chile, garlic, soy sauce,
and hot bean sauce and stir-fry briefly. Pour in the
egg mixture, do not stir for 15 seconds, and then
reduce the heat to medium. Cook, stirring slowly
and gently, until the eggs begin to set, about
1 minute. Add the bean curd and cilantro, salt to taste,
and the pepper, if using, and continue to gently stir-
fry until the egg is softly cooked and the bean curd
is warmed through, 1½–2 minutes.

⚜ Transfer to a warmed serving plate and serve
immediately.

serves 4

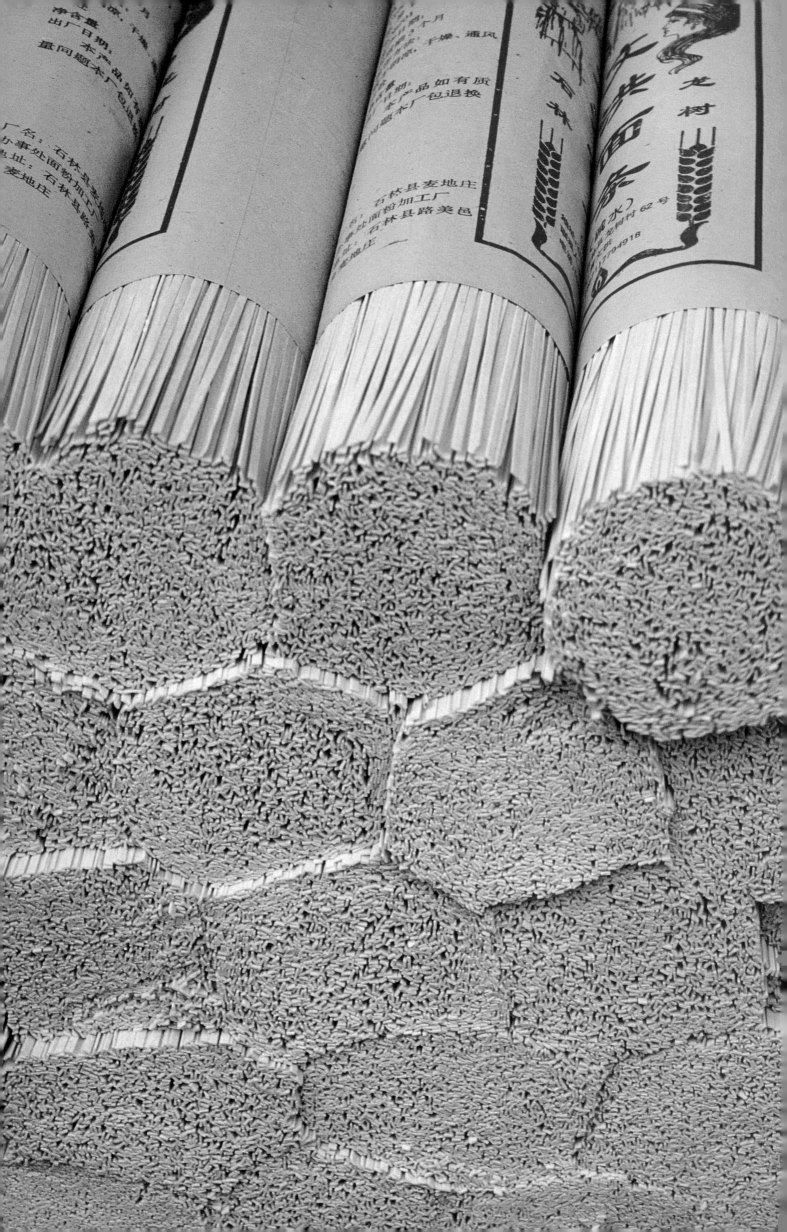

NOODLES, RICE, AND BREAD

Myriad noodles,
featherlight buns,
and sticky rice are
the foundation of
many dishes.

NOODLES ARE THE SUBJECT of an ongoing debate that may never be won. Was the origin of pasta in China or Italy? Certain food historians argue volubly that Marco Polo took the concept of pasta making back to his homeland after his extensive travels in China in the thirteenth century. The opposition stands firm in its conviction that pasta was definitely in use in the south of Italy well before that. No matter, really: Italy adores its pasta and the Chinese equally revere their noodles. No arguments will change that.

I have to confess to an irrepressible addiction to noodles. I can't live without them for long, and I know I'm not alone in my obsession. Noodles are a mainstay in the day-to-day diet of most Chinese—eaten with meals, in soups and clay pots, and as a satisfying snack whenever hunger strikes.

Eating habits in any country are dictated by geographic and climatic factors. Across the vast tracts of China's agricultural regions—in the north and central west—wheat and other dry-grown grains dominate. In the southeastern and central states, from Guangdong through to the rich farming basin of Sichuan, rice flourishes in irrigated paddies, and rice terraces pattern hillsides and gorges.

Some rice is grown for local demand in the north, but rice does not come automatically with a meal, as it usually does in the south. Instead, meals may be accompanied by soft and spongy buns, while crisp-fried or baked flat breads and thin handmade crepes are served with spicy meats and roast duck, to wrap or fill and eat out of hand. Fine textured, white, and soft as down, traditional steamed bread has an appeal all of its own. Bread makers use techniques perfected over thousands of years to achieve the rise and even-grained texture that is favored. Shapes

Preceding pages: Flat wheat-flour noodles are stacked for sale in Yunnan. **Top:** The Dragon's Backbone rice terraces climb their way up a string of 2,500-foot (800-m) peaks near Longsheng in Guangxi. The terraces were constructed over seven hundred years ago. **Left:** A chef prepares savory rolls filled with green (spring) onions for the lunchtime rush hour. **Right:** On the waterways of the scenic Li River, cormorant fishing has been practiced for centuries.

range from simple round balls to coiled "snails" to thread rolls in which fine strings of dough are rolled like wool into a ball. Some breads are folded around slices of salty Yunnan ham or sausage, resulting in a cooked sandwich to accompany soup. Some griddle-cooked and baked breads resemble the flat breads of India, an inspired borrowing from Muslim cuisine.

Ever practical, the Chinese find multiple uses for their valuable grain commodities. Rice is the most widely used grain food, and rice flour is invaluable for breads, desserts, and the noodle industry. Wheat is milled into flour for bread and pastry baking and for noodle making. Together with rice and sorghum, millet is essential to the wine industry and is boiled to make a nourishing gruel in the rural north, the counterpart of the rice breakfast soup—*zhou juk*—of the south. Barley and wheat are important in beer brewing and in the fermenting process for soy sauce and seasoning pastes.

Noodles are a lengthy subject, if you'll forgive my pun. In the Chinese language of symbolism, noodles represent longevity, so bowls of super-long noodles are served at New Year and on festive occasions. Each region has its

Left: A mound of freshly made wheat noodles sits in a restaurant kitchen. **Top:** Muslim street-stall holders sell tasty snacks wrapped in bamboo leaves on the pavements of Hohhot in Inner Mongolia. **Above:** Lake Kunming, in the Summer Palace Gardens near Beijing, is a favorite spot for all types of recreation. Kites were invented in China over two thousand years ago and the butterfly is now one of the most popular types sold. Flying a kite and then letting it go is believed to dispel bad luck or illness.

Below: Qingdao, on the edge of the Yellow Sea, is surrounded by deepwater bays perfect for local fishermen.
Bottom: Shanghai's financial district runs alongside the Huangpu River. The British occupied Shanghai by force in 1841 and many European-style buildings were built during the city's time as a treaty port. The clocktower of the British Customs House still dominates the scene today.
Right: "Silver thread" snail bread and plain bread are steamed to accompany meals in a Chengdu restaurant.

specialties and its preferences. Wheat-flour noodles are favored in the north and rice noodles in the south. Egg noodles know no territorial boundaries. Noodles can be served soft or crisp, floating in soup, or glazed with a tasty sauce. They can be the main feature of a dish or the starch base for meat and vegetable dishes. Legends and poetry attempt to explain the origin of many popular noodle dishes, such as the famed crossing the bridge noodles of Yunnan, the evocative ants climbing a tree, and the spicy *dandan mian*—the peddler's noodles of Sichuan.

Noodles are multiform—thick or thin, round or flat, single strand or bundled, fresh or dried, plain or flavored with ingredients such as spinach or dried shrimp. White wheat noodles are simply flour and water, while egg noodles are made with hard flour and whole eggs in the manner of pasta, the eggs giving them a yellow tinge and extra flavor. Dried rice noodles are made from a dough of rice flour and water that is extruded to size, or rolled and cut. Fresh rice noodles come cut in a variety of widths for noodles or in sheets to use for rice sheet rolls. They are fragile, cook quickly, and spoil easily, so should be used on the day of purchase.

Interesting, and less well known, are the bean flour, buckwheat and root vegetable noodles for which Sichuan is particularly famed. They are processed from ground mung beans and other legumes, and pastes of starch-fortified sweet potato, yam, and indigenous root crops such as the farinaceous kudzu root. When packaged they look like strips

of semitransparent plastic. When cooked they have a pleasing chewy yet soft texture, which marries well with the typically exuberant sauces of Sichuan cuisine.

In the south, no meal at the table is complete without rice. *Women zhongwu yiban chi mifan he shucai* (we must not waste a grain of rice) is a rule for life that follows through onto the table, where it is considered an insult to the host to leave uneaten rice in the bowl. Rice is usually served plain—steamed by the absorption method—and is eaten with chopsticks from a small bowl. Small portions of the main course are served into the bowl so that each bite can be accompanied by rice. At a banquet it would be a breach of etiquette to serve rice with the main courses. It comes later, sometimes also with noodles, to "fill the gaps" and ensure the guests depart satisfied.

Rice can be the backdrop to a meal or share top billing—fried rice full of meaty chunks, onions, and bean sprouts; one-pot chicken and rice with taro or *lap cheong* sausages; a plate of steaming white rice topped with a grilled pork chop and a fried egg; or sliced red roast pork

and a drizzle of oyster sauce. These are the kinds of satisfying family snack meals eaten by millions every day in China.

Snacking is intrinsic to life in China. Anywhere you go, an array of tasty snacks beckons, and many of them are noodles, rice, or breads. Walk through a food market or crowded pedestrian street and you'll pass food stalls where plump, meat-filled *baozi* buns or sweet pork *cha shao bao* are steaming in towering stacks of bamboo baskets. Doughnut sticks and green onion pastries puff and crisp in bubbling oil, noodles are tossed energetically in huge black woks over roaring fires, and rice breakfast soup simmers in a pot. Perched on a rickety, fold-out stool, shoulder to shoulder with hungry workers, shoppers, and holiday makers, there is no ceremony—merely friendly, casual eating at its most inexpensive and satisfying.

Left: A wooden footbridge 350 feet (120 m) in length traverses a deep ravine near the hot springs of Longsheng, Guangxi. **Above:** Versatile bamboo has many uses: here, a village woman cooks rice inside lengths placed over a fire.

Southern

Gong Bao Ji Mifun

spicy chicken and vegetables "on a cloud"

When rice vermicelli hits hot oil, it instantly expands into a snow white, crisp mass, as featherlight as a cumulus cloud. As the bed to nestle ingredients glazed with a smooth sauce, it provides appealing textural contrast. Rice vermicelli is sold as flat bundles, wrapped four or five to a pack, and is sometimes labeled as fine rice sticks. It is a versatile ingredient to float in soups and replace rice on a snack plate with roast duck or grilled pork. Crisp-fried, it adds crunch and visual appeal as a garnish. Stir-fried with pickled vegetables and curry spices, it becomes a popular noodle dish, that originated in Singapore but is now a hit on Hong Kong menus. Several varieties of squash are used in Chinese cooking. Luffa has hard, lateral ridges, and fuzzy melon a coating of fine hairs.

6 oz (185 g) boneless chicken breast,
very thinly sliced, then cut into 1½-by-½-inch
(4-cm-by-12-mm) pieces

1 teaspoon rice wine

1 teaspoon cornstarch (cornflour)

1¾ oz (50 g) rice vermicelli

vegetable oil for deep-frying

1½ cups (12 fl oz/375 ml) water

¼ cup (1½ oz/45 g) sliced green or long beans

½ cup (2 oz/60 g) sliced carrot

½ cup (2 oz/60 g) diced fuzzy melon, luffa
squash, or English (hothouse) cucumber

¾ cup (1¾ oz/50 g) small broccoli or
cauliflower florets

½ cup (2 oz/60 g) sliced red bell pepper
(capsicum)

½ cup (2 oz/60 g) sliced celery

⅓ cup (2 oz/60 g) sliced bamboo shoot

⅓ cup (¾ oz/20 g) cut-up garlic chives
(1½-inch/4-cm lengths)

2 tablespoons light soy sauce

2 teaspoons thick black bean sauce or garlic-chile
sauce

1–2 tablespoons sweet chile sauce (optional)

¾ cup (6 fl oz/180 ml) chicken stock (page 250)

2 teaspoons cornstarch (cornflour) dissolved in
1 tablespoon water

In a bowl, combine the chicken pieces, rice wine, and cornstarch, mix well, and set aside while you prepare the remaining ingredients.

Lightly break up the bundle of rice vermicelli. Pour the oil to a depth of 1½ inches (4 cm) into a wok, and heat to 375°F (190°C), or until a length of noodle dropped into the oil puffs up and floats immediately. Add half of the rice vermicelli and fry, turning once, until crisp and white, about 3 seconds on each side. Using a wire skimmer, lift the noodles from the oil, drain briefly over the wok, and then place on a flat plate lined with paper towels to drain. Fry the remaining rice vermicelli in the same way.

Pour off the oil from the wok into a heatproof bowl and set aside. Carefully add the water to the wok and bring to a boil over high heat. Add the beans and carrot and cook for 1 minute. Add the fuzzy melon, luffa squash, or cucumber and broccoli or cauliflower and cook for 1 minute. Using the wire skimmer, transfer the blanched vegetables to a plate. Discard the water and dry the wok.

Return 2 tablespoons of the hot oil to the wok and heat over high heat. When the oil is hot, add the chicken mixture and stir-fry until the chicken turns white, about 40 seconds. Using the wire skimmer, transfer to a plate.

Add the blanched vegetables, bell pepper, celery, bamboo shoot, and garlic chives to the wok and stir-fry until the vegetables are crisp-tender, 30–40 seconds. Season with the soy sauce and the black bean or garlic-chile sauce and stir-fry for 10 seconds. Add the sweet chile sauce to taste, if using, and the stock and simmer for 20 seconds to blend the flavors. Stir in the cornstarch mixture and stir gently until lightly thickened, about 1 minute.

Return the chicken to the wok and warm gently but briefly in the sauce. Arrange the noodles on a platter, pour the chicken and vegetables over the top, and serve at once.

serves 2–4

Food that pleases the eye is sure to please the stomach.

Southern

Cha Shao Bao

roast pork buns

Although she now only rarely revisits Hong Kong, her birthplace, my daughter Isobel still retains her childhood reverence for yum cha *("taking tea"). She has several favorites that must be ordered every time. Cha shao bao probably tops her list. The silky sponginess of the bread and the sweet saltiness of the roast pork filling are tastes and textures that instantly transport her back to magical moments in her childhood. They recall a winter morning funicular ride to the mist-shrouded Peak with a box of freshly steamed pork buns warming her knees. They also bring back the time, sitting in one of Hong Kong's vast dim sum restaurants amid hundreds of dark-haired Chinese, when she asked me why her hair was blonde and not black like that of everyone else born in Hong Kong, and failed to understand the significance of her father's sandy hair and obvious English looks.* Yu jiao, *which the Cantonese call* wu gok, *with their lacy coating of fried taro over a filling of shrimp (prawn), black mushrooms, and pork, is another dumpling high on her priority list, as are* xia shui jiao, *filled with pork, dried shrimp, and salt-pickled turnip in a chewy casing of rice-flour dough.*

Bread is as much a part of a Chinese meal in the north as rice is in the south. Vast grainfields in the northern provinces provide the wheat needed for the noodles and the many varieties of baked, fried, and steamed breads served from dawn to dusk in homes and restaurants, and by street-corner vendors. Bread is eaten by itself as a snack and served with meals. As Chinese kitchens traditionally were not equipped with ovens, steaming and dry cooking on a griddle were the economical and effective ways to cook breads. Ammonium carbonate is a high-powered leavening agent used by professional bread makers to produce the soft, textured dough that makes steamed Chinese buns so delectable.

DOUGH STARTER

1 cup (5 oz / 155 g) all-purpose (plain) flour

¼ cup (2 oz / 60 g) superfine (caster) sugar

1½ teaspoons active dry yeast

¾ cup (6 fl oz / 180 ml) lukewarm water

FILLING

10 oz (315 g) Red Roast Pork (page 115), diced

1½ tablespoons hoisin sauce

1 tablespoon cornstarch dissolved in 3 tablespoons water

DOUGH

1¼ cups (7½ oz / 230 g) all-purpose (plain) flour

2 teaspoons baking powder

1½ tablespoons melted lard or vegetable oil (optional)

⅓ cup (3 fl oz / 80 ml) lukewarm water

❧ To prepare the dough starter, in a bowl, stir together the flour, sugar, and yeast. Make a well in the center. Pour the lukewarm water into the well and stir with a fork to mix thoroughly. Cover with plastic wrap and set aside in a warm place until bubbly and doubled in size, about 3 hours.

❧ To prepare the filling, in a small saucepan over medium-low heat, combine the pork, hoisin sauce, and cornstarch mixture and heat gently, stirring, until the meat is glazed with the sauce, about 1 minute. Remove from the heat and let cool.

❧ To prepare the dough, in a bowl, sift together the flour and baking powder. Make a well in the center. Add the lard or vegetable oil, if using, the dough starter, and the lukewarm water to the well and, using your fingers, work the mixture into a smooth dough.

❧ Shape the dough into a ball and transfer to a lightly floured work surface. Using your palms, roll the dough into a log 20 inches (50 cm) long. Cut crosswise into 20 pieces each 1 inch (2.5 cm) long.

❧ To make the buns, working with 1 piece at a time, gently roll it into a ball, then, using your fingers or a rolling pin, flatten it into a 3-inch (7.5-cm) round that is thinner on the edges than in the center. Place about 2½ teaspoons of the filling in the center and pull the dough up and around the filling, twisting and pinching the edges together at the top.

❧ Cut out 20 pieces of waxed (greaseproof) paper or parchment (baking) paper each 1½ inches (4 cm) square. Place a piece of paper beneath each bun. Place the buns in 2 steamer baskets, or on 2 racks of a metal steamer, spacing them ¾ inch (2 cm) apart to allow for expansion during steaming. If you do not have 2 baskets or a double-tiered steamer, cook the buns in 2 batches. Let rise for 10 minutes.

❧ Bring water to a simmer in the steamer base. Place the steamer baskets or racks over the simmering water, cover, and steam until well expanded and dry on the surface, about 8 minutes. Serve at once.

makes 20

Eastern

Shanghai Mian

shanghai noodles

*Temperatures in northern China can plunge to
freezing in the winter months, and elevate to scorching
in summer as hot, dry winds blow across from the
plateaus of the west. As a river-port city, astride the
dark waters of the Huangpu, a tributary of the
Changjiang (Yangtze River), Shanghai's climate is
less extreme. Nonetheless, the cuisine of this energetic
city is one of full-bodied, warming, and sustaining
dishes, based on rich brown sauces and often
pungently laced with white pepper.*

*Noodles are a way of life in Shanghai, and the
local preference is for plump, chewy, handmade noodles
made from a wheat-flour dough. In some noodle
preparations, whole eggs or egg yolks are used in an
age-old formula that Marco Polo, visiting from Italy
in the thirteenth century, found little different from
the recipe for traditional Italian pasta. A plain
dough of finely milled, bleached white flour,
kneaded with water, yields the soft-textured
noodles many locals prefer.*

¼ cup (2 fl oz/60 ml) dark soy sauce

2 tablespoons oyster sauce

1 tablespoon superfine (caster) sugar

2 teaspoons peeled and grated fresh ginger

7 oz (220 g) pork tenderloin, thinly sliced

1 lb (500 g) fresh thick round egg noodles

1½ cups (12 fl oz/375 ml) water

3 tablespoons vegetable or peanut oil

4 cloves garlic, thinly sliced

1 green (spring) onion, including tender
green tops, cut into 2-inch (5-cm) lengths
and julienned lengthwise

¼ small head napa cabbage, sliced and
white and pale green parts kept separate
(about 2½ cups/7½ oz/235 g total)

2 teaspoons cornstarch (cornflour) dissolved
in ½ cup (4 fl oz/125 ml) chicken stock
(page 250)

1 tablespoon sesame oil (optional)

ground white pepper to taste

☀ In a bowl large enough to hold the pork, stir together the soy sauce, oyster sauce, sugar, and ginger until the sugar dissolves. Add the pork, stir to coat evenly, and set aside for 10 minutes. Pour into a sieve placed over a bowl, reserving the pork and marinade separately.

☀ Bring a large saucepan half full of water to a boil. Add the noodles and bring back to a boil. Add 1 cup (8 fl oz/250 ml) of the water and bring back to a boil. Add the remaining ½ cup (4 fl oz/125 ml) water and again bring back to a boil. Cook until the noodles are barely tender, 2–3 minutes. Tip into a colander in the sink, rinse with hot water, and leave to drain well.

☀ In a wok over high heat, warm the vegetable or peanut oil until smoking. Add the pork and stir-fry until lightly colored and half cooked, about 40 seconds. Using a slotted spoon, transfer to a plate.

☀ With the wok still over high heat, add half of the garlic, all of the green onion, and the white parts of the cabbage and stir-fry until the garlic and cabbage are slightly softened, about 30 seconds. Add the half cooked pork, the reserved marinade, and the green parts of the cabbage and stir-fry until the cabbage is slightly wilted, about 20 seconds.

☀ Add the noodles to the wok and then pour in the cornstarch mixture. Stir over high heat until the noodles are evenly coated, about 40 seconds. Transfer to a large serving dish.

☀ In a small saucepan over medium-high heat, warm the sesame oil to smoking. Add the remaining garlic and fry for 15 seconds until fragrant. Pour the oil and garlic evenly over the noodles and season generously with the pepper. Serve at once.

serves 4–8

Shanghai restaurant chefs meld the classic dishes of Wuxi, Suzhou, and Hangzhou to create a distinctive table of their own.

Handmade Noodles

For the food enthusiast, I don't believe a trip to China is complete without seeing a demonstration of noodle making. Some of the leading restaurants offer it as a tourist attraction. But seeing a noodle maker at work, framed in the window of a small restaurant, is a scene that might be glimpsed unexpectedly on a walk down any city street. With a series of deft tosses and stretches, and mere seconds of magical, culinary sleight of hand, the noodle maker transforms a blob of dough into a skein of tender noodles as thick as a pencil, or as slender as a pine needle. Hand-pulled noodles are made from the simplest dough of finely milled wheat flour and water. Texture is all important. The dough must be soft enough to stretch, but not to break or clump.

In the north, many home cooks prefer to make their own noodles rather than buy them. They use a rolling stick the diameter of a broom handle to roll the dough into a sheet, before wielding their versatile cleavers to slice it into narrow, even strips that go straight into a pot of simmering water.

Eastern

Taohua Fan Yu Xia

sizzling rice with seafood in garlic-tomato sauce

Authentic or not, I do enjoy the divine justice of this tale. The cook of a wealthy merchant was dragged from bed late one night to prepare a meal for his master, who had returned home drunk, belligerent, and hungry. Seething with spite, the cook stirred a fiercely hot chile sauce through leftovers scavenged in the kitchen, then tossed old rice from the bottom of the unwashed rice pot into hot oil. The sizzle of the sauce hitting the rice and its spicy taste so delighted the merchant that he declared the dish a masterpiece and richly rewarded the cook.

1¾ cups (12 oz/375 g) medium-grain white rice

3½ cups (28 fl oz/875 ml) water

½ cup (2½ oz/75 g) English peas

¼ cup (1½ oz/45 g) diced carrot

2 tablespoons vegetable oil, plus oil for deep-frying

2 teaspoons sesame oil

½ cup (2 oz/75 g) chopped yellow onion

½ cup (2½ oz/75 g) diced celery

¼ cup (1¼ oz/40 g) diced red bell pepper (capsicum)

¼ cup (1¼ oz/40 g) diced bamboo shoot

1½ tablespoons peeled and finely julienned fresh ginger

1 small, hot red or green chile, seeded and sliced

1 teaspoon crushed garlic

3 cups (1 lb/500 g) diced, cleaned mixed seafood such as squid, shrimp (prawn) meat, fish fillet, and scallops

⅓ cup (3 fl oz/80 ml) tomato ketchup

2 tablespoons light soy sauce

1 tablespoon red vinegar or cider vinegar

2 teaspoons garlic-chile sauce

2 teaspoons superfine (caster) sugar

1 tablespoon cornstarch dissolved in 1 cup (8 fl oz/250 ml) chicken or fish stock (page 250)

salt and ground white pepper to taste

2 tablespoons sliced green (spring) onion tops

☗ Begin preparing the rice several hours or as long as overnight before you plan to serve the dish. Place the rice and 2½ cups (20 fl oz/625 ml) of the water in a heavy saucepan, cover, and bring rapidly to a boil. Reduce the heat to the lowest possible setting and allow the rice to cook gently without uncovering the pan for 12 minutes. Remove from the heat and let the rice stand, tightly covered, for 10 minutes.

☗ Preheat the oven to 200°F (95°C). Brush a baking sheet with vegetable oil, and spread the rice evenly over the baking sheet. Place the baking sheet in the oven and leave to dry for several hours or as long as overnight.

☗ In a wok over high heat, bring the remaining 1 cup (8 fl oz/250 ml) water to a boil. Add the peas and carrot and boil until just tender, about 2½ minutes. Drain and set aside on a plate.

☗ In the wok over high heat, warm the 2 tablespoons of vegetable oil and the sesame oil. When the oil is hot, add the yellow onion, celery, bell pepper, bamboo shoot, ginger, chile, and garlic and stir-fry until crisp-tender, about 1 minute. Using a slotted spoon, transfer to the plate holding the other vegetables.

☗ Return the wok to high heat. When the oil is hot, add the mixed seafood and stir-fry until all the seafood is just firm, 1–1½ minutes. Return the vegetables to the wok and add the ketchup, soy sauce, vinegar, garlic-chile sauce, and sugar and stir-fry for 30 seconds. Pour in the cornstarch mixture and cook, stirring slowly, until lightly thickened, about 1½ minutes. Season with salt and pepper. Remove from the heat and keep warm.

☗ Pour the oil to a depth of 2 inches (5 cm) into another wok or a deep, heavy saucepan, and heat to 375°F (190°C), or until a small piece of the dried rice dropped into the oil sizzles immediately. Break the rice into 4-inch (10-cm) squares. Add the rice to the hot oil and fry until golden and crisp, about 1½ minutes. Using a slotted spoon, lift the rice from the oil and drain briefly over the pan.

☗ Place the rice in a large, deep serving dish. Pour the hot seafood-sauce mixture into a separate bowl, and have the sliced green onion ready. At the table, pour the seafood-sauce mixture over the hot rice, and sprinkle on the green onion tops. Serve immediately.

serves 4–6

Western

Dandan Mian

spicy sesame noodles

Sesame paste makes a deliciously nutty sauce for these noodles, served warm in winter, cold in summer.

1 cup (8 fl oz/250 ml) vegetable or peanut oil

⅓ cup (2 oz/60 g) raw peanuts

7 oz (220 g) fresh flat wheat noodles

SAUCE

¼ cup (2½ oz/75 g) sesame paste

¼ cup (2 fl oz/60 ml) vegetable oil

2 tablespoons chile oil or 2–3 tablespoons sweet chile sauce

2 tablespoons sesame oil

2 tablespoons light soy sauce

1 teaspoon salt, or to taste

½ cup (4 fl oz/125 ml) hot water

½ cup (1½ oz/45 g) chopped green (spring) onion, including tender green tops

1 hot red chile, seeded and chopped

❧ In a wok over high heat, warm the oil until nearly smoking. Add the peanuts and fry, stirring continually, until golden, about 1 minute. Using a slotted spoon, immediately transfer the peanuts to a cutting board. Let cool, then use a cleaver or sharp, heavy knife to chop finely, or place in a food processor and pulse to chop finely.

❧ Bring a saucepan three-fourths full of lightly salted water to a boil. Add the noodles and cook until barely tender, 3½–4 minutes. Pour into a colander to drain, then hold under running hot water to rinse. Leave in the sink to drain while you make the sauce.

❧ To prepare the sauce, in a bowl, combine the sesame paste, vegetable oil, chile oil or sweet chile sauce, sesame oil, soy sauce, 1 teaspoon salt, and the water. Stir until well mixed, then taste and adjust the seasoning with more salt. Transfer the noodles to a bowl, add the sauce, and stir and toss to mix.

❧ Divide the noodles evenly among individual bowls. Top each serving with an equal amount of the peanuts and green onion. Garnish each with a sprinkling of chopped chile and serve.

serves 4–6

Eastern

Nou Mi Ji

sticky rice in lotus leaves

The gluey texture of cooked glutinous rice explains its popular name, "sticky" rice. The raw grains are whiter and less opalescent than common rice and when cooked release their starches to become softly sticky. Glutinous rice is only occasionally used plain as the accompaniment to savory dishes. Instead, it is cooked with seasonings and flavorful ingredients to make delicious fillings and savory snacks. The steamed lotus leaf parcel filled with sticky rice and "eight treasures"—a variety of unusual ingredients, including ginkgo nuts, raisins, diced ham, red dates, dried shrimp, and diced sausage—is a favorite at celebration dinners. It provides drama and anticipation as the sealed package is carried to the table with aplomb and the leaves are peeled back to reveal the fragrant rice. In a scaled-down version, sticky rice parcels are enjoyed as a dim sum treat.

1½ cups (10½ oz/330 g) glutinous rice, soaked in cold water to cover for 1 hour

3 dried black mushrooms, soaked in hot water to cover for 25 minutes and drained

2 Chinese sausages

¼ cup (1¼ oz/40 g) dried shrimp (prawns), soaked in hot water to cover for 25 minutes and drained

5 oz (155 g) boneless chicken thigh, cut into ½-inch (12-mm) cubes

¼ cup (1½ oz/45 g) raw peanuts

2 green (spring) onions, including tender green tops, chopped

2½ tablespoons light soy sauce

1½ tablespoons peanut or vegetable oil

4 dried lotus leaves, soaked in cold water to cover for 1 hour

❧ Tip the rice into a colander in the sink to drain, and then transfer to a heatproof bowl. Bring a tea-kettle filled with water to a boil and pour about 4 cups (32 fl oz/1 l) boiling water over the rice. Let stand until cool.

❧ Remove and discard the stems from the mushrooms if necessary, and finely chop the caps.

❧ Bring water to a simmer in a steamer base. Place the sausages on a heatproof plate in a steamer basket, place over the simmering water, cover, and steam until soft and plump, about 5 minutes. Remove from the steamer and let cool, then thinly slice.

❧ Drain the rice and return it to the bowl. Add the mushrooms, sausage, shrimp, chicken, peanuts, green onions, soy sauce, and oil. Stir until all the ingredients are evenly distributed.

❧ Drain the lotus leaves, which should now be soft and flexible, and pat dry. Fold each leaf in half, ribs inward, and, using kitchen scissors or a sharp knife, cut away the thick central stem and ribs. Lay the leaves on a flat work surface with the cut-stem area facing you. Divide the mixture evenly among the 4 leaves, piling it in the center. Working with 1 leaf at a time, fold the 2 outer edges over the filling, fold up the bottom, and fold over the top, enclosing the filling completely in a neat parcel. Place the leaf parcels, seam sides down, in a steamer basket or steamer rack in which they fit snugly but not tightly.

❧ Bring water to a simmer in the steamer base. Place the steamer basket or rack over the simmering water, cover, and steam for about 40 minutes, replenishing the water as needed with boiling water to maintain the original level. To test for doneness, lift the top flap on a parcel; the rice should be partially translucent and tender.

❧ Serve directly from the steamer basket, or transfer the parcels to a serving plate and, using the scissors or a small, sharp knife, cut a cross in the top of each leaf parcel to expose the filling. Serve at once.

serves 4

Mayi Shang Shu

"ants climbing a tree"

Observing flecks of pork on a strand of noodles,
a Chinese poet saw black ants on a tree branch.

5 oz (155 g) bean thread noodles

boiling water to cover

7 oz (220 g) lean pork, coarsely minced

2 teaspoons peeled and grated fresh ginger

1 tablespoon light soy sauce

2 teaspoons rice wine (optional)

2 large dried black mushrooms, soaked in
hot water to cover for 25 minutes

1½-inch (4-cm) square dried black fungus,
soaked in hot water to cover for 25 minutes

2½ tablespoons vegetable oil

¼ cup (¾ oz/20 g) very finely chopped green
(spring) onion, including tender green tops

2–2½ tablespoons hot bean sauce

⅓ cup (3 fl oz/80 ml) water

chile oil to taste (optional)

ground Sichuan pepper to taste (optional)

☙ Place the noodles in a heatproof bowl and add boiling water to cover. Let stand for 10 minutes, then drain.

☙ Meanwhile, in a bowl, combine the pork, ginger, soy sauce, and rice wine and mix well. Let stand for 10 minutes.

☙ Drain the mushrooms and fungus and remove and discard the stems from the mushrooms and the woody parts from the fungus if necessary. Chop the mushrooms and fungus very finely.

☙ In a wok over high heat, warm the oil. When it is hot, add the pork, mushrooms, and fungus and stir-fry until the pork changes color, about 1 minute. Add the green onion, hot bean sauce, and water and stir-fry on high heat for 20 seconds. Reduce the heat slightly and continue to cook, stirring, until the liquid has evaporated and the pork is browned, about 3 minutes.

☙ Add the drained noodles and the chile oil and pepper, if using, and stir-fry until the noodles have absorbed the flavorings, 1–2 minutes. Transfer to a warmed serving plate and serve immediately.

serves 3 or 4

Rice

We think of rice as a staple of the Chinese diet, yet it is often conspicuously absent at a banquet. If rice is served at all on formal occasions, it is merely as a point of etiquette after the main courses. Yet throughout southern and central China rice is indeed the mainstay of the everyday diet of hundreds of millions of people. A simple family meal or restaurant dinner would always be accompanied by plain white rice, even when a noodle dish is part of the menu. In the northern regions, wheat-flour buns and noodles often replace rice at a meal.

Fan, the starch or carbohydrate element of the meal, is usually served in greater proportion to the *cai*, the vegetable or meat protein portion of the meal. The *cai* is usually cooked in a sauce and introduces the flavor and nutrient elements.

Rice has been cultivated in China for over three thousand years. A slightly starchy style of rice is preferred as it is easier to eat with chopsticks. Some varieties of higher yielding long-grain white rice, such as Javanica, are gaining popularity with farmers in the rice-growing southern provinces and central basin of China, while short- and medium-grain white rice are the principal varieties in the northern rice-growing areas. What is not sold for the table is milled into the fine flour used for making rice noodles and dumplings; however, the majority of Chinese bread and buns are made from wheat flour.

Cooked white rice is generally referred to as steamed, although it is actually cooked by an absorption method. Raw rice and a measured amount of water is cooked in a tightly sealed saucepan over low heat, until the water is completely absorbed and the cooked grains are plump and stick together enough to manage efficiently with chopsticks.

High-starch glutinous rice cooks into a soft and sticky mass. It has some savory applications, mainly as a stuffing, but more often is made into puddings and dessert dishes. Flour made from glutinous rice is used to fashion soft, chewy dough for wrapping savory and sweet dim sum dumplings.

Southern

Jing Ji Fan

steamed chicken rice pot

For a newlywed, the kitchen of my first home in Hong Kong was typical of the time. It had a deep, square porcelain sink and a single, tiled bench, both much too low for my above-average height. On the wall were a gas water heater and a few hooks for utensils and pots, and on the bench a small portable two-burner gas cooker. I added a tiny refrigerator, but soon learned to shop daily, and after a while bought myself an electric rice cooker. Perhaps it is because I had no oven through all of my early married years that I have never become a baker of cakes and cookies.

I did not miss the oven then, and I don't use one often now. On one occasion, my amah (housekeeper) arrived home after a day off with a spectacular apple pie for me. She had spent the day with a friend, the amah for an English family, learning to cook some of the classic British fare her friend's employer expected of their employee. For myself, I was happy for Ah Wei to teach me all she could of Chinese techniques.

If, as is said, necessity is the mother of invention, then a sparsely appointed kitchen gave me the impetus to learn any one-pot dish my cheerful amah wanted to share with me. I often replace the chicken legs with plump pork meatballs, and if you can't find taro where you shop for vegetables, replace it with sweet potato or yam.

12 small dried black mushrooms, soaked in 1 cup (8 fl oz/250 ml) hot water for 15 minutes

6 whole chicken legs, about 2 lb (1 kg) total weight

¼ cup (1 oz/30 g) dried shrimp (prawns), soaked in hot water to cover for 10 minutes and drained (optional)

1-inch (2.5-cm) piece fresh ginger, peeled and roughly chopped

2 tablespoons light soy sauce

1 teaspoon salt, or to taste

4 cups (32 fl oz/1 l) water

2 cups (14 oz/440 g) medium-grain white rice

1¼ cups (7 oz/220 g) cubed, peeled taro (½-inch/12-mm cubes)

2 green (spring) onions, including half of the tender green tops, cut into 1-inch (2.5-cm) lengths

♛ Drain the mushrooms, reserving the soaking water. Trim off and discard the woody stems if necessary.

♛ Rinse the chicken legs (drumsticks and thighs) and drain well. Place the legs in a saucepan. Pour the mushroom water through a fine-mesh sieve over the chicken. Add the whole mushrooms, drained shrimp, ginger, soy sauce, and salt. Add the water and bring to a boil over high heat. Reduce the heat to medium and simmer gently, uncovered, until the chicken is half cooked, about 25 minutes.

♛ Remove from the heat and, using a slotted spoon, lift out the chicken legs and mushrooms. Pour the rice into a large, flameproof Chinese clay pot or a heavy saucepan, arrange the chicken legs, mushrooms, and taro cubes over the rice, and then scatter the green onions over the surface. Pour the chicken cooking liquid through the sieve held over the rice.

♛ Place the clay pot or saucepan over high heat and bring to a rapid boil. Reduce the heat to very low, cover tightly, and cook until the stock has been absorbed and the taro and the chicken are tender, about 15 minutes.

♛ Remove from the heat, and serve directly from the clay pot or saucepan. Alternatively, carefully lift out the chicken legs, stir up the rice to incorporate the taro, and transfer to a deep serving dish. Arrange the chicken legs on top and serve.

serves 6

Northern

Ya Mian Tang

duck noodle soup

If you have access to a Chinese roast meat shop, this could be one recipe you will use time and time again. This fragrant soup is delicious, but even more delectable when made from the neck and bones of a roast duck—a half duck would do. Careful trimming should give you enough meat for the soup bowls, and you would cook the roast duck bones in the same way as the uncooked, but reduce the cooking time to 20 minutes.

SOUP

2 lb (1 kg) uncooked duck bones and necks

boiling water to cover

1½-inch (4-cm) piece fresh ginger, cut into chunks

2 star anise, broken into points

1 or 2 pieces cassia bark, each about 1 inch (2.5 cm) square, or 1 small cinnamon stick

3–4 tablespoons light soy sauce

8 large dried black mushrooms, soaked in cold water to cover for 5–6 minutes and drained

1 tablespoon rice wine

½ teaspoon salt, plus salt to taste

DUCK

2 teaspoons honey

2 teaspoons dark soy sauce

½ teaspoon five-spice powder

1 boneless duck breast or thigh, skin on, 6–7 oz (185–220 g)

7 oz (220 g) fresh fine wheat noodles or egg noodles

1 or 2 green (spring) onions, tender green tops only, thinly sliced

12 small fresh cilantro (fresh coriander) sprigs

To prepare the soup stock, break or chop the duck bones into manageable pieces, if necessary, and place in a large saucepan. Add boiling water to cover, then pour off immediately. Pour in warm water to cover the duck generously (8–9 cups/64–72 fl oz/2–2.25 l), and add the ginger, star anise, cassia bark or cinnamon stick, and 1 tablespoon of the soy sauce. Slowly bring to a boil over medium-high heat, then reduce the heat to low and simmer, uncovered, for about 45 minutes to create a well-flavored stock.

Pour the stock through a fine-mesh sieve into a clean saucepan and add the mushrooms, rice wine, 2 tablespoons of the light soy sauce, and the ½ teaspoon salt. Place over low heat and bring to a simmer. Cook for about 20 minutes to reduce the soup and concentrate its flavors. Taste and adjust the seasoning with the remaining light soy sauce and/or salt.

Meanwhile, prepare the duck: In a small dish, stir together the honey, dark soy sauce, and five-spice powder. Brush the mixture thickly over the duck breast or thigh. Place on a rack on a baking sheet and let stand for 10–15 minutes. Preheat an oven to 400°F (200°C).

Place the baking sheet in the oven and roast the duck until medium-rare, 8–10 minutes for the breast, 10–12 minutes for the thigh. Remove from the oven and let rest for 5–6 minutes, to firm up the meat. Thinly slice against the grain.

Bring a saucepan three-fourths full of lightly salted water to a boil. Add the noodles and cook until barely tender, about 2½ minutes. Drain, rinse under running hot water, and drain again. Divide the noodles evenly among individual soup bowls and set aside.

To finish the soup, scoop out the mushrooms from the soup and set aside. Pour about 1½ cups (12 fl oz/375 ml) of the soup through a fine-mesh sieve into each bowl. Add 2 of the mushrooms and an equal amount of the duck to each serving. Garnish each serving with some of the green onion tops and 3 cilantro sprigs. Serve at once.

serves 4

In the north, any occasion is reason enough to celebrate with duck.

Southern

Niulijirou Luxun Mei Fan

beef and asparagus on rice noodles

Rice noodles are a popular ingredient in southern China. They are made fresh and sold precut or in flat sheets to be cut at home. Fresh rice noodles should be used within one or two days of purchase, and, as they are coated with oil to prevent the dough sticking together, should be rinsed before use. They are somewhat fragile and cook quickly, so if mishandled or overdone will break up into a gummy mass.

BEEF

1 tablespoon light soy sauce

1 tablespoon rice wine

1½ teaspoons cornstarch (cornflour)

½ teaspoon superfine (caster) sugar

6 oz (185 g) tender rump or sirloin steak, very thinly sliced into strips 1¾ inches (4.5 cm) long by ½ inch (12 mm) wide

6 to 8 asparagus, tough ends removed and sliced on the diagonal ½ inch (12 mm) thick

½ cup (4 fl oz / 125 ml) vegetable oil

1 lb (500 g) fresh flat, wide rice noodles, rinsed in cold water and drained

3 tablespoons oyster sauce

1 tablespoon light soy sauce

2 teaspoons cornstarch (cornflour) dissolved in ¾ cup (6 fl oz / 180 ml) chicken stock (page 250)

½ teaspoon superfine (caster) sugar

2 teaspoons sesame oil

1 green (spring) onion, including tender green tops, thinly sliced

☙ To prepare the beef, in a bowl, stir together the soy sauce, rice wine, cornstarch, and sugar. Add the beef and stir to coat evenly. Let stand for 15 minutes, stirring occasionally.

☙ Bring a small saucepan three-fourths full of water to a boil. Add the asparagus and blanch for 1 minute. Drain and place in ice water to maintain crispness and color.

In a wok over high heat, warm the vegetable oil. When the oil is hot, add the beef and stir-fry until partially cooked but still pink, about 30 seconds. Using a slotted spoon, transfer the beef to a plate.

Still over high heat, add the noodles to the hot oil and stir-fry, turning carefully to avoid breaking up the noodles, until warmed through and evenly coated with the oil, about 1 minute. Carefully pour off the excess oil, then slip the noodles onto a warmed serving plate.

Add the oyster sauce, soy sauce, cornstarch mixture, sugar, and sesame oil to the wok and simmer, stirring slowly, until lightly thickened, about 1 minute. Drain the asparagus and add to the wok along with the beef. Mix well and stir just until heated through.

Spoon the contents of the wok over the noodles, scatter the green onion evenly over the top, and serve at once.

serves 2–4

Northern

Zhen Zhu Qiu

"pearl" balls

Rice grains stick to these meatballs like pearls sewn onto a velvet purse. Even the simplest of ingredients can be glamorized by the clever and practical Chinese cook.

14 oz (440 g) ground (minced) fat pork such as pork butt

1 tablespoon light soy sauce

1½ teaspoons rice wine

1 teaspoon superfine (caster) sugar

½ teaspoon salt

1 egg

2 tablespoons finely chopped green (spring) onion

1½ teaspoons peeled and grated fresh ginger

¼ cup (1 oz /30 g) cornstarch (cornflour)

2 tablespoons water or chicken stock (page 250)

1 cup (7 oz /220 g) glutinous rice

1 tablespoon vegetable oil

light soy sauce or garlic-chile sauce

In a food processor, combine the pork, soy sauce, rice wine, sugar, and salt and process to a paste. Add the egg, green onion, ginger, cornstarch, and water or stock and process until blended. Set aside.

Pour the rice into a fine-mesh sieve and rinse well under running cold water. Bring a teakettle filled with water to a boil and pour the water over the rice. Rinse with cold water and drain well. Spread the rice on a plate.

With wet hands, form the pork mixture into 1-inch (2.5-cm) balls. Roll the meatballs in the rice, covering evenly. Brush the oil over a large heatproof plate and arrange the meatballs on it.

Bring water to a boil in the base of a steamer. Set the plate on the steamer rack, cover tightly, and steam the meatballs over rapidly boiling water for 20 minutes. Reduce the heat to low and continue to steam over simmering water until the rice is tender, about 15 minutes longer.

Remove the plate from the steamer, and serve the balls on the plate or transfer to a serving platter. Accompany with light soy sauce or garlic-chile sauce in small dishes for dipping.

serves 4–6

Eastern

You Yuan

green onion pastries

If I had to choose a favorite Chinese snack,
this would get my vote.

2 cups (10 oz / 315 g) all-purpose (plain) flour

1 cup (8 fl oz / 250 ml) boiling water

3 tablespoons sesame oil

coarse or flaked salt for sprinkling

1¼ cups (3¾ oz / 110 g) chopped green (spring)
onion tops

vegetable oil for frying

❦ Sift the flour into a bowl, and make a well in the center. Pour the boiling water into the well. Using a wooden spoon, quickly work the water into the flour to make a fairly stiff, but not dry dough. Knead lightly in the bowl until the dough forms a ball. Remove from the bowl, and brush the dough lightly with some of the sesame oil. Invert the bowl over the dough and leave to cool, about 6 minutes.

❦ Knead the dough very lightly until smooth and elastic, rub with more of the sesame oil, and place in a plastic bag. Set aside for 30–60 minutes.

❦ Using your palms, roll the dough on the work surface to form a log about 10 inches (25 cm) long. Cut into 6 equal pieces. Roll each piece into a ball. Working with 1 piece at a time, roll out each ball into a very thin round about 7 inches (18 cm) in diameter. Brush generously with sesame oil. Sprinkle with salt and then cover evenly and lightly with one-sixth of the green onion. Roll up the round into a cigar shape, twist into a tight coil, and brush the top with more sesame oil. On a lightly oiled work surface, flatten the coil with a rolling pin to make a round about 5 inches (13 cm) in diameter. Try to avoid having the onions break through the pastry. Repeat until all the pastries are made.

❦ When all of the pastries are ready, pour the oil to a depth of 1 inch (2.5 cm) into a large, wide, shallow pan, and heat over medium-high heat until hot. Working with 2 or 3 pastries at a time, place them in the hot oil and fry, turning once, until golden brown, about 3 minutes on each side.

❦ Transfer to a serving platter, sprinkle with additional salt, cut into quarters, and serve immediately.

makes 6

Street Food

Snacking is a way of life in Asia, and no less in China itself where, between meals, snacks are enjoyed every day. Even aside from dim sum, with its extensive array of dumplings, buns, and pastries, there are innumerable snack foods that can be purchased on the run. Whether it's a bowl of soup noodles or rice breakfast soup, a crunchy pretzel-like twist, or a massive meat-filled steamed bun, where there's a hungry mouth there's a street stall, itinerant vendor, or food stand in a marketplace to provide a snack fresh from a wok, steamer, or portable grill.

The *baozi* found at street stalls in the north and west are huge steamed buns, heavy with a filling of seasoned ground (minced) meat. *Jiaozi* are smaller steamed or boiled pork-and-cabbage dumplings in thin dough wrappers. In Sichuan, *dandan mian* (spicy sesame noodles) are a favorite, as are won-ton dumplings in chile oil dressing. On one visit to Shanghai I discovered a night market selling small bowls of the most delectable little sea snails cooked with garlic and white pepper, and the plumpest, tastiest green onion pastries imaginable.

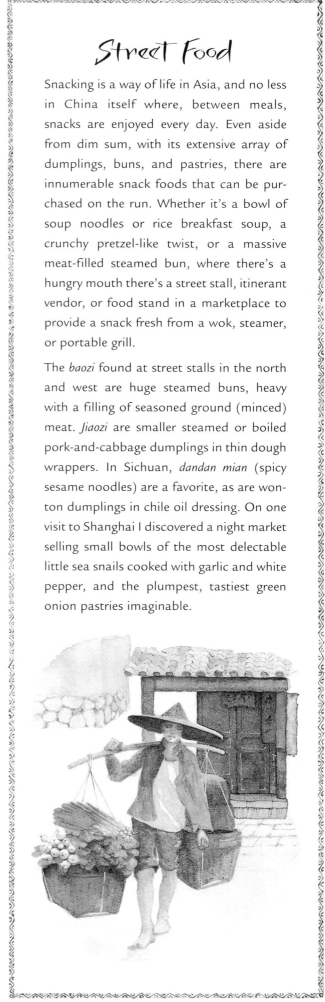

Southern

Chao Xian Mian

noodles with vegetables, meat, and seafood

Noodle dishes stir-fried with a variety of ingredients often go by the descriptive names "combination noodles" or "noodles with assortment." They are classics of the Guangdong style, the Chinese cuisine most readily recognized in restaurants around the world. In a restaurant, you may be invited to select your preferred combination of meat, seafood, and vegetables and your choice of soft or crisp noodles. Depending on the chef, soft can mean simply boiled and warmed with the sauce, or it can mean soft-fried, which calls for the noodles to be boiled, fried, and then simmered in the sauce until soft again. Crisp noodles, too, offer several possibilities. They may be softened by soaking and allowed to dry partially; they are then separated into single strands and deep-fried until crisp, to be served apart from the accompaniments so they reach the table still crunchy. Or they can be fried, like these here, in a tangled mass and topped with the ingredients so they reach the table partially crisp and partially softened by the hot sauce.

5 oz (155 g) fresh thin egg noodles

2 oz (60 g) chicken breast meat, cut into small, thin strips

1½ teaspoons peeled and grated fresh ginger

1 teaspoon rice wine

2 pinches of salt

6 shrimp (prawns), peeled and deveined, or about 2½ oz (75 g) cleaned squid bodies (about 3¼ oz/100 g squid before cleaning, page 249), thinly sliced

1½-inch (4-cm) piece carrot

1 cup (8 fl oz/250 ml) vegetable oil

8 pieces red bell pepper (capsicum), each ¾ inch (2 cm) square

1 green (spring) onion, including tender green tops, cut into 1½-inch (4-cm) lengths, then finely julienned, plus 1–2 tablespoons thinly sliced green onion tops

¼ cup (1¼ oz/40 g) sliced bamboo shoot

¼ cup (1¾ oz/50 g) sliced canned straw mushrooms

1 or 2 small heads bok choy, quartered lengthwise, blanched in boiling water for 1½ minutes, and drained

2 tablespoons light soy sauce

ground white pepper to taste

1 tablespoon cornstarch (cornflour) dissolved in 1 cup (8 fl oz/250 ml) chicken stock (page 250)

¾ cup (1½ oz/45 g) bean sprouts (optional)

1½ oz (45 g) Red Roast Pork (page 115), cut into small, thin strips (¼ cup) (optional)

♛ Bring a large saucepan three-fourths full of water to a boil. Add the noodles and cook until barely tender, about 3 minutes. Drain and rinse under running cold water. Drain well and spread on a tray to allow to dry partially.

♛ In a small bowl, mix together the chicken, ginger, rice wine, and pinch of salt and let stand for 10 minutes. In another small bowl, season the shrimp or squid with the remaining pinch of salt.

♛ Peel the carrot and, using a carving tool or sharp knife, remove 5 or 6 V-shaped strips along the length. Slice the carrot thinly crosswise to create flower-shaped pieces.

♛ In a wok over high heat, warm 1½ tablespoons of the oil. When it is hot, add the carrot and bell pepper and stir-fry for 30 seconds until the vegetables begin to soften. Add the chicken and shrimp or squid and stir-fry until white and firm, about 30 seconds. Add the julienned green onion, bamboo shoot, mushrooms, and bok choy and stir-fry for 20 seconds. Season with the soy sauce and pepper and stir-fry briefly. Add the cornstarch mixture and continue to stir over high heat until the sauce thickens, about 1½ minutes. Transfer to a bowl and set aside.

♛ Rinse and dry the wok. Place over high heat and add the remaining oil. When the oil is very hot, add the noodles and fry in a layer until lightly browned on the underside, about 30 seconds. Turn and fry on the second side until lightly browned, about 40 seconds longer. Lift the noodles from the wok with a wire skimmer and let drain over the wok for a few moments, then place on a warmed serving platter.

♛ Pour off the oil from the wok and return the wok, unrinsed, to high heat. Return the stir-fried ingredients to the wok, add the bean sprouts and pork, if using, and stir until heated through, about 30 seconds.

♛ Tip the contents of the wok over the noodles, garnish with the thinly sliced green onion tops, and serve at once.

serves 2–4

Western

Guoqiao Mian

"crossing the bridge" noodles

There are as many stories about how this dish was named as there are burned lips from tasting its steaming hot soup too soon. One version concerns a status-conscious merchant whose son had failed to pass the annual examinations and therefore forfeited his chance to win a place as assistant to an official. In shame, the son was banished to a small cottage across a stream on the family estate. Feeling sorry for him, one of the housemaids decided to smuggle a pot of soup to the boy. She floated chicken fat on the surface of the soup to hold in the heat while she made the long walk through the gardens to the bridge leading to the cottage. Another version is told by a restaurant in Kunming, which takes the name Cross the Bridge. The original restaurant was on an island and, as the story goes, the dish had acquired such a reputation that crowds thronged to cross the bridge to sample the piping-hot soup noodles.

NOODLES

1¾ cups (9 oz/280 g) all-purpose (plain) flour

3 small eggs

SOUP

6 oz (185 g) skinless, boneless chicken breast

1 teaspoon rice wine

1 teaspoon peeled and grated fresh ginger

1 teaspoon plus 1 tablespoon light soy sauce

6 cups (48 fl oz/1.5 l) chicken stock (page 250)

salt and ground white pepper to taste

2 or 3 green (spring) onions, including tender green tops, thinly sliced and white and green parts kept separate

2–3 tablespoons rendered chicken or duck fat, gently warmed

❦ To prepare the noodles, sift the flour onto a work surface and make a well in the center. Break the eggs into the well. Using your fingers, slowly work the eggs into the flour to make a soft dough, then shape it into a ball.

❦ Lightly dust a work surface with flour, and place the dough on it. Knead until the dough is smooth, 5–6 minutes. Cover the dough with a piece of oiled plastic wrap and let rest for about 20 minutes.

❦ Meanwhile, begin preparing the soup: Thinly slice the chicken against the grain, then cut the slices into 1½-inch (4-cm) squares. Place the chicken in a dish and add the rice wine, ginger, and the 1 teaspoon soy sauce. Mix well and set aside.

❦ On the same lightly floured work surface, lightly knead the dough again until elastic, 3–4 minutes. If rolling and cutting on a hand-cranked pasta machine, divide into 2 or 3 equal pieces. Working with 1 piece at a time, shape the dough into a log about 1 inch (2.5 cm) in diameter, and flatten with a rolling pin. Set the machine to the widest setting. Lightly dust the flattened dough and pass through the rollers. Reset the rollers a width narrower, fold the dough into thirds, dust if needed, and pass through the rollers again. Repeat, decreasing the setting each time, until you have a wide, thin strip of dough (setting 2 on most machines). Switch to the cutting attachment, set it about ⅛ inch (3 mm) wide, and pass the dough strip through the cutters. Repeat with the remaining dough portion(s).

❦ If rolling out the dough by hand, lightly dust a large, smooth work surface with flour. Roll out the dough into a large, thin sheet (or cut in half and roll out 2 sheets), and dust lightly with flour. Roll up lightly into a cylinder and, using a sharp knife, cut crosswise into noodles ⅛ inch (3 mm) wide.

❦ Toss the hand- or machine-made noodles lightly in flour to prevent them from sticking together. You should have about ¾ lb (375 g) noodles.

❦ To continue making the soup, pour the chicken stock into a saucepan and bring slowly to a boil over medium heat. Reduce the heat to low and keep at a gentle simmer.

❦ While the stock is heating, bring a large saucepan three-fourths full of lightly salted water to a boil. Add the noodles and cook until barely tender, about 2 minutes. Drain, rinse under running hot water, and drain again. Divide the noodles evenly among individual soup bowls and set aside.

❦ To finish the soup, add the chicken to the simmering stock, season with the 1 tablespoon soy sauce, the salt, and the pepper, and add the white parts of the green onions. Simmer until the chicken is just cooked through, about 40 seconds. Ladle the hot soup over the noodles, evenly distributing the chicken and onion.

❦ Float the green onion tops and the chicken or duck fat on the hot soup. Serve immediately.

serves 4–6

Southern

You Tiau

fried doughnut sticks

I have been hooked on these since I first encountered them at a street-side food stall in Guangzhou. I'd ordered a bowl of rice breakfast soup, and it came with diced preserved egg, straw mushrooms, green onions, and two of these doughnut sticks on the side.

1¼ cups (6½ oz/200 g) self-rising flour

2 teaspoons baking powder

1½ teaspoons salt

½ teaspoon baking soda (bicarbonate of soda)

⅓ cup (3 fl oz/80 ml) plus 1–2 tablespoons lukewarm water

vegetable or peanut oil for deep-frying

In a bowl, sift together the flour, baking powder, salt, and baking soda. Make a well in the center and pour the ⅓ cup (3 fl oz/80 ml) lukewarm water into it. Stir with a wooden spoon to mix well, adding the 1–2 tablespoons water if needed to make a soft dough. Knead very lightly in the bowl for about 30 seconds to form a very soft dough. Cover the bowl loosely with a kitchen towel and set aside for 15 minutes.

Turn out the dough onto a lightly floured work surface. With lightly floured hands, knead again very lightly until smooth, about 30 seconds. Then, still on the floured work surface, roll out the dough into a strip about 4 inches (10 cm) wide and 16 inches (40 cm) long. Using a sharp knife, cut crosswise into 20 strips each ¾ inch (2 cm) wide and 4 inches (10 cm) long. Press the strips together into pairs, sealing the seam with the back of a knife along the length of each pair. Working from the center of each pair, use your fingers to stretch the dough gently to about 10 inches (25 cm) long.

Pour the oil to a depth of 2½ inches (6 cm) into a wok, and heat to 360°F (182°C), or until a piece of dough added to it begins to bubble and turn golden within 30 seconds. Place 3 or 4 doughnut sticks in the oil and fry, turning them frequently, until golden brown, about 1½ minutes. Using a wire skimmer or tongs, transfer to paper towels to drain. Fry the remaining doughnut sticks in the same way.

Serve the doughnut sticks at room temperature.

makes 10

Southern

Zhou Juk

rice breakfast soup

During my young years in Hong Kong, my amah (housekeeper) had me convinced that I shouldn't pass a day without a bowl of rice breakfast soup (congee). Congee, she would state as she ladled it liberally into my bowl, was not only nutritious but delicious. I ate obediently, thinking it plain and uninteresting. I was not to discover how tasty congee could be until, early one morning, I decided on impulse to eat congee in one of Hong Kong's many small street-side cafés. Onto the blank canvas of my bowl of piping-hot congee the cook assembled a palette of interesting accompaniments—paper-thin slices of chicken and pig's liver, a raw egg, chopped, crisp-fried green (spring) onions, diced preserved egg, and fresh cilantro (coriander) sprigs. An amazing transformation!

1⅓ cups (9 oz/280 g) medium-grain white rice

3 cups (24 fl oz/750 ml) water

4 dried black mushrooms, soaked in hot water to cover for 25 minutes and drained

6–8 cups (48–64 fl oz / 1.5–2 l) chicken stock (page 250), pork stock (page 251), or water

1½ tablespoons dried shrimp (prawns), soaked in hot water to cover for 25 minutes and drained

2 teaspoons salt

3 oz (90 g) pork liver, very thinly sliced (optional)

¼ lb (125 g) skinless, boneless chicken breast, thinly sliced

3 oz (90 g) Red Roast Pork (page 115), thinly sliced (optional)

3 tablespoons chopped green (spring) onion, including tender green tops

3 thin slices fresh ginger, peeled and finely julienned

light soy sauce

ground white pepper

Fried Doughnut Sticks (opposite) (optional)

☙ Pour the rice into a colander and rinse under the running cold water until the water runs clear. Transfer the rice to a large, heavy saucepan and add the 3 cups (24 fl oz/750 ml) water. Cover tightly and bring to a boil over high heat. Reduce the heat to very low and cook until tender, about 20 minutes.

☙ Meanwhile, remove and discard the stems from the mushrooms if necessary, and thinly slice the caps.

☙ When the rice is ready, add 6 cups (48 fl oz/1.5 l) of the stock or water, the mushrooms, the shrimp, and the salt to the rice and bring to a boil over high heat. Reduce the heat to medium-low and simmer until the rice is very soft, about 15 minutes. To test, press a single grain between a finger and thumb; it should mash to a paste. The soup should also have a reasonably thin consistency. If it does not, add as much of the remaining 2 cups (16 fl oz/500 ml) stock or water as needed to achieve the correct consistency.

☙ Bring a small saucepan three-fourths full of lightly salted water to a boil. Add the pork liver and boil for 30 seconds to remove the pinkness. Add the chicken and boil, stirring to separate the pieces, for 30 seconds longer. The liver and chicken should be half cooked. Drain and divide the pieces among individual soup bowls.

☙ Ladle the soup into the bowls. Serve the roast pork (if using), green onion, ginger, soy sauce, pepper, and doughnut sticks (if using) in separate containers at the table for each diner to add as desired.

serves 4–8

Dried Foods

Familiar scenes along China's vast ocean fore-shore are the row upon row of lines and poles hung with flattened squid and bisected fish pinned out to dry. Beside them, on racks of enormous woven bamboo trays, a harvest of shucked shellfish slowly turns amber under the golden sun. Inland, as the harvesting seasons ebb, the eves, walls, and doorways of houses, mud-brick barns, and cattle sheds are festooned with a colorful bunting of drying corn and cabbages, and strings of scarlet chiles, fleshy black mushrooms, and exotic frilled fungi.

The dried food industry has flourished in China for millennia. Ancient culinary documents reported salt curing and sun drying among the oldest records of food preservation. Yet in earlier times there were other benefits to drying foodstuffs. Lightweight dried goods could be more easily transported on precarious rivers and primitive roadways within the vast country, and along the legendary Silk Road trade route.

Equally importantly, as a visit to a dried food store will attest, drying produces wondrously intense aromas. And it concentrates the flavors of seafoods and some vegetable ingredients, particularly cabbages and herbs, and a variety of mushrooms and other edible fungi. So, while the Chinese cook considers freshness a cardinal requisite for his or her ingredients, dried foods provide the emphatic aromas and tastes that their fresh counterparts simply cannot emulate. Even with access to the freshest seafood, a canny cook might add a sun-dried sea product as a flavor enhancer, and prefer dried mushrooms to the blandness of freshly harvested ones.

Certain dried products are so revered they are among the most expensive ingredients in Chinese cuisine. Shark's fin, abalone, gelatinous gray sea slugs, scallops (known in Guangdong and Hong Kong as *conpoy* and as *ganbei* elsewhere), the finest black mushrooms, and lacy sheaves of bamboo fungi are showcased on banquet menus. They are also appreciated as gifts. At New Year, dried food shops enjoy an active trade, wrapping gifts in the lucky colors of hot pink and red trimmed with gold.

Eastern

Yangzhou Chao Fan

yangzhou fried rice

Why fried rice became associated with the city of Yangzhou is something I have never been able to reliably discover, although over the years I have been offered many opinions. The cuisine of the city where Marco Polo—thirteenth-century explorer, diplomat, merchant, and gourmet—lived for years does, however, have something of a reputation for dumplings. And its chefs are known for their skills in producing finely diced ingredients to stuff into them. Perhaps adding colorful diced ingredients to rice was an obvious next step.

On special occasions, fried rice is served as the last course at banquets. It is the "filler" after the featured dishes, so the hosts can bid everyone farewell confident they have been generous in their hospitality. Yet it has made some pretense to fancifulness. One court chef gave it star status at a state dinner by presenting colorfully seasoned rice beneath an edible cover of a delicate golden egg crepe. Another wrapped the rice in softened lotus leaves, the fragrant contents to be dramatically revealed at the table, while one clever cook presented it in the carved shell of a winter melon.

For practical cooks, fried rice is a sensible use of leftover rice and various bits and pieces in a light, single-course meal, and as such is a homely dish enjoyed around the world.

1½ cups (10½ oz/330 g) long-grain white rice

3 tablespoons dried shrimp (prawns), soaked in ½ cup (4 fl oz/125 ml) boiling water for 10 minutes

2¾ cups (22 fl oz/680 ml) water

½ cup (2½ oz/75 g) English peas

½ cup (3 oz/90 g) corn kernels

3 tablespoons vegetable oil

2 eggs, beaten

½ cup (3 oz/90 g) diced bacon or ham

½ cup (2 oz/60 g) diced yellow onion

1 small, hot red chile, seeded and chopped

1 tablespoon light soy sauce

1 teaspoon salt

Rinse the rice well in a sieve held under running cold water, then drain well.

Pour the shrimp and its soaking water through a sieve held over a heavy saucepan. Set the shrimp aside. Add the rice and 1¾ cups (14 fl oz/440 ml) of the water, cover tightly, and bring quickly to a boil over high heat. Reduce the heat to the lowest possible setting and allow the rice to cook gently until tender without uncovering the pan, 16–18 minutes.

Meanwhile, in a wok over high heat, bring the remaining 1 cup (8 fl oz/240 ml) water to a boil. Add the peas and corn and boil until just tender, about 2½ minutes. Drain and set aside on a plate.

Wipe out the wok, add 2 tablespoons of the oil, and place over high heat. When it is hot, pour in the eggs and cook, without stirring, until lightly set, about 30 seconds. Break up the eggs with a spatula, and then transfer to the plate holding the vegetables. Return the wok to high heat, add the bacon or ham, onion, and chile, and stir-fry until the onion is golden, about 1½ minutes. Transfer to the plate.

When the rice is ready, add the remaining 1 tablespoon oil to the wok and place over high heat. When hot, add the reserved shrimp, all the cooked ingredients except the rice, and the soy sauce and salt and stir-fry briefly to reheat. Add the rice and stir-fry over high heat until thoroughly mixed.

Transfer to a warmed serving bowl and serve immediately.

serves 4

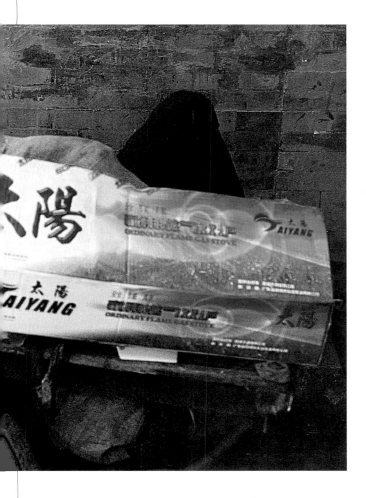

but this is not necessarily the case. Sweet tastes emerge through the savory courses of the cuisine, in the ingredients themselves, and in the sauces, dressings, and accompaniments. The use of sweet flavors in appetizers and main dishes can make the dessert course somewhat superfluous. But, as always, the principle of balance, or yin and yang, comes into play. Sweet tastes during the main meal can be harmonized by tart tastes in the fruit or dessert that follows.

In devising their sweet dishes, Chinese chefs had to work around what, to western eyes, might seem to be two insurmountable obstacles. They had no ovens for baking and no dairy cattle (except in Muslim communities) to provide the butter, cream, and milk we naturally associate with dessert cooking. Desserts were steamed or griddle-cooked. Lard, oil, and occasionally duck fat were used instead of butter, and where creaminess was desired—in the southern states at least—the coconut added its richness to steamed rice and fruit puddings.

Chinese chefs did have at their disposal fruit, nuts, rice, eggs, honey and sugar, unusual indigenous foods—and ingenuity. I can say,

Preceding pages: A swirl of pastel-colored cream is applied to a western-style cake in a Beijing cake shop. **Left:** The Hu Xin Ting (Heart of the Lake) restaurant takes pride of place in the Yuyuan Gardens in the heart of old Shanghai. **Above center:** A farmer seizes the chance for a short nap during a busy market day. **Above:** Tea bushes, grown to provide green tea, thrive amid the rocky outcrops in Shandong.

Top: China's basket makers are renowned for their skill, and their creations are put to all kinds of uses.
Above: Mangosteens and rambutans are two of the popular fruits grown in China's subtropical regions.
Right: The Summer Palace near Beijing is a reminder of Chinese imperial grandeur. The delicate, tiered Tower of Buddhist Incense stands atop its own massive plinth.

without reservation, that some of the most innovative and delicious desserts and sweet pastries I have ever eaten were served in restaurants and homes on my visits to China. Who but the Chinese would think to float white fungi or tomatoes in a clear, sweet soup as they do in Sichuan, or to glaze fingers of sweet potato with honey and sugar as they do in Kaifeng? Who but the Chinese find ways to make their desserts both delicious and medicinally beneficial, as they do with the use of the scarlet wolfberry served in syrup with white fungi as a delicious tonic for lungs and eyes, or gelatinous bird's nest for the complexion? What imagination went into the creation of a glutinous rice ball filled with the nutty sweetness of mashed lotus seeds, or fried bean curd skins with sesame and candied osmanthus flowers, a dish poetically named "sparrow heads"?

Fruit is an important element in Chinese sweet cuisine, and this vast nation has an impressive spectrum of products to draw on:

Top: A farmer carries fresh fruits to a village market.
Above: Colorful communist figurines are available to buy in Shanghai's busy antique streets. **Right top:** A Yao tribal woman embroiders traditional handicrafts for sale. Around 2 million Yao people live in the hilly regions of southwestern China, their home for thousands of years. Some are still ruled by village headmen and use antiphonal singing for courtship. **Right bottom:** Chrysanthemum flowers are often added to tea for their supposed medical benefits.

plums, apricots, cherries, hawthorn fruits, glossy red-skinned apples, tart crabapples, and sweet-crunchy snow pears, a relative of the nashi grown in the northern and central regions. From the east come citrus fruits, and from the west come white and golden yellow peaches and fragrant sweet melons. In the south, luscious tropical fruits, including bananas and pineapples, are cultivated.

Scarlet hawthorn jelly is as versatile a garnish and sweet-tart flavor note as the western classics, angelica and candied cherries. In fact, many kinds of preserved fruits are used in dessert preparation. Candied or dried green plums, winter melons, apples, tangerines, and black and red dates are ingredients of the classic "eight treasures" dishes, a popular concept in dessert preparations. Dried fruits, nuts, and glutinous rice combine as a richly flavored, textural stuffing for fruits such as apples, white pears, or melons.

Sweet foods have long been part of the Chinese diet. The Chinese began refining cane sugar more than a millennium ago and

have a history of making a wide range of
confectionery, sweet pastry, and candied fruit.
Although one early food historian claimed
sweet things were preferred by "barbarians
and country folk," there is ample evidence
of sophisticated city folk enjoying them as
well. Cameos depicted in brush paintings and
played out in old romantic novels had candied
confections and iced fruit on banquet tables
and at the scene of lovers' trysts. Sugar syrup
is the base for many Chinese sweet dishes.
Hot, spun sugar candy coats apple, yam, and
banana. Honey, on its own or in combination
with sugar, makes a deliciously sweet glaze
for fruit and vegetable desserts.

Chinese pastry makers have an important
weapon in their armory—lard. With sweet,
richly flavored pork fat, pastry is short and
crumbly, incomparably rich, and yet light as
a silk scarf. The pastry is wrapped around
sweet fillings of mashed red beans and black
dates, puréed lotus or chestnuts, or layered
beneath an egg custard of superlative delicacy
to make the famous *dan ta* (egg tarts)—
delicious bites that are more often than not
enjoyed as a between-meals snack, but can
serve to replace a dessert at the conclusion
of a banquet dinner.

Iced sweet dishes have an interesting and
lengthy history as well. The Chinese have
used refrigeration and freezing to preserve
and serve food for thousands of years. In
the far north, as far back as the Han dynasty
(202 BC–AD 220), *bingshi* (ice chambers) were
chipped into solid ice banks and rivers to
make cold rooms for food storage. Block ice,
packed in straw, was transported to the imperial residences and the homes of high officials
in the south and west, so nobles in all parts
of the country could serve exotic fruits
over crushed ice. The notion of serving
fruit studded into a cone of shaved ice that
is now found throughout Asia, from the
Indonesian archipelago to Japan, had its
beginnings in that far-off time in northern
China. In common with these countries, too,
are gelled sweet snacks, which use seaweed-
derived agar agar to set fruits and juices in
crunchy-firm jellies that won't melt in the
subtropical heat.

Walnuts, imported from western Asia, are used frequently in Chinese cuisine—in stir-fries and casseroles, fried and candied as a snack and appetizer, and as a principal ingredient in puddings. *Xuehua taoni,* or "snow-white walnut pudding," is a classic banquet dish in which chopped walnuts and mashed bread are fried with lard over a medium flame until they form a fragrant mass that smells toasty and appetizing. Candied fruit and esoteric additions, such as candied rose petals, candied olives, and osmanthus blossoms, are stirred through before a mantle of meringue is spread over the top.

Peanuts, which grow profusely in central China, and almonds, brought to China from the Middle East thousands of years ago via the Silk Road, are also used extensively in desserts. Nut soups, served hot in the colder months and iced in summer, are popular sweets.

Chinese desserts invite you to think beyond the everyday. Spooning canned lychees over ice cream might be easy, but wouldn't it be more interesting to serve lotus and tangerines in a sweet soup instead?

Left: A woman knits in the doorway of her house in Chongqing, one of the hottest and largest cities in China. **Top:** A bicycle with a trailer is the best way to get both the farmer and produce to the local market. **Above:** Peaches are native to China, originating near Xian. They have been cultivated for over three thousand years, but wild peach trees can still be found in remote areas of China.

Northern

Basi Pingguo

candied apples

I can blame apples for some unhappy moments in China. The first time I was offered this dish, at a banquet, I blistered my lip on a hot piece of candied apple, not understanding the function of the bowl of iced water on the table. On another occasion, a market vendor threatened me with his peeling cleaver for handling the tiny, bright red apples on his stall before I made a purchase, and, on one visit to the Summer Palace, I was fined for littering by an officious guard. I'd purchased a toffee-coated crabapple from a vendor at the site, and did not think twice about spitting the seeds. Unfortunately, the guard had another opinion, and the fine wasn't half as painful as his verbal dressing down.

But, aside from those negatives, apples have delighted me on occasions, too. On one visit to Shaanxi province, I could see a vendor walking the streets some distance away, carrying what appeared to be an enormous lamp with many red bulbs. Moving closer, I discovered it to be a frame on a pole, laden with candy-lacquered apples. I am delighted when, in Shanghai and Nanjing, I come across a street-side merchant selling little apple-filled buns or apple fritters stuffed with sweet red bean paste.

Before red eating apples were introduced to China, quinces, crabapples, and thorn apples—the tart fruit of an indigenous hawthorn tree—were all available. In Kaifeng, the sugared and honeyed fruit was being sold by street vendors one thousand years ago, and a few hundred years before that, in the Tang dynasty, crabapples steeped in honey and cinnabar were eaten as an elixir of life.

2 tart apples, peeled, cored, and cut into wedges ⅓ inch (9 mm) thick

⅔ cup (3½ oz/100 g) all-purpose (plain) flour

1 egg

⅓ cup (1½ oz/45 g) cornstarch (cornflour)

½ cup (4 fl oz/125 ml) water

oil for deep-frying

⅓ cup (2½ oz/75 g) superfine (caster) sugar

2 teaspoons sesame oil

2 teaspoons lard (optional)

1½ tablespoons water

ice cubes

✾ Fill a bowl three-fourths full of lightly salted water, add the apple wedges, and let soak for 10 minutes. Drain and spread to dry on a kitchen towel.

✾ Place ⅓ cup (1¾ oz/50 g) of the flour in a paper or plastic bag, add the apple wedges, close the top of the bag, and shake well to coat the apple wedges evenly with the flour.

✾ In a bowl, beat the egg lightly until well blended. Beat in the remaining ⅓ cup (1¾ oz/50 g) flour, the cornstarch, and the water to make a thin batter.

✾ Pour the oil to a depth of 2 inches (5 cm) into a wok or deep, heavy frying pan, and heat to 350°F (180°C), or until a few drops of the batter dropped into the oil almost immediately float to the surface. Dip half of the apple wedges into the batter, coating evenly, and add to the oil. Fry, stirring and turning the pieces with a slotted spoon to prevent them from sticking together, until golden, about 1½ minutes. Using a wire skimmer or slotted spoon, transfer to a serving plate. Repeat with the remaining apple wedges and batter and add to the first batch.

✾ Pour off the oil into a heatproof container. Add the sugar, sesame oil, and the lard, if using, to the pan and cook, stirring continually, until the sugar is golden brown, 3–4 minutes. Carefully add the water and allow it to bubble briefly, then add the fried apple wedges and quickly turn to coat them with the toffee. Using the wire skimmer or slotted spoon, return the apple wedges to the plate.

✾ Immediately place the ice cubes in a bowl, fill it with water, and set the bowl on the table with the plate of apple wedges. Each guest selects a piece of hot apple, holds it in the iced water for 10 seconds until the toffee hardens, and then eats it.

serves 6–8

When the dessert plates are cleared, the wine can be served again.

Southern

Ba Bao Xing Dong

almond bean curd with fruit

When the yin and yang principle is applied to food, yang relates to drinking, yin to eating. Yang also relates to foods that are strongly flavored and heating, while yin indicates bland, cooling foods. Smooth, slippery, soft and delicate, almond-flavored bean curd is the epitome of a cooling yin food to enjoy in hot weather, and when something soothing is needed. Try it chopped finely and added to iced coconut milk.

SUGAR SYRUP

¼ cup (2 oz/60 g) superfine (caster) sugar

¾ cup (6 fl oz/180 ml) water

2 cups (16 fl oz/500 ml) soybean milk or cow's milk

½ cup (3½ oz/105 g) superfine (caster) sugar

2½ teaspoons almond extract (essence)

1 cup (8 fl oz/250 ml) water

2 tablespoons powdered agar agar

3 cups (1¼ lb/625 g) drained, canned tropical fruit

☙ To prepare the sugar syrup, in a small saucepan over medium-high heat, combine the sugar and water and bring to a boil. Reduce the heat to medium-low and simmer for 10 minutes.

☙ In a saucepan over low heat, gently warm the soybean or cow's milk, sugar, and almond extract, stirring to dissolve the sugar. In a small saucepan over high heat, combine the water and agar agar. Bring to a boil, reduce the heat to medium, and simmer, stirring occasionally, until the agar agar has dissolved, 2–3 minutes. Pour the agar agar mixture through a fine-mesh sieve into the warm milk and stir.

☙ Wet a 6-by-8-inch (15-by-20-cm) pan with sides 1½ inches (4 cm) high and pour out the water. Pour the milk mixture through the sieve into the dampened pan, and let stand in a cool place or in the refrigerator until set, 40 minutes or longer.

☙ When the curd is set, use a knife to cut the curd into ¾-inch (2-cm) diamonds, or use a cookie cutter to cut into decorative shapes. Divide evenly among small dishes, and add the fruit and sugar syrup, again dividing evenly. Serve cold or at room temperature.

serves 6–8

Western

Niunai Huasheng Lao

sweet peanut cream

Chinese red dates—zao—the fruit of the jujube tree, are used in sweet and savory cooking. Strips of candied (glacé) hawthorn fruit are sold in China as a candy and dessert ingredient.

6 cups (48 fl oz/1.5 l) water

½ cup (4 oz/125 g) crushed rock sugar

12 Asian red dates, pitted, soaked for 25 minutes in hot water, and drained, or 2 tablespoons chopped dried hawthorn fruit

2 cups (10 oz/315 g) raw peanuts

½ cup (4 fl oz/125 ml) sesame oil

1 teaspoon salt

3 tablespoons cornstarch (cornflour)

☙ In a nonreactive saucepan over medium-high heat, combine 3 cups (24 fl oz/750 ml) of the water and the rock sugar. Bring to a boil, stirring to dissolve the sugar. Add the red dates, return the syrup to a boil, then reduce the heat to low, and simmer, uncovered, until the dates are almost tender, about 25 minutes. If using the hawthorn fruit, reserve for use later.

☙ Meanwhile, pour the peanuts into a wok or heavy saucepan and add the sesame oil. Place over medium heat and cook the peanuts slowly, stirring constantly, until golden brown, about 4 minutes. Remove from the heat, drain, and let cool for 10 minutes.

☙ In a food processor, combine the cooled peanuts and 1½ cups (12 fl oz/375 ml) of the water and process until smooth and creamy, about 1½ minutes.

☙ When the dates are ready, add the peanut cream and simmer gently, stirring occasionally, until thick and creamy, about 10 minutes.

☙ In a small bowl, stir together the salt, cornstarch, and the remaining 1½ cups (12 fl oz/375 ml) water. Pour the cornstarch mixture into the date mixture. Raise the heat to medium and bring the soup to a boil, stirring occasionally. Reduce the heat to low and simmer, stirring occasionally, until the soup is heated through and smooth, 3–4 minutes.

☙ Pour the soup into a deep dish. If using the hawthorn fruit, sprinkle it over the surface of the soup. Serve warm.

serves 6–8

Southern

Yezi Zhi Dongfen

coconut jelly

Coconut palms proliferate in the semitropical, southern coastal regions of China, where the milk is used in a number of popular dishes, and the water from inside the coconut is drunk as a refreshing beverage. When Zhao Reiyan became empress two thousand years ago, she insisted some of the dishes of her childhood on Hainan Island be served at court. Warm coconut and sago puddings, coconut custard baked in a young coconut shell, and sweetened coconut cream over crushed ice with beads of sweet jelly were favorites. Agar agar, a gelatin obtained from seaweed, sold as powder and strips, is the preferred gelling agent in the hot south, as it sets firm and does not melt.

2¼ cups (18 fl oz/560 ml) coconut cream
½ cup (3½ oz/105 g) superfine (caster) sugar
1 tablespoon powdered agar agar
1 cup (8 fl oz/250 ml) water
1 teaspoon almond or macadamia nut oil

In a bowl, whisk the coconut cream until smooth and creamy, about 1 minute.

In a small saucepan over high heat, combine the sugar, agar agar, and water and bring to a boil, stirring occasionally. Reduce the heat to medium-low and simmer for 5 minutes. Pour through a fine-mesh sieve into the coconut cream, then immediately whip for about 1 minute with a wire whisk or an electric mixer.

Brush a 6-by-8-inch (15-by-20-cm) pan with sides 1½ inches (4 cm) high with the oil. Pour the coconut cream mixture through the sieve into the mold. Let stand in a cool place or in the refrigerator until set, about 30 minutes.

Using a small, sharp knife, cut the jelly into about 1½-inch (4-cm) cubes. Serve on small plates.

makes about 18 pieces; serves 6

Southern

Ma La Gao

steamed sponge cake

Anyone trained in the conventional baking arts may be surprised at the light texture of this steamed sponge cake. Beneath its delicate honey taste is a subtle flavor drawn from the bamboo steamer. This classic dish appears on the varied and extensive menu in many dim sum restaurants.

2 teaspoons plus ½ cup (4 oz/125 g) butter or margarine, at room temperature

½ cup (3½ oz/105 g) superfine (caster) sugar

½ cup (6 oz/185 g) honey

4 eggs

1 teaspoon vanilla extract (essence)

2½ teaspoons baking powder

1½ cups (7½ oz/235 g) all-purpose (plain) flour

½ cup (4 fl oz/125 ml) milk, at room temperature

☼ Cut out a piece of parchment (baking) paper to fit the bottom of a 9-inch (23-cm) steamer basket precisely, place in the basket, and thickly grease the parchment with the 2 teaspoons butter or margarine.

☼ Set a steamer base half filled with hot water over high heat, and bring to a boil.

☼ Meanwhile, in a food processor, combine the sugar, honey, eggs, the ½ cup (4 oz/125 g) butter or margarine, and the vanilla extract and blend until smooth. Add the baking powder, flour, and milk and beat until a smooth, thick batter forms. Pour into the prepared steamer basket.

☼ Place the basket over the boiling water, cover, and reduce to a steady simmer. Cook, replenishing with extra boiling water as needed to maintain the original level, until the cake looks spongy and well risen and feels dry on the surface, about 30 minutes.

☼ Remove from the steamer, allow to cool for about 5 minutes, and then cut into wedges to serve.

serves 6–8

Bai Li Tian Tang

snow pears poached in rock sugar syrup

The round, crisp-fleshed, sweet and juicy snow pear of Sichuan is one of the finest of China's several species of native pear, and equates with the best of the Japanese nashi varieties. The superb white and yellow peaches native to China can also be cooked in this way. Peaches are symbolic of wisdom and longevity. At Chinese New Year, peach blossoms are everywhere, and peach-shaped "long life" buns are eaten and offered to the gods.

3 cups (24 fl oz / 750 ml) water

½ cup (4 oz / 125 g) crushed rock sugar

1 cinnamon stick

2 star anise

4 thin slices fresh ginger

4 pears, about 1¼ lb (625 g) total weight, peeled

In a nonreactive pan over medium heat, bring the water to a boil. Add the sugar, cinnamon, star anise, and ginger and simmer, stirring, until the sugar has dissolved, about 4 minutes.

Add the peeled pears, and, when the liquid has returned almost to a boil, reduce the heat to medium-low and simmer gently, uncovered, until the pears are tender when pierced with a knife, 15–20 minutes. Remove from the heat and let the pears cool to room temperature in the syrup.

Divide the pears among individual serving bowls. Spoon some of the cooled syrup over each pear. Serve at room temperature.

serves 4

China wakes up early, its merchants stocking market stalls with fruits still damp with morning dew.

The Lotus

The lotus is an elegant water plant that pro-liferates in lakes throughout China, some of the most majestic growing in the famed West Lake waterways beside the city of Hangzhou. Buddha ascribed a sacred sta-tus to the lotus, making it a symbol of puri-ty and fertility. Purity can be attained from the lowliest beginnings, as shown by the beautiful lotus growing from the sludgy mud of a pond or lake. That it is highly pro-lific is indisputable. One small plant can grow to cover a massive waterway in a very short time.

But if the lotus plant takes something for itself, it gives back tenfold. Blossoms of fragile beauty in yellow, pink, white, blue, and lavender are inedible, but are used as garnishes. Leaves as big as rafts can be employed as umbrellas against a sudden downpour, or dried for use as food wrap-pers. Delve beneath the mud in which the lotus has taken root, and you will find long, hollow tubers that can be cooked as a ten-der but crunchy vegetable, or sugar-coated as candy. As if all of that was not enough, the edible seeds of the plant have many culinary uses. The nutty flavor of lotus seeds is appre-ciated in both sweet and savory dishes, and they can be boiled with sugar and mashed to a thick paste to fill sweet buns and pastries.

Eastern

Zhima Lianzi Qiu

sesame lotus balls

The seedpods of the lotus plant are studded with edible oval seeds, the core (or embryo) of which is bitter in taste and can be mildly toxic, so should be removed. These versatile edibles are hard and dry, and need to be soaked or cooked before use. They are also ground and cooked with sugar to make sweet lotus seed paste to use as the filling for sweet buns, pancakes, and pastries, and the festive moon cakes eaten during the midautumn Moon Festival. Lotus seed paste is sold ready-made in cans.

2 cups (8 oz/250 g) glutinous rice flour
3 tablespoons superfine (caster) sugar
¾ cup (6 fl oz/180 ml) water
1 cup (10 oz/315 g) sweetened lotus seed paste
⅔ cup (2 oz/60 g) sesame seeds
vegetable oil for deep-frying

✥ In a large bowl, combine the rice flour, sugar, and water and stir until well mixed. Then, using your hands, knead the dough in the bowl until it is soft and smooth. Turn out onto a lightly oiled work sur-face and, using your palms, roll the dough into a log 15 inches (38 cm) long. Cut into 15 equal pieces each 1 inch (2.5 cm) thick. Roll out each piece into a round about 2½ inches (6 cm) in diameter.

✥ Divide the lotus paste into 15 equal pieces, and roll each piece into a ball. Place a ball of paste in the center of each dough round, and draw the dough up around it to form a ball, pinching the edges together at the top. Lightly oil your hands and gently roll each ball into a smooth, round sphere.

✥ Spread the sesame seeds on a plate. One at a time, roll the balls in the sesame seeds to coat evenly.

✥ Pour the oil to a depth of 2 inches (5 cm) into a wok or deep, heavy frying pan, and heat to 325°F (165°C), or until a small cube of bread dropped into the oil begins to turn golden after about 1 minute. Add the balls all at once and fry until puffed and golden, about 2½ minutes. Using a wire skimmer or slotted spoon, transfer to paper towels to drain.

✥ Serve the balls warm or at room temperature.

makes 15

Southern

Mang Guo Buding

mango pudding

Although Chinese cuisine is indisputably the most expansive cuisine in the world, little attention is paid to desserts. Members of the younger generations, however, have more of a sweet tooth. This pudding, an inspired borrowing from the kitchens of South Asia, has been absorbed into the dim sum repertoire in Hong Kong and Guangdong. Some particularly luscious fruits grow in southern China, among them mangoes, soursops, custard apples, and the odoriferous durian. Their counterpart in the north is the persimmon, its ripe red flesh so honeyed as to be almost cloying.

½ cup (3 oz/90 g) small pearl tapioca or sago

1 can (14 oz/440 g) sliced mango, drained, with liquid reserved, and the flesh puréed

½ cup (4 fl oz/125 ml) water

⅓ cup (3 oz/90 g) superfine (caster) sugar

½ cup (4 fl oz/125 ml) coconut cream

☙ Pour the tapioca or sago into a saucepan and rinse well with cold water. Drain. Measure out 1 cup (8 fl oz/250 ml) of the reserved mango liquid and add it to the saucepan (discard the balance) along with the water and sugar. Bring to a boil over medium-high heat, reduce the heat to medium-low, and simmer, stirring frequently, until almost all of the tapioca or sago pearls are translucent, about 20 minutes.

☙ Add the coconut cream and simmer gently until the pudding is thick and no white pearls remain, about 6 minutes.

☙ Stir in the mango purée, divide the mixture evenly among small individual serving bowls, cover, and refrigerate until firm.

☙ Serve the pudding chilled.

serves 4–6

Northern

Hong Dou Sa Biang

red bean pancakes

*Red beans boiled with sugar make
a sweet dessert soup, or a stuffing for sweet
pastries, pancakes, and buns.*

1 egg

1 cup (8 fl oz/250 ml) water

½ cup (2½ oz/75 g) all-purpose (plain) flour

3 tablespoons cornstarch (cornflour)

2 tablespoons vegetable oil, plus 2–3 teaspoons

2 teaspoons sesame oil

*6 oz (185 g) sweetened red beans or
red bean paste*

1 tablespoon confectioners' (icing) sugar

☼ In a food processor, combine the egg and water and process briefly to blend. Add the flour, cornstarch, and the 2 tablespoons vegetable oil and process until a thin batter forms. Let stand for 10 minutes.

☼ Place a cast-iron or heavy, nonstick frying pan over medium-high heat. When it is hot, add ½ teaspoon each vegetable and sesame oil, and rub the inner surface of the pan with a ball of paper towel to moisten evenly.

☼ Pour one-fifth of the batter into the pan and tilt and swirl the pan to spread the batter evenly and thinly over the bottom. Cook over medium-high heat until set on the bottom, about 30 seconds. Carefully spread one-fifth of the red beans or bean paste across the center of the pancake, then fold the sides and ends over it to form a rectangle. Using a flat spatula, press on the surface to spread the filling evenly. Cook for 20 seconds to brown the underside, then turn and cook, again pressing gently, to brown the other side, about 30 seconds. Using the spatula, transfer the pancake to a plate. Use the remaining batter and red beans or bean paste to make 4 more pancakes in the same way.

☼ Cut the pancakes into slices ¾ inch (2 cm) wide, arrange on a serving platter, and dust with the sugar. Serve warm or at room temperature.

serves 8

Northern

Fengmi Shanyao

honey sweet potato

Honey from Kaifeng was one of the prime seasonings in Chinese cooking in the Sung dynasty (AD 960–1279).

1 lb (500 g) sweet potatoes, peeled and cut
into sticks 1½ inches (4 cm) long by ½ inch
(12 mm) wide by ¾ inch (2 cm) thick

1 tablespoon sesame seeds

vegetable oil for deep-frying

HONEY SYRUP

⅓ cup (3 oz/90 g) superfine (caster) sugar

⅔ cup (5 fl oz/160 ml) water

¼ cup (3 oz/90 g) honey

1 tablespoon cornstarch (cornflour) mixed with
⅓ cup (3 fl oz/80 ml) water

❦ Fill a bowl three-fourths full of lightly salted water, add the sweet potato sticks, and let soak for 10 minutes. Drain and spread on a kitchen towel to dry.

❦ Heat a wok over medium-high heat. When hot, add the sesame seeds to the dry pan and toast, stirring frequently, until golden brown, about 1 minute. Pour into a dish and set aside to cool.

❦ Wipe out the wok. Pour oil to a depth of 1 inch (2.5 cm) into the wok, and heat to 350°F (180°C), or until a small cube of bread dropped into the oil turns golden in about 1 minute. Add the sweet potato sticks and fry, stirring occasionally, until softened and lightly colored, about 5 minutes. Using a slotted spoon, transfer to a plate.

❦ To prepare the honey syrup, pour off all but 3 tablespoons of the oil into a heatproof container. Return the wok to medium heat, add the sugar, and cook until golden brown and melted, 3–4 minutes. Carefully add the water and bring to a boil. Boil for 1 minute, stirring to dissolve any lumps that may have formed. Add the honey and simmer briefly, then add the sweet potato strips and carefully turn and stir in the syrup until glazed. Cook over medium heat for 2 minutes, until the sweet potato has absorbed some of the syrup. Add the cornstarch mixture and the toasted sesame seeds and boil, stirring slowly, until the sauce thickens and glazes the sweet potato strips, about 2 minutes.

❦ Transfer to a serving plate and serve immediately.

serves 6–8

Eastern

Juzi Lianzi Xingren

lotus and tangerine sweet soup

Clear sweet soups, based on a syrup of rock sugar and water, are an important aspect of Chinese desserts. They are considered cooling, and in many instances are medicinally beneficial. An imaginative variety of ingredients are floated in sweet soups. Among the most popular are crunchy-textured white fungus, often in combination with scarlet wolfberries, and gelatinous edible bird's nest, which is sometimes served sprinkled with crushed pearls. Ginkgo nuts, red dates, cherries, crabapples, and hawthorn fruits are favorite additions, too. Indeed, just about any fresh fruit can be served in a sweet soup, including indigenous litchis and longans.

Some of China's best citrus fruits are grown in Fujian province, and lotus plants proliferate in the waterways around Hangzhou. Together these two eastern specialties make an elegant and refreshing soup. Fresh lotus root must be well scrubbed and thickly peeled before use. If unavailable, substitute water chestnuts.

⅓ cup (1½ oz/45 g) dried lotus seeds, soaked
in water for 2 hours and drained

4 cups (32 fl oz/1 l) cold water

¾ cup (6 oz/185 g) crushed rock sugar or
superfine (caster) sugar

3-oz (90-g) piece lotus root, peeled and thinly
sliced crosswise

3 tangerines, peeled and sectioned

❦ In a small saucepan over high heat, combine the soaked lotus seeds with hot water to cover. Bring to a boil, reduce the heat to low, and simmer, uncovered, until partially tender, about 15 minutes.

❦ In another saucepan over medium heat, combine the cold water and sugar and bring to a boil, stirring to dissolve the sugar. Add the drained lotus seeds and simmer, uncovered, for 15 minutes. Add the lotus root and continue to simmer until the lotus root and seeds are tender, 10 minutes longer.

❦ Carefully remove all the white pith and seeds from the tangerine sections, and add the sections to the lotus syrup. Simmer over low heat, uncovered, until the tangerine is slightly transparent, about 10 minutes. Let cool and serve at room temperature, or chill before serving.

serves 6–8

Eastern

Babao Pingguo

eight treasures apples

*Satisfying as a fresh fruit, in the winter months apples
are highly appreciated when served hot like this
at the conclusion of a banquet menu.*

*Their shiny, scarlet skins make apples symbolic of good
fortune. Like golden citrus fruits, they are offered to
the gods at temples and are associated with auspicious
events. Red apples cooked in their skins are, therefore,
an impressive and much-loved banquet dish.*

*Several varieties of native apples have been grown since
early times in far western china, and scientists recently
identified the slopes of the Tian Shan mountain range,
which forms China's border with Kyrgyzstan, as the
possible location of the original apple from which
all modern apples have developed.*

*Crisp-fleshed, sweet, and juicy Chinese round pears,
also called white or snow pears, can be prepared in the
same way with a rich stuffing of nuts and dried fruit
as a warm dessert, or with a mixture of diced
fresh fruit as a cooling summer sweet.*

4 round red apples

¼ cup (1½ oz/45 g) glutinous rice

3 tablespoons superfine (caster) sugar

1 cup (8 fl oz/250 ml) water

8 blanched almonds

8 toasted cashew nuts

4 maraschino cherries

1 tablespoon raisins

4 teaspoons sweetened red beans

1 teaspoon sesame seeds

½ cup (4 fl oz/125 ml) water

Fill a high-sided dish three-fourths full with
lightly salted water. Using a sharp knife, cut off the
top from each apple, about ½ inch (12 mm), and
place the tops in the water.

Using a small knife or teaspoon, remove the core
and a portion of the flesh from each apple, to form a
cavity in the center of each. Be careful not to cut
through the blossom end. Place the apples upside
down in the salted water.

☸ In a small saucepan over medium-high heat, combine the rice, 1 tablespoon of the sugar, and the 1 cup (8 fl oz/250 ml) water and bring to a boil. Cook until the water is absorbed, about 10 minutes.

☸ In a small bowl, mix together one-fourth of the rice, 2 almonds, 2 cashews, 1 cherry, several raisins, 1 teaspoon red beans, and ¼ teaspoon sesame seeds. Stuff the mixture into the cavity of an apple. Repeat to make 3 more batches, stuffing 1 batch into each of the remaining 3 apples. Stand the apples upright in a small heatproof dish and replace their tops.

☸ In a small saucepan over medium heat, combine the remaining 2 tablespoons sugar and the ½ cup (4 fl oz/125 ml) water and bring to a simmer, stirring until the sugar has dissolved, 2–3 minutes. Pour into the dish with the apples.

☸ Bring water to a simmer in a steamer base. Place the dish in a steamer basket or rack over the simmering water, cover, and steam until the apples are tender when pierced with a knife and the rice is cooked, about 30 minutes. Add boiling water as needed to maintain the original level.

☸ Remove the dish from the steamer and let the apples cool completely. Divide among individual serving plates and serve at room temperature.

serves 4

Come, god of the kitchen, whose surname is Chang, now here is your pudding, and here is your tang (soup). When you get up to heaven it will make us all glad, if you tell what is good, and omit what is bad.

Fresh Fruits

China covers a vast territory, with climate ranging from semitropical to near-Arctic, and its native and cultivated crops reflect this diversity. Fruits that may be commonplace in the hot and sultry south are an expensive rarity in the north and far west.

You'll find an abundance of commonly known tropical fruits in the fresh food markets in Guangdong and Guangxi, but also such lesser-known exotics as litchis and longans, rambutans and mangosteens. In Fujian and Jiangxi, superb citrus fruits compete for space on market shelves, while some of the country's best melons and grapes are brought in from the far western provinces, and superb stone fruits and pears are harvested in the central-western Sichuan basin. As you travel northward, temperate to cold conditions dictate the dominance of cooler-climate fruits, such as cherries and hawthorn fruits, persimmons and apples.

Hainan Island, China's southernmost region, enjoys a near-tropical climate where coconuts and pineapples grow readily, and exotics include the gargantuan, fleshy jackfruit and the spiny-skinned durian. This latter tropical treat is so odoriferous that it is banned from transport on public vehicles, and is said to be an aphrodisiac.

GLOSSARY

The following entries cover basic recipes and key ingredients called for throughout this book. Chinese ingredients may be obtained from Chinese grocery stores, specialty-food stores, well-stocked supermarkets, and by mail order. For information on items not listed here, please refer to the index.

AGAR AGAR

A powdered gelatinous substance processed from seaweed, agar agar must be dissolved by boiling. Desserts and sweets set with agar agar have a firm, crisp texture and will not melt. Agar agar also comes in strips. It can be used as a vegetarian alternative to gelatin.

BAMBOO SHOOTS

The edible shoots of certain types of bamboo are known as *qingsun*. Fresh, untreated shoots have tough, outer leaves over a golden-colored, horn-shaped, tender shoot of layered construction. Ready-to-use shoots are sold fresh, frozen, or canned in whole pieces, slices, or shreds, and what is not used can be kept fresh in the refrigerator in lightly salted water for up to a week. Winter bamboo shoots (*dongsun*) are small and tender. Salted dried bamboo shoots should be soaked and rinsed thoroughly before use.

BEAN CURD

Protein-rich bean curd (*doufu*) is a bland-tasting, jellylike substance produced by adding a coagulating ingredient to a liquid of crushed and boiled dried yellow soybeans and water. Soft or "silk" fresh bean curd has a smooth and fragile texture, suited to soups and some stir-fries. Firm fresh bean curd has been compressed to extract water, giving it a firmer texture and slightly stronger taste suited to stir-fries, deep-frying, and slow-cooked dishes. Fresh bean curd is packed in water and sold in blocks, packs, or squares, and should be used within 2 to 3 days of opening. The water should be changed frequently. Fried bean curd is the fresh product cut into blocks, strips, and slices and deep-fried to crisp the surface. It is suited to slow-cooked dishes and should be rinsed before use. Bean curd sheets (*youpi*) are made by drying the firm, thin skin that coagulates on the top of heated soybean milk, and is also sold folded into sticks (*fuzhu*). As dried ingredients, they last indefinitely, and both must be soaked to soften before use in stewed dishes and as wrappers for fried foods. *Jiangdoufu* is bean curd "cheese," a pungent seasoning for braised dishes made by fermenting bean curd in salty water, chile, and alcohol.

BEAN SPROUTS

The edible mung bean sprouts (*ludouya*) are slender, silver-cream colored shoots growing to about 2 inches (5 cm) long with a seedpod at one end and a tapering root at the other. Fresh sprouts are readily available and are a superior choice to canned sprouts. Both should preferably be blanched in boiling water and then crisped in ice water before use. Keep fresh sprouts in an airtight container in the refrigerator for 3 to 5 days. To make elegant "silver" sprouts, pick off and discard the root and the seedpod from each sprout before cooking. Longer, stronger-tasting soybean sprouts (*huang douya*) can be used in the same way.

BEAN THREAD VERMICELLI

These fine, transparent noodles (*fensi*), also known as cellophane or glass noodles, are made from a paste of ground mung beans and water. They should be softened in hot water before use. When stewed, the noodles retain their firm, crunchy texture, making them suitable for soups, hot pots, and vegetarian dishes. For manageability, cut them into short (4 inch/10 cm) lengths before serving.

BEAN SAUCES

Both broad beans and the versatile soybean provide the base ingredient for many Chinese seasoning pastes and sauces, including, of course, the renowned condiment and flavoring, soy sauce (see page 48). The intense flavors of these sauces are appreciated in many stir-fries and braised dishes. Store bean sauces in the refrigerator in sealed jars. They will last for at least 3 months. While each province has its specialties, the most common sauces follow.

BLACK BEAN SAUCE Crushed or chopped fermented black soybeans are suspended in a salt solution. The sauce (*huang jiang*) comes in thin and thick varieties, of which the latter has been used predominantly in these recipes.

GARLIC-CHILE SAUCE This salty and hot-tasting combination of crushed garlic, chiles, and fermented beans is known as *suan lajiang*.

HOT BEAN SAUCE Also known as chile bean paste, hot bean sauce (*douban lajiang*) is a thick, salty paste of mashed chiles, fermented yellow beans, seasonings, and oil.

SWEET BEAN SAUCE The traditional accompaniment to Peking duck, sweet bean sauce (*tianmian jiang*) comes in several varieties: for convenience we recommend the easily obtained hoisin sauce, which is slightly sweeter than the sauces made in the north. It should not be confused with the sweetened, mashed red (adzuki) beans used in some dessert recipes.

YELLOW BEAN SAUCE Fermented yellow soybeans are crushed or left whole in a salt solution to make this sauce. A thick variety may also be known as brown bean sauce.

BEANS, YARD LONG

As their name suggests, yard long beans can grow up to 3 feet (1 m) in length. Also known as snake beans or long beans, the species is native to Asia. Dark green varieties are more tender than the paler green, slightly thicker beans. Substitute green beans if yard long beans are not available. They should be stored in a plastic bag in the refrigerator and used within 4 days.

BLACK BEANS

Salted and fermented soybeans are popular in southern China, where they are used as a seasoning. The salty, wrinkled beans may be rinsed and dried before use to decrease their saltiness. They are also called dried or salted black beans, fermented black beans, or simply black beans, and will keep for many months in an airtight container in a cool storage cupboard.

BOK CHOY

Bok choy (*bai cai*) has fleshy, white stems with a delicate flavor and round green leaves, which can be steamed or used raw as a salad vegetable. It is sometimes called Chinese chard or white cabbage. Bok choy should not be confused with Shanghai cabbage, which has pale green stems and a slightly tougher texture.

CASSIA BARK

Cassia bark is an aromatic bark native to southern China and its neighbors. It is similar to and interchangeable with cinnamon sticks as a flavoring agent in slow-cooked dishes and desserts. Usually sold in pieces of about ¾ by 3 inches (3 by 7.5 cm) in length. Store in an airtight jar.

CHILE OIL

Chile oil is an infusion of fresh or dried hot red chiles in vegetable oil or sesame oil. The hot, flavored red oil is used sparingly as a condiment and seasoning. *Huajiaoyou* is an oil infused with Sichuan peppercorns that can be used instead of regular chile oil for a spicier taste.

CHILE SAUCE

Seasoned with rice vinegar, sugar, and salt, chile sauce is a fiercely hot sauce made from ground red chiles.

CHILES

Hot red and green chiles grow abundantly in the central and western provinces of China, where they feature in many dishes. Fresh, dried, pickled, and powdered chile are all commonly used.

CHINESE BROCCOLI

Chinese broccoli is also known as *gai lan* and Chinese kale. It resembles *choi sum* but is slightly more bitter and has thicker stems and small white flowers. Sliced broccoli stems are interchangeable with asparagus in Chinese recipes.

CHINESE GREENS

The Chinese cultivate a bewildering variety of unique vegetables of the genus *Brassica*, as well as the large, round-headed cabbage, an important winter vegetable in the north of China. *Dong cai* is preserved dried cabbage used in braised dishes and soups. It is sold in airtight packs, and should be rehydrated by soaking in warm water, and drained before use. When shopping for fresh Chinese greens, choose those with firm stems and fresh-looking, unblemished leaves and store them in the vegetable crisper of the refrigerator. Where Chinese broccoli and cabbages are not available, substitute ordinary cabbage or broccoli. See also bok choy, Chinese broccoli, *choi sum*, mustard greens, napa cabbage, pickled radish.

CHINESE SAUSAGE

More commonly known as *lap cheong*, these red-colored, hard, dry sausages that resemble slim salamis are made from fat pork lightly spiced to give them their distinct flavor. Another variety, known as *yun cheung* or *xiang chang*, is made from a mixture of chopped liver and pork and is a brown-red color. Both types will keep for many months in the refrigerator or a cool cupboard. Steam for 4 to 5 minutes before use to soften them.

CHOI SUM

Choi sum is a flowering cabbage with sparse leaves and tiny yellow flowers on slender green stems. Its name means "vegetable heart" and it is closely related to broccoli rabe and *B. juncea*, the rape plant used extensively in Chinese cooking as a vegetable and from which the earliest forms of cooking oil were extracted. Poached *choi sum* dressed with oyster sauce is one of the most popular vegetable dishes in Chinese cuisine. *Qing cai* is winter rape with round, dark green leaves.

CILANTRO

The distinctively aromatic fresh leaves of the coriander plant are used extensively as a fresh garnish on stir-fries and soups, and the chopped leaves and stems are an ingredient in stuffings and fillings. The roots are not used in Chinese cooking. Parsley, Vietnamese mint, or basil can be substituted if this unique pungent flavor is not appreciated. Wrap fresh coriander in moist paper or a kitchen towel and store in the vegetable section of the refrigerator. Rinse well before use.

CORN, YOUNG

Also known as miniature or baby corn, young corn are small, fully formed spears of tender sweet corn, sold fresh or canned. They require minimal cooking and add textural and visual interest to soups and stir-fries while contributing insignificantly to flavor. Fresh young corn should be used within 3 to 4 days of purchase. Canned corn can be kept in clean water in a covered container in the refrigerator for up to 4 days.

CORNSTARCH

Also known as cornflour, cornstarch is a fine-textured flour made from maize, sometimes with wheat flour added. When used in a paste with water as a thickener, it results in a glossy, translucent sauce, and gives a crisp coating to fried foods. Tapioca and arrowroot starches can substitute.

DUMPLING WRAPPERS

Wheat-flour skins (*jiaozi mian*) also known as *gow gee* or *gyoza*, are 3-inch (7.5-cm) round, thin wrappers made from wheat flour and water dough. They are used to wrap pot stickers and other folded steamed or fried dumplings. Wonton skins (*huntun mian*) are 3½-inch (9-cm) square thin wrappers made from an egg and flour dough used to wrap soup dumplings and some fried snacks. They are usually sold in blocks of 30 or 50, wrapped in plastic. Fresh skins will keep in the refrigerator for 3 to 5 days. Freeze to keep longer, and thaw until flexible before using.

DATES, CHINESE RED

The wrinkled, red-brown fruits (*zao*) of the jujube tree have a datelike texture and taste. They introduce an interesting flavor counterpoint in stews, and are used in desserts and fillings for pastries and sweet buns. Seeded black dates can substitute.

FIVE-SPICE POWDER

A finely ground aromatic condiment and seasoning, five-spice powder is made by blending Sichuan pepper, cinnamon or cassia, cloves, fennel, and star anise.

FUNGI, DRIED BLACK

Black fungi is also known as wood ear fungi (larger, thicker tree fungi) and cloud ear fungi (smaller, dark, curled fungi) as a result of the earlike shapes of this gray-black fungus, which is sold fresh in some specialty Asian stores. Its pleasing crisp texture and taste is appreciated in dishes from all regions of China, and it is extensively used in vegetarian cooking. Dried black fungus is sold whole or in pieces of approximately 2 inches (5 cm) square, or is shredded for convenient use. It must be soaked to soften and any woody root sections should be trimmed off before use. Store in an airtight container for many months. Fresh fungus should be used within 3 to 4 days of purchase.

GARLIC CHIVES

Garlic chives are related to green (spring) onions, but have flat, deep green leaves with a strong aroma of garlic. They are sold fresh in bundles to be chopped into soups, stir-fries, and stuffings. They are best kept wrapped in paper and stored in the vegetable crisper, but should be used within a few days of purchase. They grow readily in a herb garden, and a mixture of peeled, chopped garlic and green onions can substitute when garlic chives are unavailable.

GINGER

The edible root or rhizome of ginger is buff colored and smooth when young, and sometimes comes with slender, pink-tipped green shoots attached. When older, root ginger becomes a dull, deep buff color with slightly wrinkled skin; its flavor intensifies and the flesh becomes fibrous. It is peeled and grated, minced, sliced, or

WONTON WRAPPER GARNISH

vegetable oil for deep-frying

5 wonton wrappers, cut into strips ⅛ inch (3 mm) wide

♛ Pour the oil to a depth of 1 inch (2.5 cm) into a wok or heavy saucepan, and heat to 375°F (190°C), or until a wonton strip dropped into it turns crisp and golden within seconds. When the oil is ready, add the wonton strips and fry until crisp and golden, about 30 seconds. Using a wire skimmer or slotted spoon, transfer the crisp strips to paper towels to drain.

coarsely chopped for use as an edible flavoring of unique taste and appealing spiciness. Dried ginger is not a suitable substitute in Chinese cooking; however, processed ginger products packed in brine or vinegar may be appropriate substitutes, if rinsed first.

TO MAKE GINGER JUICE, peel and finely grate fresh root ginger onto a piece of fine cloth, gather up into a ball and squeeze to extract the juice. The pulp can be discarded or used in a soup or stir-fry. One tablespoon of grated ginger will produce approximately 1½ teaspoons of ginger juice. Ginger wine is a seasoning and marinade made by combining 1 part ginger juice with 2–3 parts rice wine.

HAIR VEGETABLE

Hair vegetable is a highly nutritious freshwater algae unique to Chinese cooking. Also known as black moss, it grows as fine, black, hairlike strands in mountain springs in northern Gansu province, abutting Mongolia. Its Chinese name, *facai*, forms part of the New Year greeting wishing wealth, happiness, and longevity. Its length and obscurity make it an essential symbolic ingredient in New Year's festive dishes. Hair vegetable should be soaked to soften before use and has a pleasing crunchy texture.

JICAMA

Jicama is a root vegetable with white, crunchy flesh that can be eaten raw or used in braised dishes and soups. It has buff-colored skin and a round, semiflattened, fluted shape. It is also known as yam bean.

LILY FLOWERS

The dried flower buds of the tiger or day lily are known as golden needles or lily buds. They are slender, ochre-golden slips about the size of a bean sprout, with a delicate flavor and a musky fragrance. They are used in braised dishes, as an ingredient in classic "eight treasures" combinations, and are highly appreciated in vegetarian cooking. They are sometimes tied into a knot before cooking to symbolize unity. In an airtight jar, away from heat and damp, dried lily flowers will keep for many months.

LOTUS

The beautiful lotus has many practical applications in the kitchen, providing several important ingredients for savory and sweet dishes, petals for decoration on plates and tables, and leaves for wrapping steamed dishes.

LOTUS LEAVES When purchased dried, lotus leaves are soaked to soften, and the hard stem junction should be trimmed away before use. Fresh and dried lotus leaves are used to wrap steamed rice and other ingredients in tantalizing parcels: the leaves can then impart their unique fragrance to the food.

LOTUS PASTE Mashed, sweetened lotus paste is a popular filling for sweet buns and pastries and is sold canned or frozen. Unused lotus paste can be stored in the refrigerator for several weeks in a covered container.

LOTUS ROOT A crisp-textured vegetable, lotus root (*lian ou*) is sold fresh, canned, or frozen, and is used in stir-fries, soups, and simmered dishes. It can be used as a substitute for water chestnuts.

LOTUS SEEDS The seeds (*lianzi*) are purchased dried or canned, and are used as a nutty-textured ingredient in sweet and savory dishes. The slender inner core should be removed before use.

MELONS

China cultivates numerous varieties of sweet and savory melons, gourds, and squashes—the long, ridged silk squash or angled luffa; the bitter-tasting, knobbly green bitter melon appreciated for its medicinal benefits; the fuzzy or hairy melon, which looks somewhat like a thick zucchini; and the giant, white-fleshed, bland-tasting winter melon (*donggua*). Melons, with the exception of bitter melon, are interchangeable in Chinese recipes, or can be replaced by chayote (choko) or zucchini or, in some instances, by giant white radish or jicama.

MUSHROOMS

China's central-western mountain ranges are a prolific habitat for many types of unique, indigenous mushrooms and, in addition, a number of popular varieties are cultivated to meet local fresh food market and export demands. Fresh mushrooms should be used within 2 to 3 days of purchase, and should be rinsed and drained or dried before use. Once opened, unused canned mushrooms can be stored in fresh water in a small covered container in the refrigerator. If the water is changed daily, they will remain fresh for up to a week.

ABALONE MUSHROOMS A buff colored, irregular-shaped fungi, the abalone mushroom has thick flesh, a meaty texture, and a taste not unlike the seafood after which it is named. Fresh abalone mushrooms have a less intense taste than the canned variety.

BUTTON MUSHROOMS These common small, fresh mushrooms may also be known as champignons. They are bland in taste, and may be used as a substitute for straw mushrooms. They are also sold in cans.

DRIED BLACK MUSHROOMS Intense flavor and a meaty texture are the standout features of dried black mushrooms (*xianggu*). Dried mushrooms should be reconstituted by soaking in cold water, generally for about 25 minutes, before use. If dried mushrooms have stems, these should be trimmed off close to the caps after they have softened in the soaking water. The strongly flavored soaking water can be strained through a fine-mesh strainer and used in soups and braised dishes. Keep dried mushrooms in an airtight container away from damp and heat and they will last for many months.

GOLDEN MUSHROOMS These elegant mushrooms have tiny, round caps on long, slender stems. They are harvested in small clumps, and when fresh are a light cream color and very delicate in taste. Canned golden mushrooms are deeper in color and slightly more intense in flavor. They are attractive in soups and stir-fries.

OYSTER MUSHROOMS Used mostly in soups and stir-fries, oyster mushrooms have fragile, uneven caps on fleshy, white stems. They are generally sold fresh, and are appreciated for their delicate texture and taste.

STRAW MUSHROOMS A dark gray to brown, ball-shaped mushroom, which when halved reveals a layered construction. Straw mushrooms are slippery and gelatinous in texture, and are frequently used in soups, stir-fries, and braised dishes. They are generally sold in cans, but are sometimes available fresh. The fresh mushrooms should be used within a day of purchase as they do not keep well. Button mushrooms are interchangeable with straw mushrooms in most recipes.

MUSTARD GREENS

Gai choi and *daigai choi* (*gai lan cai tai/jie cai*) are mustard greens with scraggly green leaves along fleshy pale green or white ribbed stems. The bitter taste of mustard greens is appreciated as a fresh vegetable, but they are more commonly dried or pickled as a dietary mainstay.

NAPA CABBAGE

Napa cabbage, also known as Peking or Tianjin cabbage, has a large head of tightly packed leaves with fleshy white bases and crinkled, pale green tops. Its mild flavor, crunchy stems, and tender leaves make it a versatile ingredient in soups, stir-fries, and stuffings.

NOODLES

Rice vermicelli (*mi fen*) are extruded dried fine strands of rice flour and water dough, firm and creamy white. Soak in cold water to soften before use and cut into manageable lengths. They should not be confused with rice stick noodles, also called *mi fen*, which are semitransparent, plastic-looking, flat, rice-flour noodles ⅛ to ¼ inch (3–6 mm) wide used in soups and stir-fries, or bean thread vermicelli (see page 244). Rice ribbon noodles (*fen*) are fresh noodles made from a dough of finely ground rice flour and water. Rinse gently in warm water to remove surface oil before use. They require brief cooking only. Rice sheets are the same dough cut into large squares, which can be used as edible wrappers for rolls and snacks or cut up into noodles. Rice noodles are favored in the south of China, while wheat-flour noodles are the preference in the northern wheat-growing regions. Wheat-flour noodles (*mian*) vary from fine to thick and are made from a dough of wheat flour and water, sometimes with eggs. *E fu* noodles are flat wheat noodles that have been fried and dried, giving them a light texture.

NUTS

Peanuts are an important crop in China, being used extensively for cooking oil production and as an ingredient in stir-fries and stuffings for buns and pastries, particularly in central and southern cuisines. Boiled and salted, or sugar-glazed shelled peanuts are enjoyed as an appetizer with pre-dinner drinks. Roasted cashew nuts and almonds are occasionally used in the south in stir-fries, and chopped as an ingredient in sweet "eight treasures" desserts.

OILS AND FATS

Polyunsaturated vegetable and seed oils are the predominant oils used in Chinese cooking. For stir-fries, "fried" oil (oil that has been previously used for deep-frying) is preferred for its extra flavor. Favored oils are peanut and corn, with rapeseed, cotton seed, safflower, sunflower, and soybean oils all used. Rendered animal fats are used in pastry making and occasionally in stir-frying. They can also be heated and splashed over finished dishes for extra flavor and gloss. Chicken fat, duck fat, and pork fat (lard) are the most commonly used.

SESAME OIL burns easily so is unsuitable for cooking at high temperatures, although it is occasionally used to deep-fry sweet pastries. It is used extensively in marinades, sauces, and dips, and is added to vegetable oil in stir-fries and when deep-frying for its rich nutty flavor.

ONIONS

Green (spring) onions are the onion of choice in most Chinese cooking for their mild flavor and fine texture. Both the white root end and the tapering tubular green tops are used as a seasoning vegetable and garnish. Onion curls can be made, using a knife, by shredding one or both ends of a 2-inch (5-cm) section of the white end. The green tops can be made into a decorative garnish by shredding them lengthways. Both should be placed in iced water until they curl. When yellow onions are used in a stir-fry, they are usually cut into small wedges. Cut a thick slice from the top and bottom of the onion, then work around the onion, cutting right to the center, to produce wedge-shaped pieces. Separate layers before use.

OYSTER SAUCE

Oyster sauce or *haoyou* is a thick, salty, dark brown condiment and seasoning sauce made from fermented soybeans and the liquor drawn off from fermented dried oysters. It can be stored in the refrigerator for several months.

PEA SHOOTS

Pea shoots have tender, round green leaves, with thin stems and curling tendrils; substitute small spinach leaves if these are not available.

PEPPER

Finely ground white pepper is used in most stir-fries and as a condiment, particularly with Shanghai cuisine. Black pepper can substitute. See also Sichuan pepper, which is not a true pepper.

PICKLED RADISH

Pickled radish is a salty vegetable made by salt-curing shredded daikon (giant white radish, also known as Chinese turnip). It is sold in small packs and will keep for many months if transferred to an airtight jar. Pickled radish gives an appetizing, crunchy texture to stuffings for bread and buns and a pleasing flavor to soups. It may be advisable to rinse the pickled radish before using it in a recipe; if you don't, taste the dish before adding any extra seasoning. Shredded, salt-pickled radish or rutabaga, sometimes seasoned with chile, is a strongly flavored ingredient in northern and Yunnanese cooking.

PLUM SAUCE

A thick, tart-sweet conserve made from a type of small, sour, green plum native to China. It is used in braised dishes, particularly with rich meats such as pork and duck, and as a glaze on grilled meats. Plum sauce should be stored in the refrigerator in warmer climates, and will keep for many months. Apricot conserve or marmalade can be substituted in most recipes.

RICE See box, page 196.

RICE WINE

Rice wine (*liaojiu*) is indispensable to Chinese cooking, adding flavor to sauces and stir-fries, and working as a tenderizer and seasoning in marinades. Rice wine can be purchased at most Asian food stores, and those labeled "cooking wine" may contain 5 percent added salt, so check labels before seasoning a dish. Dry sherry is a substitute in most recipes, while Japanese *mirin* is the alternative choice when a mild, aromatic wine is required. Shaoxing is an excellent choice for both drinking and cooking, while *maotai* liquor is a potent spirit best reserved for toasting at banquets. As a beverage, Chinese wine is served warm in small porcelain cups.

SCALLOPS

Sea scallops feature in the stir-fries and specialty seafood dishes of the coastal Fujian province and in the cuisines of Guangdong and Hong Kong. In general, the white meat is preferred to the richer roe, which sometimes clings to the side of the fresh scallops. *Ganbei* (dried scallops, sometimes called *conpoy*) are a type of deep-sea scallop harvested off the China coast. They are cut into slices and dried into rock-hard, amber disks and can also be bought as small chips or floss.

SESAME PASTE

Sesame paste (*zhimajiang*) is made from ground whole white sesame seeds and is used to thicken and enrich sauces and dips. Substitute tahini if it is not available.

SESAME SEEDS

Sesame products are frequently used for both flavor and their nutritional value. Sesame seeds, white or black, are used as garnishes and textural elements in stir-fries and sweet dishes. To toast sesame seeds, cook them gently in a wok without oil.

SHRIMP

Dried shrimp (*haimi*) are tiny, sun-dried, shelled shrimp sold in packages or by weight, and they need to be soaked to soften before use. The best will be bright orange-pink and have a fresh, pungent aroma. They add flavor to stuffings and rice dishes and a subtle hint of seafood to sauces and stocks. Store in an airtight container in the refrigerator. Shrimp balls are precooked, bite-sized balls of mashed shrimp; they can be purchased from the frozen food department of Asian food stores and added to soups, stir-fries, and braised dishes. Squid balls and fish balls are also available.

SICHUAN PEPPER

Sichuan pepper grows and is used extensively in the province of Sichuan. The small, red-brown berries from the prickly ash tree are also known variously as *Xanthoxyium piperitum*, fagara, wild peppercorn, or Chinese pepper. Spicy rather than hot, it can have a numbing effect if used to excess. When buying whole peppercorns, look for a bright red-brown color. Store in an airtight jar. Buy only small quantities of ground Sichuan pepper and use within a few weeks for the freshest flavor. *Huajiaoyan* is pepper-salt, a mixture of finely ground Sichuan pepper and fine salt.

SQUID AND CUTTLEFISH

Cuttlefish and squid are different animals, although they can be used interchangeably in recipes. Squid is slimmer and less fleshy than cuttlefish, which is more rounded and squat in the body, but both are cleaned and prepared in the same way.

TO CLEAN SQUID, pull the head and tentacles from the body pouch, then discard the clinging innards. Just below the eyes, cut off the tentacles and reserve them, discarding the eye portion. Squeeze the cut end of the tentacles to expel the hard, round beak, discarding it. Pull out and discard the long, transparent quill from inside the body pouch. Rinse the pouch and tentacles thoroughly under running cold water. Peel the gray membrane from the pouch, taking with it the two side flaps. Cut the body or leave whole as directed in individual recipes.

SOY SAUCE See box, page 48.

STAR ANISE

Star anise is a star-shaped, dried seedpod with five points, each containing one shiny black seed. Its pronounced licorice flavor has a particular affiliation for duck and other rich meats such as game and pork. It is used whole, broken into individual points, or crushed in a spice grinder. Store in an airtight jar.

SUGAR

Baitang is Chinese brown sugar, compressed into round, flat cakes or sticks of layered light and dark brown sugar. It is used for flavoring and coloring. Palm sugar or brown sugar can be substituted.

ROCK SUGAR *Bingtang* or rock sugar—chunks of crystalline sugar—is used to make a clear, sweet syrup for soups and sauces. Crystal sugar can often be substituted.

TAMARIND CONCENTRATE

Tamarind concentrate is a tart seasoning produced by scraping the flesh from dried tamarind pods. It is readily available where Asian foods are sold. Lemon or lime juice, or pickled limes can substitute.

TANGERINE PEEL

The thin skin of tangerines (*chenpi*) can be torn into strips and dried in the sun or oven. The resulting hard brown pieces add a delicious fresh flavor to stewed and braised dishes, and the boldly flavored stir-fries of Sichuan. Sold in small packs, tangerine peel should be kept in a cool, dry cupboard, or frozen. Alternatively, dried mandarin orange peel can be used.

TAPIOCA STARCH

Tapioca starch is used as an alternative to cornstarch as a thickener for clear sauces and as a coating for fried food.

TARO

Taro is a starchy root vegetable that is useful in vegetarian cooking, and as an alternative to sweet potato.

VINEGAR

Three main types of Chinese vinegar are distilled from fermented rice. White rice vinegar (*micu*) is a clear, mild vinegar for general use. Cider or distilled white vinegar can replace it, using 5 to 10 percent less than the recipe calls for. Black (also labeled brown) vinegar is a dark-colored, subtly flavored vinegar used as a flavoring and condiment, while red vinegar is amber-colored and slightly spicy in taste; it is used as a condiment with soups, noodles, and dumplings. Balsamic vinegar can replace black and red vinegar; adjust the amount to taste.

WATER CHESTNUTS

Water chestnuts are small, round white tubers with sweet, crisp flesh. Sold fresh or canned, they add texture to sweet and savory dishes. Stored in fresh water, they can be refrigerated for up to 3 days. Fresh water chestnuts should be scrubbed and peeled before use.

STOCKS

When required, freshly made or purchased stock gives best results. Fresh chicken stock is indispensable in the Chinese kitchen, as is the so-called superior stock. The latter combines chicken and pork bones to produce a subtle, rich flavor with a gelatinous quality that brings a silken smoothness to sauces and a pleasing texture to soups. Chinese grocers stock a variety of instant stock bases and flavor boosters, such as chicken essence (used where an intense chicken flavor is called for) and spiced beef stock base, which contains star anise and cassia.

If powdered chicken stock, also known as bouillon granules, is used instead of fresh stock it may be necessary to decrease the amount of salt and/or soy sauce in a recipe to allow for its saltiness. In some recipes, chicken stock powder is used in addition to fresh stock to intensify the flavor of a sauce or soup.

Freshly made stocks will keep in the refrigerator for up to 3 days and may be frozen for up to 2 months, with the exception of fish stock, which can be kept in the refrigerator for up to 1 day and frozen for up to 1 month.

BEEF STOCK

3 lb (1½ kg) meaty beef soup bones, such as shank

2½ qt (2.5 l) cold water

2-inch (5-cm) piece fresh ginger, unpeeled, scrubbed, and cut into cubes

1 yellow onion, unpeeled and quartered

2 star anise

2 pieces cassia bark or 1 cinnamon stick

½ teaspoon salt (optional)

6 white peppercorns (optional)

♨ Place the beef bones in a large pot. Bring a kettle filled with water to a boil, and pour the boiling water over the beef bones. Place the saucepan over high heat and bring the water back to a boil. Immediately remove from the heat and tip the contents of the pan into a colander in the sink to drain.

♨ Return the beef bones to the saucepan and add the cold water. Place over medium heat and bring to a boil, skimming the surface occasionally to remove any froth. Add the ginger, onion, star anise, cassia bark or cinnamon stick, salt (if using), and peppercorns (if using) to the pan. Reduce the heat to low so the water is barely bubbling and simmer, uncovered, for 3 hours, skimming occasionally.

♨ Remove from the heat and strain through a fine-mesh sieve into a clean saucepan. Discard the contents of the sieve and simmer the stock for 1 hour to con-centrate the stock. Let cool, then lift off the surface fat. Use the stock immediately or store until needed.
Makes about 4 cups (32 fl oz/1 l)

CHICKEN STOCK

2 lb (1 kg) chicken necks, wings, and uncooked bones

3 qt (3 l) cold water

1-inch (2.5-cm) piece fresh ginger

1 green (spring) onion, trimmed

½ teaspoon salt

6 white peppercorns (optional)

♨ Place the chicken pieces in a saucepan. Bring a kettle filled with water to a boil, and pour the boiling water over the chicken. Place the saucepan over high heat and bring the water back to a boil. Immediately remove from the heat and tip the contents of the pan into a colander in the sink to drain.

♨ Return the chicken to the saucepan and add the cold water, ginger, green onion, salt, and peppercorns (if using). Place over medium heat and bring to a boil, skimming the surface occasionally to remove any froth. Reduce the heat to low so the water is barely bubbling and simmer, uncovered, for 1½ hours.

♨ Remove from the heat and strain through a fine-mesh sieve into a clean jar or other container. Let cool, then lift off the surface fat (reserve, if desired, for stir-frying). Use the stock immediately or store until needed.
Makes about 7 cups (56 fl oz/1.75 l)

FISH STOCK

1½ lb (750 g) fish heads and frames

1 tablespoon vegetable oil

½-inch (12-mm) piece fresh ginger

1 small yellow onion, cut in half, peeled

1 small clove garlic, unpeeled

1 tablespoon rice wine

½ teaspoon salt

6 white peppercorns (optional)

1½ qt (1.5 l) water

♨ Cut the fish heads in half and remove the gills. Rinse the fish heads and frames thoroughly under cold running water.

♨ In a heavy saucepan over medium heat, warm the oil. Add the fish heads and frames, ginger, onion, and garlic, and cook, stirring and turning, for 5 minutes to draw out the flavors. Add the wine and cook briefly until it evaporates. Add the salt, peppercorns (if using), and water and bring slowly to a boil, skimming the surface occasionally to remove any froth. Reduce the heat to medium-low as soon as the water reaches a boil and simmer for 20 minutes, skimming occasionally.

☀ Remove from the heat and strain through a fine-mesh sieve into a clean jar or other container. Use the stock immediately or store until needed.

Makes about 6 cups (48 fl oz / 1.5 l)

PORK STOCK

1 pork hock with skin intact, 1½ lb (750 g), or 1½ lb (750 g) pork shank or similar flavorful cut

3 qt (3 l) cold water

1-inch (2.5-cm) piece fresh ginger

1 piece dried tangerine peel, about ¾ inch (2 cm) square (optional)

1 green (spring) onion, white part only

½ teaspoon salt

6 white peppercorns (optional)

☀ Place the pork in a saucepan. Bring a kettle filled with water to a boil, and pour the boiling water over the pork. Place the saucepan over high heat and bring the water back to a boil. Immediately remove from the heat and tip the contents of the pan into a colander in the sink to drain.

☀ Return the pork to the saucepan and add the cold water. Place over medium heat and bring to a boil, skimming the surface occasionally to remove any froth. Reduce the heat to low so the water is barely bubbling and simmer, uncovered, for 1½ hours.

☀ Add the ginger, tangerine peel, green onion, salt, and peppercorns (if using) to the pan and continue to simmer gently for 2 hours longer, skimming occasionally.

☀ Remove from the heat and strain through a fine-mesh sieve into a clean jar or other container. Let cool, then lift off the surface fat. Use the stock immediately or store until needed.

Makes about 8 cups (64 fl oz / 2 l)

SUPERIOR STOCK

2 lb (1 kg) chicken necks, wings, and uncooked bones

1 pork hock with skin intact, 1½ lb (750 g)

4 qt (4 l) cold water

1-inch (2.5-cm) piece fresh ginger

2 green (spring) onions, white part only

2 points from star anise

1-inch (2.5-cm) piece cassia bark

¾ teaspoon salt

6 white peppercorns (optional)

☀ Place the chicken and pork in a large saucepan. Bring a kettle filled with water to a boil, and pour the boiling water over the chicken and pork. Place the saucepan over high heat and bring the water back to a boil. Immediately remove from the heat and tip the contents of the pan into a colander in the sink to drain.

☀ Return the chicken and pork to the saucepan and add the cold water. Place over medium heat and bring to a boil, skimming the surface occasionally to remove any froth. Reduce the heat to low so the water is barely bubbling and simmer, uncovered, for 1½ hours.

☀ Using a slotted spoon, remove and discard the chicken bones, retaining the necks and wings. Add the ginger, green onions, star anise, cassia bark, salt, and the peppercorns (if using) to the pan and return to low heat. Continue to simmer gently for 2 hours longer, skimming occasionally.

☀ Remove from the heat and strain through a fine-mesh sieve into a clean jar or other container. Let cool, then lift off the surface fat. Use the stock immediately or store until needed.

Makes about 8 cups (64 fl oz / 2 l)

VEGETABLE STOCK

2 tablespoons vegetable oil

1 yellow onion, unpeeled and quartered

1 daikon, peeled and cut into cubes

2 cups (6 oz / 185 g) sliced white stems of napa cabbage, or bok choy

6 cups (48 fl oz / 1.5 l) cold water

½ teaspoon salt (optional)

6 white peppercorns (optional)

☀ In a large saucepan over medium-high heat, warm the oil. Add the onion, daikon, and cabbage or bok choy and stir-fry until lightly browned, about 6 minutes.

☀ Add the water, salt (if using), and peppercorns (if using) and bring to a boil over high heat. Reduce the heat to medium-low, and simmer, uncovered, for about 30 minutes.

☀ Remove from the heat and strain through a fine-mesh sieve into a clean jar or other container. Use the stock immediately or store until needed.

Makes about 6 cups (48 fl oz / 1.5 l)

INDEX

ACKNOWLEDGMENTS

Jacki Passmore would like to thank the following individuals and organizations for their assistance:
I would like to thank the chefs of China for their efforts individually and collectively in maintaining
the long tradition of culinary excellence and inventiveness in a country to which I have a deep
personal and professional attachment.

I wish to acknowledge and recommend the masterly work published by the Yale University Press,
Food in Chinese Culture, edited by K. C. Chang. This invaluable reference book, offering a long-range
perspective on the history of China's food and culinary culture, has been in part my inspiration to
continue with my own efforts at documenting the culinary traditions of this fascinating country.
I would like to thank Kevin for transplanting me into life in a Chinese community, Allan Amsell
for giving me the confidence to compile my first major work on Chinese cooking,
Paul for our marriage in Hong Kong and our beautiful daughter Isobel.

And, most importantly, I extend my heartfelt thanks and gratification to the many officials,
managers, secretaries, and personnel in restaurants and hotels, and in government departments
and agencies throughout China who have aided, encouraged and assisted me in so many ways
over almost thirty years of travel and research.

Jason Lowe thanks Gaye, Miranda, and Angela.

Jason Lowe sends his thanks to all at Weldon Owen Australia ("although we never met")
and thanks Lori and Rae for their love.

Andre Martin wishes to thank Sally Parker for propping and styling; Jacqueline Richards
for art direction; and his wife, Nikki, and children, Benito, Pablo, and Isabella, for their patience
and support.

Sally Parker wishes to thank Christine Sheppard, Andre Martin, and Jacqueline Richards for being
such a wonderful team to work with, and Orient House, 45 Bridge Road, Glebe, Sydney,
for their willing assistance.

OXMOOR HOUSE INC.

Oxmoor House books are distributed by Sunset Books
80 Willow Road, Menlo Park, CA 94025
Telephone: 650-321-3600, Fax: 650-324-1532

Vice-President/General Manager: Rich Smeby
Director of Special Sales: Gary Wright

Oxmoor House and Sunset Books are divisions of
Southern Progress Corporation

WILLIAMS-SONOMA INC.
Founder and Vice-Chairman: Chuck Williams

WELDON OWEN PTY LTD.
Chief Executive Officer: John Owen
President: Terry Newell
Publisher: Hannah Rahill
Art Director: Sue Burk
Project Editor: Angela Handley
Design: Jacqueline Richards, PinchMe Design
Editorial Assistant: Kiren Thandi
Consulting Editor: Sharon Silva
Production Manager: Caroline Webber
Production Coordinator: James Blackman
Calligraphy: Jane Dill
Vice President International Sales: Stuart Laurence
European Sales Director: Vanessa Mori

pp 4–5: A buffalo roams the rice terraces that spiral around a mountain near Longsheng, Guangxi. **pp 6–7:** Brightly colored and embroidered clothing marks this woman as a member of one of the hill tribes of Yunnan. **pp 8–9:** Village stalls stock every possible type of red-glazed meat, from ducks to pig snouts. **pp 12–13:** The tranquil Li River, near Yangshuo, is the focus of many traditional farming and fishing activities.

THE SAVORING SERIES
conceived and produced by Weldon Owen Inc.
814 Montgomery Street, San Francisco, CA 94133
Telephone: 415-291-0100, Fax: 415-291-8841

In collaboration with Williams-Sonoma Inc.
3250 Van Ness Avenue, San Francisco, CA 94109

A WELDON OWEN PRODUCTION
Copyright © 2003 Weldon Owen Inc.

First printed 2003
10 9 8 7 6 5 4 3 2 1

Library of Congress Cataloging-in-Publication Data is available.

ISBN 0-8487-2644-8

Separations by Colourscan Overseas Co. Pte. Ltd.
Printed in Singapore by Tien Wah Press (Pte.) Ltd.

Savoring is a registered trademark of Weldon Owen Inc.